# HEBREW FOR
# BIBLICAL INTERPRETATION

## Society of Biblical Literature

## Resources for Biblical Study

Steven L. McKenzie
Editor

Number 48
HEBREW FOR
BIBLICAL INTERPRETATION

# HEBREW FOR
# BIBLICAL INTERPRETATION

by
Arthur Walker-Jones

Society of Biblical Literature

Atlanta

# HEBREW FOR
# BIBLICAL INTERPRETATION

## Arthur Walker-Jones

The Hebraica and Hebraica II fonts used to print this work are available from Linguist's Software, Inc., PO Box 580, Edmonds, WA 98020-0580 USA
tel (425) 775-1130 www.linguistsoftware.com.

**Library of Congress Cataloging-in-Publication Data**

Walker-Jones, Arthur.
  Hebrew for biblical interpretation / by Arthur Walker-Jones.
     p. cm. — (Resources for biblical study ; no. 48)
  Includes bibliographical references and index.
  ISBN 1-58983-086-5 (pbk. : alk. paper)
  1. Hebrew language—Grammar. 2. Bible. O.T.—Criticism,
interpretation, etc. I. Title. II. Series.
PJ4567.3 .W35 2003
492.4'82421--dc22

                                    2003015640


     08 07 06 05 04 03      5 4 3 2 1

Printed in the United States of America
on acid-free paper

To Carrie, David, and Katherine

# Contents

# Acknowledgments

I am indebted to many people. I would like to thank my students in the South Pacific for whom I began to write this book. Partly because of my experience working with students for whom English is a second or third language, I have tried to write clearly and concisely. To all the students over the last eight years ·who have used earlier versions of this textbook I am grateful, particularly those who have pointed out errors, made constructive criticisms, and encouraged me to publish it.

I would like to acknowledge my indebtedness to two of my professors: Patrick D. Miller with whom I studied biblical interpretation and C. L. Seow for many of the concerns and much of the description of Hebrew grammar. I inherited from him a desire to simplify the teaching of Biblical Hebrew and relate it to exegesis. Those who are familiar with Bonnie Kittel's work will recognize that I am indebted to her for the use of indicators and charting.

Charles William Miller was kind enough to test an early version of this book in class. His detailed comments resulted in an extensive revision and helped clarify my thinking about pedagogical principles. I am grateful to my colleagues Eleanor Stebner and Peggy Day for reading drafts and providing corrections and suggestions.

The University of Winnipeg provided funds for copyediting and a research assistant. John Kutcher's hard work and attention to detail improved almost every aspect of this book. It was gratifying to work with someone who had learned Hebrew from this textbook and believed in the method.

Because of the nature of this work, I have tried to avoid extensive documentation. The bibliographies at the end are intended as guides to further reading and documentation of the sources of the chapters. The Bibleworks™ software was a tremendous help in researching and writing this book. I would also like to thank Deutsche Bibelgesellschaft for permission to reproduce passages and text-critical notes from *Biblia Hebraica Stuttgartensia* (fourth revised edition 1990, © 1967/1977 Deutsche Bibelgesellschaft Stuttgart) and Oxford University Press for permission to reprint an entry from Brown, Driver, and Briggs' *Hebrew and English Lexicon of the Old Testament* (1907).

With so much support and assistance, I am all the more responsible for the errors that may remain and would appreciate corrections and suggestions for future editions.

# Introduction

Why write yet another Hebrew textbook? In brief, because existing Hebrew grammars tend to focus on only a few aspects of language, and studies in applied linguistics show that their educational approach does not work well. This textbook integrates some of the best features of existing Hebrew grammars with a new approach designed to promote better learning outcomes. The first two sections of this introduction explain the linguistic and educational reasons for this paradigm shift. They will be of interest to teachers. Students may want to skip to the third section on the use of the book.

## Language and Learning

Almost all Hebrew grammars use what applied linguists refer to as a Grammar-Translation Method. It originated with the teaching of Latin in seventeenth-century English "grammar" schools. Grammar Translation organizes the chapters of a textbook according to a logical description of Hebrew grammar. Translation exercises at the end of each chapter illustrate and reinforce the grammar rules taught in the chapter.

According to applied linguists, Grammar Translation "is a method for which there is no theory. There is no literature that offers a rationale or justification for it or that attempts to relate it to issues in linguistics, psychology, or educational theory."[1] Moreover, studies have shown that it does not work well as an educational method. No matter how well they are explained and how thoroughly they are drilled, students do not learn forms in the

---

[1] Jack C. Richards and Theodore S. Rodgers, *Approaches and Methods in Language Teaching* (Cambridge Language Teaching Library; Cambridge: Cambridge University Press, 2001), 7.

logical order of the textbook.[2] In an age when teaching is becoming increasingly learner-centered, the Grammar-Translation Method tends to be teacher-centered. Janice Yalden suggests that "the relationship between teacher and learner is that of the classical teacher-centred methodology." It does "not dwell on the learning process, on individual needs, or on any of the other considerations that teachers and materials writers take for granted now."[3] Memorization is the predominant learning method. This appeals to a limited number of learners, and seems out of place in contemporary academic settings that prize critical thinking and recognize a variety of intelligences and learning styles. In brief, Grammar Translation tends to be teacher-centered and has been shown not to work well as an educational method.

The awareness seems to be growing in biblical studies that yearlong grammar courses do not prepare students adequately to read the Hebrew Bible. Ehud Ben Zvi expresses the experience of many when he says that "after finishing an introductory Hebrew course, the intermediate reader often finds that there is still a gap between his or her reading ability and the demands of the biblical texts."[4] He wrote his textbook for a second year course designed to bridge that gap. Others have added a few exegetical elements to already long first-year grammars. Because of the many new

---

[2] Catherine Doughty, "Acquiring Competence in a Second Language: Form and Function," in *Learning Foreign and Second Languages: Perspectives in Research and Scholarship*, ed. Heidi Byrnes (Teaching Languages, Literatures, and Cultures; New York: Modern Language Association, 1998), 128–133; P. Skehan, "Second Language Acquisition Research and Task-Based Instruction," in *Challenge and Change in Language Teaching*, eds. J. Willis and D. Willis (Oxford: Heinemann, 1996), 18, cited in Richards and Rogers, 249.

[3] *Principles of Course Design for Language Teaching* (New Directions in Language Teaching; Cambridge: Cambridge University Press, 1987), 52.

[4] Ehud Ben Zvi et al., *Readings in Biblical Hebrew: An Intermediate Textbook*, (Yale Language Series; New Haven and London: Yale University Press, 1993), vii.

demands in the curriculum of theological schools, few theological students will be willing to dedicate more time to learning Hebrew. Many students and faculty in religious studies programs may also welcome a shorter and more effective route to proficiency in Hebrew exegesis.

In addition, the theory of language that Grammar Translation appears to assume is problematic. Contemporary linguists have extensively criticized the idea of a universal, logical grammar (largely identified with English grammar), question the centrality of syntax, and generally use broader definitions of language that include things like semantics and pragmatics. No linguistic reasons exist for focusing almost exclusively on grammar.

In contemporary North American culture, it is common for students and even faculty to think language learning is unnecessary to understand literature from another culture. In theological schools, many faculty and students think learning biblical languages is largely irrelevant to theological education. Unfortunately, Hebrew grammars tend to confirm this suspicion by teaching grammar with little reference to wider issues of language and meaning.

Hebrew grammars do show some limited influences from applied linguistics in three areas: the organization of the grammar from simple to complex, references to "inductive" learning, and the teaching of vocabulary in descending order of frequency. First, the idea of organizing grammatical forms from simple to complex was introduced in 1899 by Henry Sweet, one of a number of linguists advocating reform.[5] Thus in Hebrew grammars the noun comes before the verb and strong verbs before weak verbs. However, in other respects, Hebrew grammars retain a logical order. For example, verb stems or *binyanim* are usually taught in the logical order they appear on a verb chart. The problem with this is that the most commonly occurring verbs in Hebrew are weak verbs (to say, to be, to do, etc.) and some appear exclusively or frequently in derived stems (to speak, to command, to make known, to save). The effect of keeping these frequent and

---

[5] *The Practical Study of Language*, cited in Richards and Rogers, 10.

meaningful aspects to the end of a yearlong course is to prolong and make more difficult the learning of real Hebrew. In addition, the detail and complexity of the discussion of each topic often makes even the supposedly simple aspects of grammar complex for the learner. This text begins teaching weak verb forms and derived stems early in the book so that, by the end of the book, with frequent encounter, they are no longer difficult.

Second, some Hebrew grammars claim to be partially inductive because they use genuine biblical passages in the exercises. These are more realistic and meaningful than the artificial sentences of older grammars. By inductive learning of grammar, however, applied linguists normally mean that learners are exposed to grammar before they have learned or been taught it. This is not the case when the biblical exercises have been chosen and edited so that they do not contain anything students have not already been taught deductively.

The third area of limited influence is the learning of vocabulary in descending order of frequency. In the 1950s and 60s the use of frequency counts to structure the learning of vocabulary was an important feature of the Oral/Situational Approach. *Hebrew for Biblical Interpretation* is one of the few Hebrew textbooks that extends this principle to the learning of grammar in descending order of frequency.

Although I have tried to state as clearly as possible the problems with Grammar Translation, I am not advocating the wholesale rejection of the method. Communicative Language Approaches in contemporary applied linguistics are primarily for developing fluency in modern languages. Grammar Translation works against fluency, but has its advantages in biblical studies where scholarly literature often discusses vocabulary and grammar. Grammar Translation is a quick way for some learners to understand and engage in those discussions. This textbook retains many of the best features of the Grammar-Translation Method. Chapters are organized according to a systematic description of Hebrew grammar and the descriptions are clear and concise. Examples and exercises are from the Hebrew Bible and include both narrative and poetic texts. Verb charts are included.

Vocabularies include all words occurring one hundred times or more and are organized in descending order of frequency. The grammar and vocabulary chapters have been kept separate from the exegesis chapters so that those using the Grammar-Translation Method can skip over the exegetical chapters. I have tried to include some of the best aspects of Grammar Translation, and enhance it with another approach designed to provide better learning outcomes.

## Integrating Exegesis

Studies in applied linguistics show that people learn a language, even the grammar, better in the context of meaningful communication. One way to apply this in biblical studies would be to have students learn Modern Hebrew either before or during the learning of Biblical Hebrew. For biblical studies, a more direct approach is to integrate the learning of grammar into the meaningful, communicative context of interpretation. The word "interpretation" in the title refers to exegesis, by which I mean the critical methods of interpretation used by biblical scholars.

Integrating exegesis makes the learning of grammar relevant and more interesting to students. An attempt has been made to choose reading exercises from passages of broad cultural significance that will be of interest to both general education and theological students. They are then motivated to continue to use Hebrew and retain or expand their skills. However, even if students take only one Hebrew course, they learn things of enduring value about the use of Hebrew in biblical interpretation.

Integrating exegesis also engages a broader range of learning styles. Students who are less able at memorizing grammar rules and vocabulary may be able to engage critical, exegetical skills. At the same time, for those who do further study, the textbook lays a solid foundation. My experience in combining the teaching of Hebrew and exegesis is that a broader range of students is able to become more capable and knowledgeable in the use of Hebrew for exegesis in a shorter period of time.

Teaching grammar in the context of exegesis also assumes a better theory of language. It is neither necessary nor desirable in an introductory course to introduce the technical language of semantics, pragmatics, or discourse analysis to do this. Biblical scholars have traditionally discussed the broader meaning of language in relation to exegesis. For example, historical, genre, and tradition criticism discuss the social and historical context of language. Form and rhetorical criticism discuss the way larger discourses join units together to create meaning. Integrating the teaching of Hebrew with the teaching of exegesis, therefore, presupposes better linguistic theory.

## How to Use This Textbook

This textbook integrates the learning of grammar and exegesis in order to make the learning of grammar more interesting and so that learners can develop more rapidly the ability to engage in exegesis themselves.

In order to simplify the learning of Hebrew, and make room for discussions of exegesis, this book teaches **indicators**. Many Hebrew teachers have students memorize the Qal stem of the strong verb and then point out the differences in the other stems and weak verbs. The indicators are not all differences between paradigms, only those that occur on almost all forms. They correspond not to all identifying features of a paradigm, but to those few features that experienced readers come to recognize intuitively as indicating a verb form or a weak root most consistently.

The textbook notes exceptions to the indicators that might confuse learners.[6] I recommend memorizing the Qal stem of the strong verb, but thereafter the use of indicators should reduce the need for memorization and get learners reading and identifying forms faster.

In order to begin reading Hebrew as quickly as possible, the organization of the book is according to frequency and significance for understanding. For this reason I pass quickly over Masoretic

---

[6] Even in full paradigms, there are ambiguous forms. In addition, the logical consistency verb charts appear to present is misleading because they often leave out alternate forms.

pointing and move quickly to verb conjugations. Because the most frequently occurring verbs in Hebrew (to say, to be, to do, etc.) are all weak verbs, these are introduced from the beginning. This means that early chapters, like Chapters 6 and 7 on the Imperfect, are challenging because they cover a lot of difficult material. But students usually have more time and energy early in the term and, with practice, these essential aspects of the language will no longer seem so difficult.

As well as being organized in descending order of frequency and meaning, the chapters are organized for easy reference, because people do not learn forms in logical order. In this regard, it is important for students to realize that they do not need to memorize everything in a chapter before moving on. Each chapter usually indicates the most important points, by placing them at the beginning of the chapter or section, and includes many details and exceptions later in the chapter that learners may encounter in reading and need to look up again to refresh their memory.

Because dictionaries are mines of exegetical information, the book begins early teaching the use of a Biblical Hebrew dictionary. For this reason, there is no English to Hebrew glossary and exercises in the early chapters have a few words that have not been in the vocabulary lists, so students learn to use a dictionary. In later chapters, when the vocabularies ask them to memorize the word, then they have already begun to learn it in context. Similarly, exercises include some forms and constructions not yet introduced (often with explanatory footnotes to avoid too much confusion). When students later learn the theory, they are able to recognize its relevance in practice.

This book tries to use simple English and avoid technical terms. Some textbooks contain so many difficult English words and technical terminology that students almost have to learn two new languages. Technical terms have their place. When they are necessary and useful, the text includes a definition with the first use of grammatical or technical terms. The book also lists more technical or alternative names in case the reader encounters these in other books.

While this textbook was initially written to address educational needs in the theological curriculum, I have designed it in a way that allows for use in a variety of different contexts, courses, and approaches. The exegetical chapters and exercises focus on historical and literary methods widely used by biblical scholars in both theology and religion. This should allow for its use by people from a range of perspectives in theology and religion. These chapters are also intentionally brief so that teachers can add perspectives and exercises relevant to them and their students.

This textbook was originally designed for a yearlong introduction to Biblical Hebrew course, but with the growing variety of intensive and short language courses being offered by theological schools in mind. It is well suited to intensive, summer courses because it is concise, uses indicators to reduce memorization, and is designed to get students reading Biblical Hebrew as quickly as possible. If the exegetical chapters were supplemented with exegetical articles and handbooks, it could be used as a textbook in language tools for exegesis courses. Because it teaches the most frequent and significant aspects of Hebrew in the beginning, it is sufficient for shorter courses. Even if a course covered only the first fifteen chapters, students would have learned many of the most important features of Hebrew and exegetical skills of enduring value. The final chapter could then be used to integrate these skills.

In my own development as a teacher of Biblical Hebrew, I found it difficult to give up some of the content of the Grammar-Translation Method by which I had learned, even if it was for better learning outcomes. I was encouraged along this road as I discovered that learners were better able to remember grammar rules when taught in the context of exegesis. I therefore understand that it may be tempting for teachers and certain types of learners to skip over the exegetical chapters. I would encourage you to use them to make the teaching and learning of Hebrew more interesting and relevant and thereby promote deeper learning.

# Chapter 1

## Consonants

The sounds of a language can be divided into consonants and vowels. Vowels are sounds that involve a continuous stream of air with only slight friction. Consonants are sounds that involve closing or partial closing of the flow of air. In English, the vowels are *a, e, i, o, u,* and sometimes *y*. All other letters are consonants. Hebrew was originally written only with consonants. You will learn about how the vowels are indicated in the next chapter. The following consonants make up the Hebrew alphabet:

| Letter | Name | | Sound |
|---|---|---|---|
| א | ʾaleph | (awlef) | a stoppage of air |
| ב | bet | (bayt) | b *or* v |
| ג | gimel | (geemel) | g |
| ד | dalet | (dawlet) | d |
| ה | heʾ | (hay) | h |
| ו | vav | (vawv) | v |
| ז | zayin | (za-yin) | z |
| ח | ḥet | (chayt) | ch as in "loch" |
| ט | ṭet | (tayt) | t |
| י | yod | (yod) | y |
| ך כ | kaph | (kahf) | k *or* ch as in "loch" |
| ל | lamed | (lahmed) | l |
| ם מ | mem | (maym) | m |
| ן נ | nun | (noon) | n |
| ס | samech | (sawmech) | s |

| ע | ʿayin | (a-yin) | a stoppage of air |
|---|---|---|---|
| ף פ | peh | (pay) | p *or* ph |
| ץ צ | tsade | (tsawday) | ts as in "cats" |
| ק | qoph | (qowf) | q as in "plaque" |
| ר | resh | (raysh) | r |
| שׂ | sin | (seen) | s |
| שׁ | shin | (sheen) | sh |
| ת | tav | (tahv) | t |

In parentheses are approximations of how the names of the letters of the alphabet sound in English. The dot under the *h* in ḥet distinguishes it from the Hebrew letter heʾ and distinguishes the sound from the English letter *h*. The ḥet's sound occurs rarely in English and never at the beginning of words.

**Final Forms**

Five consonants in the table have two forms. The forms on the left side of the alphabet column (ץ ף ן ם ך) are called final forms because they appear whenever the letter occurs at the end of a word. Note that all but one of the final forms seem like pulled down versions of the letter. The forms on the right (צ פ נ מ כ) appear when the letter is anywhere else, namely, at the beginning or in the middle of the word.

**BeGaD KePhaT Letters**

BeGaD KePhaT is a memory aid. The six capital letters in English represent the six letters (בגד כפת) that each had two pronunciations in Medieval Hebrew. Medieval Jewish scholars used a dot in the center of each letter to indicate the different pronunciations. This dot is called a **dagesh**. With the dagesh, the movement of air stopped during pronunciation of the letter. For this reason these letters with the dagesh are called **stops**. Without the dagesh, the movement of air did not stop during the pronunciation of the letters. For this reason these letters without the dagesh are called **spirants**. In Modern Hebrew only three of

the BeGaD KePhaT letters are pronounced differently (פ כ ב).
You might use BaK Pak to help remember them.
   **BeGaD KePhaT letters** are pronounced as follows:

| With Dagesh hard | | Without Dagesh soft | |
|---|---|---|---|
| Letter | Pronunciation | Letter | Pronunciation |
| בּ | b | ב | v |
| גּ | g | ג | g / gh |
| דּ | d | ד | d / dh |
| כּ | k | כ | ch as in "Bach" |
| פּ | p | פ | ph / f |
| תּ | t | ת | t / th |

## Printing Hebrew Letters

   Hebrew is written and read from right to left across a page.
The reader of the Hebrew Bible also turns the pages in the opposite
direction from English. The following is an example of how the
letters are printed by hand. The small arrows show the direction the
pen moves. Pen strokes move from top to bottom, right to left in
preparation for writing the next letter.

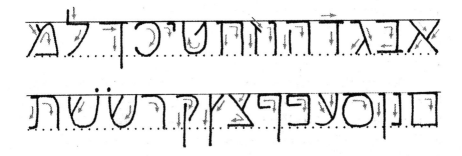

Hebrew is printed hanging down from the line. Do not write the
ʾaleph as an X. Several letters are easily confused. In your reading
and writing, you should be careful to distinguish the letters that
appear together in the following table:

| ב כ נ | ה ח | ס ם |
|---|---|---|
| ג נ | ו ז י ן | ע צ |
| ד ד ר | ד ו | שׁ שׂ |

One letter extends above the line—lamed (ל). Several letters extend below the dotted line (ק ץ ף ן ך).

## Using a Dictionary

You may want to begin learning the alphabet and do exercises 1, 2, and 3 before reading this section.

Once you have learned the alphabet, you know enough to begin learning to use a dictionary. One of the exercises at the end of this chapter is to look up several commonly occurring words.

The best one-volume dictionary of Biblical Hebrew is F. Brown, S. R. Driver, and C. A. Briggs, *Hebrew and English Lexicon of the Old Testament*. (A **lexicon** is a dictionary of an ancient language.) Although this work is quite old and the authors did not have the benefit of much new information, it still contains an impressive presentation of the considerable data then available. It is a mine of information for interpretation. The abbreviation commonly used for this work in biblical studies is **BDB**.

BDB lists words under **roots**. These are usually three-letter roots. Verbs, nouns, adjectives, and so forth, listed under a three-letter root add different prefixes, suffixes, and vowel patterns to the root. The meanings of all the parts of speech listed under the root are related to the **root meaning**. The three-letter root and the root meaning are an abstraction created by scholars. Speakers of the language would determine the meaning primarily from where and how a word was used. But the root meaning is helpful in learning the language because many words do have related meanings. For example:

| | |
|---|---|
| דִּבַּרְתִּי | I spoke |
| דָּבָר | word |
| דִּבְרָה | cause |
| מִדַּבֵּר | mouth |

The three-letter roots are usually printed in the largest letters in BDB. Some letters are susceptible to change with the addition of prefixes, suffixes, or vowel patterns. For example, under the root בוא (go in, enter, come) BDB lists a noun, בָּאָה (entrance). The vav has disappeared.

Roots with the same letters in the same positions tend to change in the same ways. For this reason it is convenient to classify roots according to the letter and whether it is the first, second, or third letter of the root. For example, of the roots you will look up in the exercise, בוא, מות, and שוב are II-vav, because their second letter is a vav.

The words at the tops of columns in BDB are the first and last words on the page. When looking up a root, the words at the tops of columns may be confusing because they may appear to be out of alphabetic order. Thus on page 99 of BDB, the top of the second column has מבוא because it is derived from בוא, not because this is the beginning of roots beginning with מ. Words may add letters to the beginning, middle, or end of a root or omit root letters. For the moment, focus on the three root letters that are in the largest print in the body of the columns.

When you do exercise 4, try not to be intimidated by all you see on a page. Look only at the words in the largest Hebrew print and the definitions that immediately follow them.

As you move toward the end of the alphabet, beware that BDB has an **Aramaic** section at the back.

If you have trouble finding a root or word in BDB, you may want to try using William L. Holladay, *A Concise Hebrew and Aramaic Lexicon of the Old Testament*. It lists words alphabetically, exactly as they are spelled. Because it abridges a multi-volume German dictionary that is a classic in biblical studies, Holladay is a useful resource. However, it does not contain as much information as BDB. In Holladay, the meanings of words are in bold print.

Sometimes the same three letters have such different meanings that lexicons list them as separate roots (with the same letters), usually listed as I., II., III., and so on. For example, in the exercises for this lesson, Holladay lists I. דבר ... **turn away** ... II. דבר ... **speak**.

## Exercises

1. Practice writing and saying the alphabet until you have it memorized.

2. Read the following similar letters making sure that you can identify them correctly. Practice writing them, and make sure that your writing clearly distinguishes them. For example, check that there is a gap in your heʾ (ה) and no gap in your ḥet (ח).

a. ב כ נ

b. ד ן

c. ג נ

d. ם ס

e. ד ר ך ז

f. ע צ

g. ה ח

h. שׁ שׂ

i. ז ו י ן

3. Match the letters in the left column with their final forms in the right column.

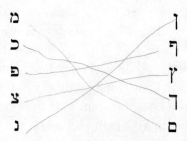

4. Once you have learned the Hebrew alphabet sufficiently, copy the following commonly occurring roots to practice writing and then look up the basic meaning in BDB. In order to help you get started, the first word in the following list (אכל) is on page 37

of BDB. The abbreviation immediately following indicates that this form is a verb. The root means "eat." (If you glance at page 38, you will see a number of nouns from the same root meaning food, a meal, even a knife.)

| Hebrew | Gloss | Hebrew | Gloss |
|---|---|---|---|
| יָשַׁב | to sit, remain, dwell | אכל | to eat, consume |
| לקח | to take | אמר | to utter, say |
| מות *(môt)* | to die | בוא | to come, go in |
| נתן | to give, put, set | דבר | to speak |
| עשה | to do, make | היה | ~~to come to pass, become~~ (to be) |
| ראה | to see | הלך | ~~hapless, unfortunate~~ to walk, to go |
| שוב *(šûb)* | to turn back, return | ידע | to know (also biblically) |
| שמע | to hear | יצא | to go, come out forth |

*middle vav roots*

## Chapter 2
### Vowels

Originally, Hebrew used only consonants in writing. The reader supplied the vowels from their knowledge of the language and the context. In some cases, different possibilities could create confusion. By the rise of the Israelite monarchy, at the beginning of the ninth-century B.C.E., scribes were using some consonants to represent vowels on the end of words: ' for final long i, ו for final long u, and ה for the remaining vowels. The Latin name for these consonantal markers of vowels is *matres lectionis*, "mothers of reading." In the eighth-century B.C.E. these consonants began to be used within words to represent vowels. From 600 to 1000 C.E. families of Jewish scholars added marks to the consonantal text to indicate the pronunciation. These scholars are called **Masoretes**, and the marks to indicate the pronunciation are called **vowel points**.

Hebrew vowels can be divided into three groups or classes: *a*, *i* (which includes e), and *u* (which includes *o*). The chart on the next page uses the letter מ to illustrate the position of the vowel points.

The chart lists only the most frequently occurring combinations of **vowels** and **vowel letters**. Other less commonly occurring combinations are מֹה מֶה מֵי מֹ. The last is an older spelling that holem vav replaced.

Most vowel points appear under the consonant and are pronounced after it. The **holem** appears at the top left corner of the consonant after which it is pronounced. If a holem and the dot of שׁ occurred together, then the Masoretes often wrote only one dot instead of two:

יֹשֵׁב instead of יֹשֵׁב

In some manuscripts, the Masoretes did the same with שׁ:

שְׂנֵא instead of שָׂנֵא

| Class | Sign | Sound | Name |
|-------|------|-------|------|
| a | מַ | short *a* as in "man" | pataḥ |
| | מָ | long *a* as in "father" | qamets |
| | מָה | long *a* | qamets heʾ |
| i | מֶ | short *e* as in "met" | segol |
| | מֵ | long *e* as in "they" | tsere |
| | מֵי | long *e* | tsere yod |
| | מִ | short *i* as in "lid" *or* long *i* as in "machine" | ḥireq |
| | מִי | long *i* | ḥireq yod |
| u | מָ | short *o* as in "hot" | qamets ḥatuph |
| | מֻ | short *u* as in "bud" *or* long *u* as in "flute" | qibbuts |
| | מוּ | long *u* | shureq |
| | מֹ | long *o* as in "mole" | ḥolem |
| | מוֹ | long *o* | ḥolem vav |

A **syllable** in Hebrew is a word or part of a word consisting of *either* a consonant and a vowel (Cv), *or* a consonant, a vowel, and a consonant (CvC). ("C" stands for any consonant and "v" stands for any vowel.) A syllable usually does not start with a vowel in Hebrew (vC) or involve consonant clusters (CvCC). When a syllable ends in a vowel it is **open**. When a syllable ends in a consonant it is **closed**.

**Stress.** Syllables may be either **stressed** or **unstressed**. In reading Hebrew the last syllable of a word is normally the stressed or emphasized syllable. When this is not the case, this work will indicate the stressed syllable with an accent ( ´ ) until you learn the accents in Chapter 8. The biblical text has accents for every stressed syllable.

Vowels are **short** or **long**. Vowels tend to be short when they are in closed, unstressed syllables (CvC). They tend to be long in unstressed, open (CV), stressed, open (CV), and stressed, closed (CVC) syllables. Hebrew seldom has an open syllable with a short, unstressed vowel (Cv) or a closed syllable with a long, unstressed vowel (CVC). This is important for various rules of pronunciation that follow.

**Qibbuts** and **ḥireq** are normally short. They are long in open or stressed syllables. For example, in the word בִּנְיָמִן "Benjamin," the first ḥireq is short. The second is long because it is in the final syllable, which is stressed.

The same vowel point ( ָ ) can stand for a *long a*, in which case its name is **qamets**, or for a *short o*, in which case its name is **qamets ḥatuph**. Qamets is more common than qamets ḥatuph, so the issue in reading is to identify the few times when qamets should be pronounced as a short *o*. Qamets ḥatuph occurs in closed, unstressed syllables. In the word וַיָּקָם "he arose" the first qamets is pronounced as a long *a*, because it is stressed, but the second is pronounced as a short *o* because it is in a closed, unstressed syllable.

## Silent and Vocal Sheva

One vowel point, the **sheva**, may be either silent or vocal. When vocal, it may appear in conjunction with other short vowels.

| Vowel Point | Name | Pronunciation |
|---|---|---|
| : | silent sheva | none |
| : | vocal sheva | reduced short *e* |
| ֲ | ḥateph pataḥ | reduced short *a* |
| ֱ | ḥateph segol | reduced short *e* |
| ֳ | ḥateph qamets | reduced short *o* |

A sheva is **vocal** and is pronounced as a short "uh" sound when it is under the first consonant of a syllable. A sheva is under the first consonant of a syllable when:

1. It comes after a long vowel:

שֹׁפְטִים      judges

2. It is the second of two shevas:[1]

יִרְמְיָה      Jeremiah

↑

3. It is under the first letter of the word:[2]

יְהוּדָה      Judah

In all other cases, a sheva is **silent**.

## Gutturals

The gutturals are א ה ח ע. The name comes from the Latin, *guttur*, "throat," because they are pronounced in the throat. Remembering them and their character will help explain many of the peculiarities of Hebrew. With the frequent exception of א, they prefer a-class vowels underneath and before them. The gutturals and ר cannot be doubled (see below). They never take a vocal sheva and prefer composite shevas—hateph patah ( ֲ ), hateph segol ( ֱ ) or hateph qamets ( ֳ ).

א is not pronounced when it ends a syllable. That means it does not take a silent sheva. For this reason it is said to be **quiescent** (it goes quiet).

---

[1] The first sheva ends a syllable and is silent.

[2] An exception to this rule and the rule about consonant clusters are the forms of the number two: שְׁתַּיִם and שְׁתֵּי, pronounced *shtayim* and *shtey*.

## "Sneaky" Pataḥ

Most grammars call this a **furtive pataḥ**. (Furtive means "sneaky.") When one of the gutturals ע ח ה appears at the end of a word and is not preceded by an a-class vowel, an additional pataḥ appears under the guttural. It is not considered a true vowel. It is pronounced before the guttural. To indicate this, it may appear under and slightly before the letter:

הַ rather than הַ

Examples:

רוּחַ       spirit, wind

אֱלוֹהַּ       Eloah, God

## Dagesh and Mappiq

The dot in the above ה is not a dagesh but a mappiq and indicates the ה is a consonant and not a vowel letter.

Dagesh has two uses. The first, already noted, is to indicate that a BeGaD KePhaT letter is a stop. This is a **weak dagesh**. (It is also called dagesh *lene*. *Lene* is Latin for "weak.")

בָּבֶל       Babel

The second use is to indicate the doubling of a letter. Instead of writing the same letter twice, the Masoretes put a dagesh in the letter. This is called a **strong dagesh**. (It is also called dagesh *forte*. *Forte* is Latin for "strong.")

שַׁבָּת       Sabbath

Note: The sheva under a strong dagesh will be vocal. Because the letter is doubled, there are really two shevas. The first sheva is silent and the second is vocal according to the second rule for vocal shevas.

In BeGaD KePhaT letters the dagesh can represent a stop only (weak) or a stop and doubling (strong). A dagesh in a BeGaD KePhaT letter is:

1. Strong when following a short vowel in the middle of a word:

עַמּוֹן        Ammon

2. Weak anywhere else:

יַרְדֵּן        Jordan

**Full and Defective**. Several vowel points occur with or without vowel letters (*matres lectionis*). When a word is written with a vowel letter, the spelling is **full**. When the same word is written without the vowel letter, the spelling is said to be **defective**.

דָּוִיד        David ("full" spelling)

דָּוִד        David ("defective" spelling)

## Vocabulary

After you have completed exercise 2 below, learn the names. Each occurs more than one hundred times in the Hebrew Bible.

**Exercises**

1. Now you should be able to read and pronounce in Hebrew the names of the letters of the Hebrew alphabet.

| | | | | | |
|---|---|---|---|---|---|
| פֵּה | פ | טֵית | ט | אָלֶף | א |
| צָדֵה | צ | יֹד | י | בֵּית | ב |
| קוֹף | ק | כַּף | כ | גִּימֶל | ג |
| רֵישׁ | ר | לָמֶד | ל | דָּלֶת | ד |
| שִׂין | שׂ | מֵים | מ | הֵא | ה |
| שִׁין | שׁ | נוּן | נ | וָו | ו |
| תָּו | ת | סָמֶךְ | ס | זַיִן | ז |
| | | עַיִן | ע | חֵית | ח |

2. Read aloud the biblical names on the next page and then see if you recognize them. For each dagesh in a BeGaD KePhaT letter, decide whether it is weak or strong. For each sheva, decide whether it is silent or vocal by consulting the rules. If you do not recognize the name, look it up in BDB, Holladay, or another lexicon. On the one hand, they may be difficult to find in BDB because you will not know what root to look under. On the other hand, trying to look them up will familiarize you with the way BDB often helps you in such situations. For example, if you do not recognize אַבְרָהָם and do not know the root, but look it up in alphabetical order in BDB, you will find on page seven (almost at the bottom of the second column, in small print) the note:

אַבְרָהָם v. אַבְרָם sub II. אבה

This means for אַבְרָהָם see אַבְרָם under the second root אבה. Hendrickson Publishers' version of BDB adds the page and column where you will find the root (p. 4b). If you look in the second column on page four, you will find these names are

"Abraham" and "Abram." Often you can look words and forms up in BDB in this way even if you do not know the root.

| | | |
|---|---|---|
| לֵוִי *Levi* | יְהוּדָה *Judah* | אַבְרָהָם *Abraham* |
| מוֹאָב *Moab* | יְהוֹנָתָן *Jonathan* | אַבְשָׁלוֹם *Absalom* |
| מְנַשֶּׁה *Manasseh* | יוֹסֵף *Joseph* | אֱדוֹם *Edom* |
| מֹשֶׁה *Moses* | יַעֲקֹב *Jacob* | אָדָם *Adam* |
| עַמּוֹן *Ammon* | יִצְחָק *Isaac* | אַהֲרֹן *Aaron* |
| פַּרְעֹה *Pharoah* | יַרְדֵּן *Jordan* | אֶפְרַיִם *Ephraim* |
| צִיּוֹן *Zion* | יְרוּשָׁלִַם³ *Jerusalem* | אֲרָם *Aram* |
| שָׁאוּל *Saul* | יִרְמְיָהוּ *Jeremiah* | בָּבֶל *Babel/Babylon* |
| שַׁבָּת *Sabbath* | יִשְׂרָאֵל *Israel* | בִּנְיָמִן *Benjamin* |
| שְׁמוּאֵל *Samuel* | כְּנַעַן *Canaan* | דָּוִד *David* |

Note: The name Adam in Hebrew is also the word for "human being." How does this affect our understanding of the story of Adam and Eve?

*theophoric names ( -el)*

---
³ The defective spelling is far more common: יְרוּשָׁלַם

## Chapter 3

## Nouns and Prepositions

**Gender** in Hebrew is either masculine or feminine. **Number** is singular, dual, or plural. In linguistics, **marking** refers to the addition of something to distinguish it from other forms.

**Masculine singular** (ms) **nouns** are unmarked. They have no additional ending.

**Masculine plural** (mp) **nouns** usually end in םי–.[1]

| | |
|---|---|
| מֶלֶךְ | king (ms) |
| מְלָכִים | kings (mp) |

In most cases, the vowels of the noun change when an ending is added. For students who are interested, the rules covering most of these vowel changes may be found in Lambdin's or Seow's grammars. Nouns that do not follow the general rules are called **irregular plurals** and are so noted in this book's vocabularies. Those that add consonants may have originally come from a different root than the singular. The plural of אִישׁ, for example, is אֲנָשִׁים.

**Feminine singular** (fs) **nouns** usually end with ה– or a ת–. (The ת may be vocalized in a number of different ways.) Various possibilities are represented in the examples below. Historically, the feminine endings all derived from ת– (at).

| | |
|---|---|
| אִשָּׁה | woman (fs) |
| שָׁנָה | year (fs) |

---

[1] The hyphen represents any final root letter to which the ending is added.

| בַּת | daughter (fs) |
| חַטָּאת | sin, sin-offering (fs) |
| בְּרִית | covenant (fs) |

Some feminine nouns look like they are masculine. They are masculine in ending:

| עִיר | city (fs) |
| נָשִׁים | women (fp) |

They may have a masculine ending only in the singular, only in the plural, or in both. Although they have a masculine form, that they are feminine is evident in reading because they take feminine adjectives and verbs.

**Feminine plural (fp) nouns** add ות–.

| חֲרָבוֹת | swords (fp) |

As with the masculine endings, some nouns may take feminine plural endings, but are masculine.

| אָבוֹת | fathers (mp) |

Both genders use the same **dual** ending םִי–, which is similar to the masculine plural form. The dual is limited in Hebrew. It is used for body parts that occur in pairs, expressions of time, and measurements.

| Body parts | עֵינַיִם | eyes |
| Time | יוֹמַיִם | two days |
| Measurements | אַמָּתַיִם | two cubits |

For a variety of reasons, some nouns have endings that appear dual, but do not have a dual meaning.

A table can summarize the endings that mark the different genders and numbers in Hebrew:

| Ending | Masculine | Feminine |
|--------|-----------|----------|
| Singular | none | ת– ‏ הָ– |
| Dual | ‏ יִם– | ‏ יִם– |
| Plural | ‏ יִם– | וֹת– |

The addition of endings may cause vowels to change:

| Without Ending | | With Ending | |
|---|---|---|---|
| נָבִיא | prophet (ms) | נְבִיאִים | prophets (mp) |
| חָכָם | wise man (ms) | חֲכָמִים | wise men (mp) |
| שֹׁפֵט | judge (ms) | שֹׁפְטִים | judges (mp) |
| אַיִל | ram (ms) | אֵילִים | rams (mp) |
| אָוֶן | trouble (ms) | אוֹנִים | troubles (mp) |

At this point, it is not necessary to understand or memorize the rules that govern these vowel changes. You should be able to recognize the word and root without knowing the rules.

More difficult to recognize is when a letter changes or disappears. With nouns ending in a heʾ (הָ–), the heʾ may change to a tav or disappear before the plural ending.

| Without Ending | | With Ending | |
|---|---|---|---|
| שָׁנָה | year (fs) | שְׁנָתַיִם | two years (dual) |
| | | שָׁנִים | years (fp) |

Ideas about what is singular and plural vary within and between languages. A **collective noun** is a noun that has a singular ending but stands for a group or collection of individuals. Army, crowd, orchestra are examples in English. Examples in Hebrew are:

צֹאן      "flock" or "flocks"

בְּהֵמָה      "beast" or "beasts"

One of the most striking differences between Hebrew and English is the use of the **plural for honor** or majesty:

אֱלֹהִים      "gods" or "God"

אֲדֹנִים      "lords" or "lord"

## The Definite Article

The definite article points to something and limits or defines it—this one and not another. (Hebrew has no indefinite article such as English "a." The absence of a definite article with a Hebrew noun indicates "a.") Hebrew prefixes the definite article to the word to which it points. The definite article is usually הַ– with doubling (a strong dagesh) in the first letter of the word.

הַכֹּהֵן      the priest

Before nouns beginning with a guttural or resh, the definite article will be הָ– or הֶ– without doubling, because the gutturals (א ה ח ע) and resh (ר) do not take doubling.

הָאֱלֹהִים      (the) God

הָאָרֶץ      the earth

הַהֵיכָל      the temple

As in the second example above the definite article may also affect the vowels of the noun it modifies. אֶרֶץ with the definite article becomes אָרֶץ.

Before חָ and sometimes הָ and עָ, the definite article is הֶ–.

עָרִים      cities

הֶעָרִים      the cities

Note: The addition of the definite article or the addition of gender and number endings to some nouns changes the vowels. As an aid to identifying these remember that BDB and other dictionaries list the gender and various forms of nouns after the etymology.

## Prepositions

Hebrew prepositions may either be **prefixed** to words or be independent words.

Hebrew prefixes to words the prepositions –בְּ "in," "at," "with," –כְּ "as," "like," and –לְ "to," "for."

לְנָשִׁים                   for women

When the word is definite, the he⁾ of the definite article disappears, but the vowel and doubling remain.

לַנָּשִׁים                   for the women

Some prepositions such as לִפְנֵי "before" are **independent** words.

לִפְנֵי יְהוָה              before the LORD

Some prepositions such as עַל "on," "upon" and אֶל "to" are typically joined to the following word with a mark called a **maqqeph**.

עַל־הָאָרֶץ                on the earth

אֶל־הָעִיר                 to the city

Some prepositions such as אֵת "with" may or may not be joined to the following word with maqqeph. The preposition אֵת has the vowel pointing אֶת־ when it is joined with maqqeph to a word and, of course, the pointing אֵת when it is not joined with maqqeph to a word.

| | |
|---|---|
| אֶת־יְהוָה | with the LORD |
| אֵת רִבְקָה | with Rebekah |

## Rule of Sheva

When a preposition comes before a word that begins with a vocal sheva, the vowel pointing under the preposition changes to a hireq.

לִמְנַשֶּׁה      for Manasseh

This is the **rule of sheva**: when two vocal shevas would appear together in Hebrew, the first changes to hireq, and the second becomes silent.

When the second sheva is under a yod, the sheva disappears.

| | |
|---|---|
| יְהוּדָה | Judah |
| לִיהוּדָה | to Judah |

## The Conjunction –וְ

The conjunction –וְ is always prefixed to a word. Its vowel pointing may be either –וְ or –וּ. The pronunciation of the first is "ve-." The pronunciation of the second is an important *exception* to the rule that Hebrew syllables always begin with a consonant. The pronunciation is "u-."

| | |
|---|---|
| וְיִשְׂרָאֵל | and Israel |
| וּמֶלֶךְ | and a king |

Before a composite sheva, the conjunction takes the corresponding long vowel. This is another variation of the rule of sheva.

וַאֲשֶׁר                    and who

The vowel pointing of the conjunction before אֱלֹהִים "God" is unique. The ʾaleph goes quiet and the vowel lengthens.

וֵאלֹהִים              and God

## Vocabulary

| | |
|---|---|
| אִישׁ | man |
| אֲנָשִׁים | men (irregular plural) |
| אֶל | to, toward |
| אֱלֹהִים | God |
| אֶרֶץ | earth, land |
| אִשָּׁה | woman |
| נָשִׁים | women (irregular plural) |
| אֵת | with, beside |
| –בְּ | in, at, with, on (preposition prefixed to the beginning of a word) |
| –הַ | the |
| –וְ | and, also; but (conjunction prefixed to the beginning of a word) |

יהוה
(YHWH = tetragrammaton)
long form of the name of God. (The rabbis kept the pronunciation secret in order to avoid profanation and either did not point the name or pointed it with the vowel points of a word to be substituted in reading, most often the vowels for אֲדֹנָי, "my Lord," as you will see in the following exercises. For this reason translations such as the NRSV often translate it as LORD in capital letters and it is normally read אֲדֹנָי in Hebrew.) Short forms of the name of God are: יָהּ and יְהֹ .

כְּ– as, like (prefixed preposition)

כִּי because, for, that, when, but; indeed, truly

כֹּל כָל all, every (This is one of the most frequently occurring examples of qamets ḥatuph. When joined with a maqqeph to a following word it loses its accent and becomes כָּל– pronounced with a short o.)

לְ– to, toward, for (prefixed preposition); Do! Yes!

מֶלֶךְ king (MLK)

לִפְנֵי before

עַל on, upon, against, over; beside

עִם with

## Exercises

1. Practice reading aloud the following verse until you can read it smoothly and fluently. Translate the words you recognize.

(Deut 6:4) שְׁמַע יִשְׂרָאֵל יְהוָה אֱלֹהֵינוּ יְהוָה אֶחָד

2. Read aloud and translate the words in the following phrases. In these early exercises, the important thing is that you translate the individual words. Until you become more familiar with Hebrew, it will be difficult to create a translation that makes

sense in English, but you should be able to identify the individual words. In the exercise, you will begin to learn by experience that word order is different in Hebrew than it is in English. In addition, you will need to add "is" to make sense of some of the phrases that do not include a verb. If you still cannot make sense of the phrases, you may consult an English translation.

(Exod 9:29) כִּי לַיהוָה הָאָרֶץ

(2 Sam 6:21) וַיֹּאמֶר² דָּוִד
אֶל־מִיכַל³ לִפְנֵי יְהוָה

(1 Sam 2:21) שְׁמוּאֵל עִם־יְהוָה

(2 Chr 6:18) אֱלֹהִים אֶת־הָאָדָם עַל־הָאָרֶץ

(Gen 6:9) אֶת־הָאֱלֹהִים הִתְהַלֶּךְ⁴־נֹחַ

(Ps 47:8 ET 7)⁵ כִּי מֶלֶךְ כָּל־הָאָרֶץ אֱלֹהִים

(Exod 35:22) הָאֲנָשִׁים עַל־הַנָּשִׁים

(Deut 22:22) אִישׁ שֹׁכֵב⁶ עִם־אִשָּׁה

(Lev 25:4) לָאָרֶץ שַׁבָּת לַיהוָה

---

² "said" (The subject, when named, normally comes after the verb rather than before it, as in English. See "Word Order" in Chapter 6.)
³ "Michal." If you have trouble with a word in the exercises, remember that it could be a name. Sound it out or look it up.
⁴ "walked"
⁵ ET = Verse number(s) in English translations
⁶ "lying"

3. Read aloud and translate the words in the following phrases. They contain a few words you have not had in your vocabulary and will need to look up in a lexicon. Again, until you know more Hebrew, you may not be able to figure out how the words fit into English translations. The important thing is to identify the individual words.

(Gen 2:4) בְּיוֹם עֲשׂוֹת[7] יְהוָה אֱלֹהִים
אֶרֶץ וְשָׁמָיִם[8]

(Judg 20:11) כָּל־אִישׁ יִשְׂרָאֵל אֶל־הָעִיר כְּאִישׁ אֶחָד

4. Some recent grammars argue that grammatical gender of nouns for living and non-living things is primarily syntactical and does not reflect social ideas about gender. Some feminists think that the gender of non-living things often does reflect and support the sexist ideas and practices of patriarchal cultures. English, for example, uses feminine pronouns (she, her) for the church, because the church is thought of as emotionally supportive and nurturing like a mother. This usage is usually unconscious. What do you think? Is gender only grammatical or does it reflect ideas about male and female?

---

[7] "made" (The next two words are the subject of this verb. See footnote 2.)

[8] You will find this word listed in BDB under the root שׁמה.

# Chapter 4

## Word Studies

**Exegesis** comes from a Greek word meaning "to lead out of." In biblical studies, it refers to the methods of historical and literary analysis of a passage that "lead out" meaning. It refers, in short, to methods of biblical interpretation. Throughout this work, there will be chapters on aspects of biblical interpretation.

In the process of interpreting a biblical passage, it may be necessary or valuable to do a word study to understand the meaning of a word. When translating from Hebrew into English, a scholar may have difficulty making sense of a Hebrew word in a particular context and may need to do a word study. While studying a passage, you may decide there are one or several words that are very important to understanding a passage and therefore may deserve a word study.

A word usually has a range of meanings within a language. These meanings may change over time within a culture. New words are created, and old words gradually stop being used. Different groups of people may assign peculiar meanings to particular words. Because the Bible was written over a long period by many groups of people, words may have different meanings in different bodies of literature and historical eras. Ancient Israelite culture was very different from our own and we look at it from a great historical distance. Word studies are like telescopes helping us to see ancient meanings from a great cultural and historical distance.

Theological terms in English may be very abstract, but have concrete meanings in Hebrew that bring them alive. For example: "Redeemer" is quite abstract in English, but in Hebrew it has a variety of concrete meanings, including a person who buys a relative from slavery.

## Lexicons

Lexicons are dictionaries of ancient languages. They provide the range of meanings of a word and much other useful information for translation and interpretation. If there is a history of scholarly discussion about the meaning of a word, a lexicon often contains a brief summary.

There are two multi-volume lexicons of classical Hebrew. The first by Koehler, Baumgartner, and Stamm was originally in German (with some English translations). It now appears in English translation as *The Hebrew and Aramaic Lexicon of the Old Testament*, and is often referred to by the abbreviation *HALOT* in biblical studies. The second multi-volume lexicon is *The Dictionary of Classical Hebrew*, edited by David J. A. Clines, and abbreviated *DCH* in biblical studies. *DCH* is influenced by contemporary linguistics and focuses on the meaning of words in the context of the Hebrew language. For this reason, it does not contain references to the meaning of roots in other Semitic languages, but does contain references to the Dead Sea Scrolls that were not available to earlier works.

Hebrew students commonly use either one of two one-volume lexicons: William L. Holladay's *A Concise Hebrew and Aramaic Lexicon of the Old Testament* or Brown, Driver and Briggs' *Hebrew and English Lexicon of the Old Testament* (BDB). Holladay is based on an earlier German lexicon by Koehler and Baumgartner (KBL) and is favored by some because the entries are in alphabetic order and therefore easier to find for beginners. BDB lists words under roots but has more information. The *New Brown-Driver-Briggs* from Hendrickson Publishers adds to the bottom of pages the Addenda and Corrigenda that were at the back of the Oxford version. Both versions lack much new information, particularly the library of Ugaritic literature, and recent advances in the understanding of Hebrew.

Although BDB is difficult to use, it contains much information. Therefore, this textbook provides helps for its use. What follows is a reproduction of the beginning of an entry from BDB. Refer to that reproduction (or page 55 in BDB) as you read the following description of how to use it.

אָמַר [5287] **vb.** utter, say (MI Ph. אמר, Aram.
אֱמַר, Eth. አመረ፡ I. 2 *shew, declare*, Ar. اَمِر *command;* perh. √ אמר orig. = *be* or *make prominent*,
hence Hithp. infr., אָמִיר: Sab. אמר *lofty*, epith.
of king J H.Mordtm [ZMG 1876, 37]; cf. Dl [Pr 23] who
thinks orig. mng. *hell, sichtbar sein*, whence
As. *amâru, see*, & *shew, declare, say*)—**Qal**
*Pf.* 'א Gn 3¹ +, etc.; *Impf.* יֹאמַר Gn 31⁸ +;
וַיֹּאמֶר Gn 1³ +; וַיֹּאמֶר Gn 14¹⁹ +; in Jb alw.
וַיֹּאמַר Jb 3² +; 3 fs. תֹּאמַר Gn 21¹² +; תֹּאמַר Pr 1²¹;
1 s. אֹמַר Gn 22² +; אוֹמְרָה ψ 42 ·⁰; וָאֹמַר Gn 20¹³ +;
וָאֹמַר Ne 2⁷·¹⁷·²⁰; 3 m. pl. יֹאמְרוּ Ex 4¹ + etc.; sf.
יֹמְרוּךָ ψ 139²⁰; 2 mpl. תֹּאמְרוּ 2 S 19¹⁴ (cf. Kö [i. p. 395]);
*Imv.* אֱמֹר (אֱמָר־) Gn 45¹⁷ +, etc.; *Inf. abs.* אָמוֹר
Ex 21⁵ +; cstr. אֱמֹר Ez 25³ +; (הֵ)אֱמֹר Jb 34¹⁸
but rd. הָאֱמֹר ⑥ 𝔙 Di, or better הֵאָמֹר *Inf. abs.*
c. ה interrog. cf. Ew [§ 328 d]; sf. אָמְרִי Jos 6¹⁰ +;
אֲמָרְכֶם Je 23³⁸; אֲמָרְכֶם Mal 1⁷ +; לֵאמֹר Gn 1²² +,
etc.; *Pt. act.* אֹמֵר Gn 32¹⁰ +, etc.; *pass.* הֵאָמוֹר
Mi 2⁷, but this grammatically indefensible, rd.
הֵאָמוֹר, *Inf. abs.* c. ה interrog., v. Dr [Expositor. April,
1887, 263.]

**1.** *Say* (subj. God Gn 3¹ + or man 32⁵,
serpent 3¹, ass Nu 22²⁸, horse הֶאָח יֹאמַר Jb
39²⁵ etc.; inanimate things, personif. Jb 28¹⁴ cf.
v²² etc.; so in allegory or fable Ju 9⁸ 2 K 14⁹
etc.; esp. in narrat., וַיֹּאמֶרetc., Gn 4⁶ + very oft.):
mostly sq. thing said, either subst. Je 14¹⁷ (c.
cl. app.) Dt 27¹⁶ᶠ· Ju 12⁶; pronoun Gn 44¹⁶
2 K 20¹⁴ +; or (usually) clause Gn 1³ 3¹ 37²⁰

The parenthesis following the root contains information on
the origin and meaning of the word. There are abbreviated
references to various scholars as well as the meanings of the word
in various **Semitic languages**. The key to the abbreviations is at
the front of BDB. Even if you do not know the alphabets of the
other Semitic languages, you can use this section because BDB
gives the translation.

After the parentheses in BDB is a dash (—) and the various
forms of the verb. Do not worry about these now. The numbered
sections that follow give various meanings of the verb and where
BDB thinks those meanings occur. (This particular entry continues
for two pages.) BDB lists various biblical occurrences under each

meaning and you may find the passage you are studying. If there is a sword (†) to the left of a word, this means the entry lists all occurrences of the word. Check other lexicons for different meanings. Various lexicons and translations may choose different meanings. Examine this range of meanings to see what best fits the context of your passage.

If there is a large Roman numeral to the left of the root, then the root has other unrelated meanings. This is important. A different meaning may fit the context you are studying as well or better.

Note: Be careful with etymologies. **Etymology** is the study of the origin and derivation of words. BDB's etymologies are sometimes fanciful. In *The Semantics of Biblical Language*, James Barr criticized the use of etymologies in biblical studies. He pointed out that context and usage determine the meaning of a word, not etymology. For example, the word "nice" originally meant "stupid" in English. Someone hearing the word "nice" used today would know from the context that it no longer means "stupid."

Barr noted another danger. The lexicons of Semitic languages, particularly Arabic, contain so many meanings for a root that an interpreter can choose any meaning that suits her or his purposes.

When a word is rare and occurs in contexts where its meaning is obscure, however, consulting the uses of the root in other Semitic languages may be necessary and provide important interpretive clues. For example, the Hebrew word מִמְסָךְ occurs only in Isaiah 65:11 and Proverbs 23:30. Neither context makes clear the meaning of the word. Since the meaning of the root מסך is "to mix," the traditional translation in Proverbs, represented by the RSV, is "those who tarry long over wine, those who go to try *mixed wine*." But a Ugaritic text has a list of vessels which includes *mmsk* listed after *spl* (bowl). Since the מִמְסָךְ is being filled, a cup or mixing bowl makes sense in the context. Thus, the New Jewish Publication Society Bible (NJPS) translates Proverbs 23:30 as: "Those whom wine keeps till the small hours. Those who gather to drain the *cups*."

Recently people who study the meaning of words have been realizing that the study of synonyms and antonyms may be as important or more important than the meanings a lexicon lists. **Synonyms** are words with the same or similar meanings. **Antonyms** are words with a contrary meaning. You should develop an understanding of how the word is and is not like its synonyms in various contexts. *DCH* is particularly helpful in studying synonyms and antonyms.

## Concordances

Lexicons are created by collecting all the occurrences of a word and grouping them according to meaning. You can do this yourself by using a concordance. A **concordance** lists the verse and a selection from the verse where a word occurs. In some cases you may want to group words yourself before studying lexicons in order to make your own discoveries without being biased by them. Three major Hebrew concordances are: Evan-Shoshan, *A New Concordance of the Old Testament*; Lisowsky, *Konkordanz zum Hebräischen Alten Testament*; and Mandelkern, *Veteris Testamenti Concordantiae Hebraicae atque Chaldaicae* (2 vols.). Each has its advantages and disadvantages, but the last is the most comprehensive.

If you find reading the Hebrew verses difficult, *The Englishman's Hebrew and Chaldee Concordance of the Old Testament* lists the verses in English under the Hebrew forms.

A number of computer programs are now the best concordances because of the speed with which they can compile customized lists of words, phrases, or grammatical forms.

As you study the occurrences of the word, you should group them according to book, genre, and historical period to understand the differences in meaning between different authors, genres of literature, and historical periods. You should also note the nearby words such as prepositions that may be indicators of a particular meaning. Compare the synonyms and antonyms of the word. If the word study is too large, you may want to limit it by studying only one form, grammatical construction, book, genre, or historical period.

## Versions

Versions are translations of the Bible into other languages. Early versions may have had insights into the meaning of words. The **Septuagint** is a collection of translations of biblical books into Greek from the second and third centuries B.C.E. The Septuagint is sometimes abbreviated by the roman numeral LXX, because of the ancient tradition that seventy-two scholars translated the Septuatint in seventy days. If you know Greek, you could look to see how the Septuagint has translated the word. If the meaning is very different, however, the Septuagint may have been using a Hebrew manuscript with a different word. The best one-volume work for purchase is Rahlfs' *Septuaginta*. Two multi-volume, critical editions of the Septuagint are also available.

## Theological Dictionaries

There are extensive and detailed discussions of words with a view to their theological meaning in *Theological Dictionary of the New Testament* (*TDNT*) and *Theological Dictionary of the Old Testament* (*TDOT*). *TDNT* includes long discussions of the Hebrew words that lie behind the NT Greek. There is a serious danger of becoming overawed by the extent and detail of information in these two works and not forming your own opinions. James Barr wrote the work mentioned earlier as a critique of the methods and conclusions of these dictionaries. In addition to criticizing the emphasis on etymology rather than context and usage, he questioned the idea that a word carries all its meanings into every context. This makes for interesting theologizing, but is not how language works. Words may bring some associations with them, but context may exclude other associations for the native speaker. Again, the way the word is used and the specific context in which it is used determine its meaning.

Less extensive but useful is Westermann and Jenni's *Theological Lexicon of the Old Testament*. Articles by forty international scholars discuss the meanings of words in their historical and religious contexts.

## Exercises

1. In Psalm 1:2, the New Revised Standard Version (NRSV) translates תּוֹרָה as "law." The New Jewish Publication Society (NJPS) or *Tanakh* translates it as "teaching." Do a word study to find out which is the better translation. תּוֹרָה is on page 435 in BDB. The root is on the previous page. You may want to focus on the use of the word in Psalms to make the study more manageable.

Some standard questions that you can ask when doing a word study are:

a. What is the meaning in other languages? (Use BDB)
b. What are the meanings that BDB lists?
c. What are the meanings that *HALOT* lists?
d. What are its synonyms and antonyms listed in *DCH* and how is it like or unlike them?
e. What meanings do you find by doing your own investigation with a concordance?
f. What is the meaning in the particular Bible passage(s)? Commentaries may be helpful to understand the use in particular passages.

Some have suggested that Psalm 1 is placed at the beginning of the book of Psalms as an introduction. If Psalm 1 is an introduction, how would the translation and interpretation of תּוֹרָה influence our understanding of the book of Psalms?

2. The meanings of biblical names often have religious or literary significance. For example, אָדָם "Adam" means "human being." The name יְהוֹנָתָן "Jonathan" means "the LORD (יהוֹ ) has given (נָתַן)." In BDB, look up the etymology (the information in parentheses about the origin of the word) for the following names you learned in Chapter 2.

| | | | |
|---|---|---|---|
| יוֹסֵף | יַעֲקֹב | דָּוִד | בִּנְיָמִן |
| שְׁמוּאֵל | יִשְׂרָאֵל | יְרוּשָׁלַ͏ִם | יִצְחָק |

# Chapter 5

## Pronouns and Demonstratives

**Pronouns** are words that substitute for nouns (this, that, he, she, they, and the like). In Hebrew, pronouns may be either independent or suffixed.

### Independent Personal Pronouns

Independent pronouns are independent because they are separate words. Personal pronouns have **person** (first, second, or third), **gender** (masculine, feminine, or common), and **number** (singular or plural). The first person is "I" or "we" in English. The second person is "you." The third person is "he," "she," and "they." Person, gender, and number are abbreviated PGN in the table below and elsewhere in this book. In Hebrew the **independent personal pronouns** are:

| PGN | Pronoun | Trans. | PGN | Pronoun | Trans. |
|-----|---------|--------|-----|---------|--------|
| 3ms | הוּא | he (hoo) | 3mp | הֵמָּה / הֵם | they (ha-mah) (haim) |
| 3fs | הִיא | she (hee) | 3fp | הֵנָּה | they (hay nah) |
| 2ms | אַתָּה / אַתְּ | you (atah) | 2mp | אַתֶּם | you (atem) |
| 2fs | אַתְּ | you (at) | 2fp | אַתֵּן / אַתֵּנָה | you (aten) (atenah) |
| 1cs | אֲנִי / אָנֹכִי | I (ani) (an-o-chee) | 1cp | אֲנַחְנוּ | we (anaknu) |

c = common

As the table indicates, several independent pronouns have alternate forms. Note also where the accents are when you learn to pronounce them.

## Suffixed Pronouns

Pronouns may also be added as suffixes to prepositions, verbs, nouns, and particles. As in the example below, the vowels of the form to which the suffixed pronoun is attached may change:

אַרְצְךָ          your land

The following table shows suffixed pronouns attached to the preposition lamed, –לְ "to."

| PGN | Suff. pron. | Trans. | PGN | Suff. pron. | Trans. |
|-----|-------------|--------|-----|-------------|--------|
| 3ms | לוֹ *(-o)* | to him | 3mp | לָהֶם *(ahem)* | to them |
| 3fs | לָהּ *(-ah)* | to her | 3fp | לָהֶן *(ahen)* | to them |
| 2ms | לְךָ *(-eka)* | to you | 2mp | לָכֶם *(akem)* | to you |
| 2fs | לָךְ *(-ak)* | to you | 2fp | לָכֶן *(aken)* | to you |
| 1cs | לִי *(-ee)* | to me | 1cp | לָנוּ *(anu)* | to us |

The dot in the 3fs suffix, a **mappiq**, indicates that this is a consonant, not a vowel letter. Taking note of this will be particularly important when distinguishing a suffixed pronoun from something else, such as a fs ending on a noun.

There are other forms of suffixed pronouns attached to other prepositions and other words. The main concern of this chapter is pronouns suffixed to prepositions. Nouns, verbs and particles, however, take the same pronoun suffixes.

The table below summarizes the different forms of **suffixed pronouns**. For beginning students, it is probably enough to memorize the pronouns on lamed in the table above and merely be familiar with the following table for future reference. The suffixed pronouns are often used as objects so that is the translation given in both tables. They may also be possessive (his, her, your . . .). The similarities between the independent and suffixed pronouns may help you remember and recognize both.

| PGN | Suff. pron. | Trans. | PGN | Suff. pron. | Trans. |
|-----|-------------|--------|-----|-------------|--------|
| 3ms | ‏–ֹו‏ ‏–הוּ‏ ‏–וֹ‏ ‏–וּ‏ ‏–נּוּ‏ | him | 3mp | ‏–ָם‏ ‏–הֶם‏ ‏–מוֹ‏ ‏–הֶם‏ | them |
| 3fs | ‏–ָהּ‏ ‏–ָהּ‏ ‏–נָה‏ | her | 3fp | ‏–נָה‏ ‏–ן‏ ‏–ָן‏ ‏–הֶנָה‏ ‏–הֶן‏ ‏–ָן‏ | them |
| 2ms | ‏–ךָ‏ ‏–כָה‏ | you | 2mp | ‏–כֶם‏ | you |
| 2fs | ‏–ך‏ | you | 2fp | ‏–כֶן‏ | you |
| 1cs | ‏–ִי‏ ‏–ִי‏ ‏–ֶנִי‏ ‏–ַי‏ | me | 1cp | ‏–נוּ‏ | us |

Vowels and consonants may arise between the suffix and the form to which it is attached. Common is the addition of a vowel to the final letter of the word and a yod before the suffix. Compare:

אָב     father

and

אָבִיו     his father.

Compare:

עַל     on

and

עֲלֵיהֶם     on them.

Some words such as the preposition ‏–כְּ‏ (like) add consonants in addition to vowels before the suffixed pronouns. For example:

כָּמוֹהוּ     like him
כָּמוֹנוּ     like us

But they may not do this for all pronouns.

כָּהֶם                              like them

## Demonstratives

In grammar, a demonstrative is a word that points to something. A demonstrative can be a **near** demonstrative, when it points to something close (this), or a **far** demonstrative, when it points to something far away (that).

| GN | Near | | Far | |
|---|---|---|---|---|
| ms | זֶה | this (*zeh*) | הוּא | that (*hoo*) |
| fs | זֹאת | this (*zot*) | הִיא | that (*hee*) |
| mp | אֵלֶּה [1] | these (*ay-leh*) | הֵם | those (*haym*) |
| fp | אֵלֶּה | these | הֵנָּה | those (*hey-neh*) |

Notice that the far demonstratives have the same form and usage as the third person independent pronouns. English makes a distinction between personal pronouns and far demonstratives that Hebrew does not. Pronouns have a pointing quality and in some instances this demonstrative meaning warrants the use of English demonstrative adjectives in translation.

Demonstratives may be predicate or attributive. A predicate is a verb and its modifiers. In English translation of a predicate demonstrative, a form of the verb "to be" is necessary. The **predicate** demonstrative agrees with the noun it modifies in gender and number. It never takes an article and usually comes before the noun.

זֹאת הָאָרֶץ              This is the land (Deut 34:4)

זֶה־הַשַּׁעַר לַיהוָה       This is the gate of the LORD
                        (Ps 118:20)

---

[1] Sometimes אֵל.

When demonstratives are **attributive,** they come after the word they modify and agree in gender, number, and definiteness. Study the way in which the two following examples are translated into English:

| | |
|---|---|
| הָאִשָּׁה הַזֹּאת | this woman |
| הַיּוֹם הַהוּא | that day |

**Vocabulary**

| | |
|---|---|
| אָב | father |
| אֵלֶּה | these |
| אֲנַחְנוּ | we |
| אָנֹכִי | I (long form) |
| אֲנִי | I |
| אַתָּה | you (ms) (אַתְּ "you" [fs]) |
| אַתֶּם | you (mp) (אַתֵּן "you" [fp]) |
| בֵּן | son |
| בָּנִים | sons (irregular plural) |
| בַּיִת | house |
| בָּתִּים | houses (irregular plural) |
| דָּבָר | word, thing, matter |
| הוּא | he, that |
| הִיא | she, that |
| הֵמָּה  הֵם | they (m) (הֵנָּה "they" [f]) |
| זֶה | this (m) |
| זֹאת | this (f) |
| יוֹם | day |
| יָמִים | days (irregular plural) |

**Exercises**

1. Read aloud and translate the following:

זֶה־הַיּוֹם (Ps 118:24)

(2 Chr 20:9) לִפְנֵי הַבַּיִת הַזֶּה וּלְפָנֶיךָ כִּי שִׁמְךָ² בַּבַּיִת הַזֶּה

(Judg 17:6) בַּיָּמִים הָהֵם אֵין³ מֶלֶךְ בְּיִשְׂרָאֵל

(2 Sam 12:7) אַתָּה הָאִישׁ . . . אָנֹכִי מְשַׁחְתִּיךָ⁴ לְמֶלֶךְ עַל־יִשְׂרָאֵל

(Zech 8:15) זַמַמְתִּי⁵ בַּיָּמִים הָאֵלֶּה
לְהֵיטִיב⁶ אֶת־יְרוּשָׁלָ͏ִם

---

² "your name"
³ "no"
⁴ "I anointed you"
⁵ "I have purposed"
⁶ "to do good"

2. Read aloud and translate the following. You will need to look up a couple of words in a lexicon.

(Deut 34:4) וַיֹּ֤אמֶר[7] יְהוָה֙ אֵלָ֔יו זֹ֚את הָאָ֔רֶץ
אֲשֶׁ֣ר נִשְׁבַּ֣עְתִּי[8] לְאַבְרָהָ֤ם לְיִצְחָ֣ק וּֽלְיַעֲקֹב֙

(Gen 6:4) הַנְּפִלִ֞ים הָי֣וּ[9] בָאָרֶץ֮ בַּיָּמִ֣ים הָהֵם֒

(Jer 30:4) וְאֵ֣לֶּה הַדְּבָרִ֗ים אֲשֶׁ֨ר דִּבֶּ֧ר[10] יְהוָ֛ה
אֶל־יִשְׂרָאֵ֖ל וְאֶל־יְהוּדָֽה

---

[7] "said"

[8] "I promised"

[9] "were"

[10] "spoke"

# Chapter 6

## Qal Imperfect, Part I

**Verbs** are words that express action, existence, or occurrence. In many languages, a verb expresses many things in a single sentence. A verb in a Hebrew sentence has more functions than in a sentence in English. Just one example is that the verb includes the subject. A separate subject is often unnecessary in Hebrew. The Hebrew verb also expresses ideas that are difficult to express in English. Because it is so important for the meaning of a Hebrew sentence, we begin early introducing the verb.

### Qal Stem

The Qal is the verbal stem (in Hebrew *binyan* "building") with the simplest construction and meaning. Qal means light. Other names for the Qal stem are G (German: *Grundstamm*, "Basic stem") or B (Basic stem). The modification of the Qal by the addition of consonants and vowels creates the various other stems with more complex meanings. This will become clearer when you study the other stems in future chapters.

### Imperfect Conjugation

For each stem, there are also two major conjugations in Hebrew. A **conjugation** is a list of the forms of a verb according to person (first, second, or third), gender (masculine, feminine, or common), and number (singular or plural). Person, gender, and number are abbreviated PGN in the table below and elsewhere in this book. Other names for a conjugation are an inflection and a paradigm.

The most common conjugation in Hebrew is the **imperfect**. Hebrew adds prefixes and some suffixes to the root to form the imperfect. A **prefix** is a consonant and a vowel (Cv) added to the beginning of a word. A **suffix** is a vowel (v) or a cluster of vowels and consonants (Cv or CvC) added to the end of the word. The root שָׁמַר (to keep, guard, or watch) will be used in this text to demonstrate the stems and conjugations for verbs. The imperfect conjugation is as follows:

| PGN | Form | PGN | Form |
|-----|------|-----|------|
| 3ms | יִשְׁמֹר | 3mp | יִשְׁמְרוּ |
| 3fs | תִּשְׁמֹר | 3fp | תִּשְׁמֹרְנָה |
| 2ms | תִּשְׁמֹר | 2mp | תִּשְׁמְרוּ |
| 2fs | תִּשְׁמְרִי | 2fp | תִּשְׁמֹרְנָה |
| 1cs | אֶשְׁמֹר | 1cp | נִשְׁמֹר |

When you are reading, these prefixes and suffixes are **indicators** that you have an imperfect. The indicators are those features that occur on most forms and are therefore the most reliable indicators that you are looking at a particular form. I would recommend that you memorize the basic conjugation in the above chart, noting especially the prefixes and suffixes. In future chapters, however, the indicators should free you from having to memorize all the consonants and vowels on conjugations.

The 3mp and 2mp forms frequently have a nun on the end:

תִּשְׁמְרוּן     יִשְׁמְרוּן

When a maqqeph (a dash) joins the imperfect to another word, the holem may reduce to a qamets hatuph.

יִשְׁמֹר becomes יִשְׁמָר־

Some verbs take an a-class or i-class vowel instead of a holem.

יִכְבַּד     he honored

These verbs are usually either from a root with a III-guttural
(ע ח ה א), because gutturals prefer a-class vowels underneath and
before them, or from roots that have a stative meaning. (For the
definition of stative, see Chapter 7).

### Use for Past Narration

The imperfect is most commonly used with a prefixed vav
(waw) to narrate past events.

וַיִּשְׁלַח

he sent (Gen 41:8)

The prefixed vav is commonly called a vav conversive or vav
consecutive. The reasons for these names will be explained in the
next chapter. This book will use the term **vav consecutive**.

Some scholars think of the imperfect with prefixed vav as a
conjugation separate from the imperfect because it has a different
usage and sometimes a different form than the imperfect without
the vav. They may therefore refer to this as the *vayyiqtol* or
*wayyiqtol*. The name comes from the 3ms form (וַיִּקְטֹל) of the root
קטל. This book uses the traditional term, imperfect, because it is
more widely used.

The pointing of the vav consecutive (-וַ) is different than the
vav conjunction (-וְ). The vav with patah and doubling in the prefix
(- וַי) is an **indicator** of the imperfect. When you see vav with
patah and doubling of an imperfect prefix, you know you have an
imperfect verb. Because ʾaleph does not accept doubling and
lengthens the preceding vowel instead, the form of the vav
consecutive with the 1cs imperfect is:

וָאֶשְׁמַע

I heard . . . (Isa 6:8)

Many versions translate the vav consecutive as "and." This
sounds childish to an English speaker, because there are so many
in past narration. Moreover, the pointing on the vav consecutive is
different than on the vav conjunction. Therefore, another word
such as "then" or, if it begins a sentence or clause, a punctuation

mark such as a period (.), semicolon (;), or a comma (,) at the end of the preceding clause, are often better translations of the vav.

## Word Order

The **subject** is the person, place, or thing that does the action of the verb. Independent personal pronouns are unnecessary and not usually used with finite verbs in Hebrew, as in the two examples in the previous section. When independent pronouns are used with finite verbs, it is usually for emphasis. When the subject is expressed as a separate word, it normally follows the verb rather than precedes it as in English.

וַיִּשְׁמַע אַבְרָם    Abram heard (Gen 14:14)

## Sign of the Definite Direct Object (אֵת or אֶת־)

The direct object is the object on which a subject and verb act directly. When the direct object of a verb is definite, Hebrew often (not always) marks it with the **sign of the definite direct object** (אֵת or אֶת־). This may help you distinguish the subject and object when they both follow a verb. When a maqqeph joins the sign of the definite direct object to a following word, the resulting shift in accent causes the tsere under the ʾaleph to change to a segol. The sign of the definite direct object is not translated in English.

וַיִּבְרָא אֱלֹהִים אֶת־הָאָדָם    God created the human
(Gen 1:27)

## Missing and Weak Letters

In order to recognize a word and look it up in BDB, you need to know the three-letter root. Sometimes, after removing the prefix and suffix of a verb, only two letters are left. One letter is missing. It requires some detective work to find the missing letter in order to identify the root and the meaning of the word. These missing letters are often called weak letters. The types of roots with weak letters are often named by the position the weak letter appears in the roots. When a verb is formed, for example, from a root with a third letter that is a ה, we call it a third heʾ verb (written III-heʾ or III-ה). Letters are often missing in the Qal imperfect when the verb root is I-nun, I-vav, II-vav or yod (also called "hollow"), or III-heʾ. Some people use the name יוֹנָה "Jonah" to help remember the missing letters.

The nun usually assimilates into the second letter of the root with **I-nun** verbs. For example, the Qal imperfect (3ms) of נתן is:

וַיִּתֵּן        he put (Gen 1:17)

The nun is assimilated into the tav. This happens in English when the prefix in- (not) is added to rational and becomes not *in*rational but *ir*rational. In Hebrew the doubling of the tav is expressed by a strong dagesh. When there are only two root letters, doubling is the **indicator** of a I-nun.

The frequently occurring verb לקח masquerades as a I-nun.

וַיִּקַּח יְהוָה אֱלֹהִים        The LORD God took (Gen 2:15)

With **III-heʾ** verbs, the heʾ may be present, replaced by a yod or absent.

וָאֶהְיֶה        I was (2 Sam 7:6)

וַיִּהְיוּ        they were (Gen 2:25)

וַתִּהְיֶינָה        they were (Num 36:11)

When the vav consecutive is added, the stress moves toward the vav and the final heʾ is lost.

וַיְהִי        he was (Gen 21:20)

Notice that there is no doubling in the first letter. A strong dagesh disappears when some consonants have a sheva under them.

I-vav verbs are verbs that in the history of the language used to begin with a vav. Most forms came to look like I-yod verbs. I-vav verbs lose the first root letter. Thus the imperfect of יָשַׁב is:

וַיֵּשֶׁב        he lived (Gen 4:16)         —

The tsere under the yod is the **indicator** of a I-vav imperfect.

The verb הָלַךְ masquerades as a I-vav in the imperfect.

וַיֵּלֶךְ              he went (Gen 12:4)

This verb occurs frequently so remember it whenever you see ־לֶךְ.

Most **I-yod** verbs retain the yod.

וַיִּיטַב           its was good (Gen 41:37)

Though יָכֹל (to be able) has תּוּכַל, יוּכַל, etc.

**II-vav** and **II-yod** verbs are also called **hollow** verbs, because they lose the vav or yod in some forms. Without the vav consecutive, the middle root letter is visible in most forms of the imperfect of the II-vav or II-yod (hollow) verbs:

יָקוּם        יָשִׂים        יָבוֹא

But hollow verbs occur more often after the vav consecutive and then the middle letter is missing:

וַיָּקֻם   he arose    וַיָּשֶׂם   he put    וַיָּבֹא   he came

When there is a qamets under the prefix of the imperfect and two root letters, this is the **indicator** that the middle root letter is ו or י.

**I-guttural** verbs have different vowels because they prefer a-class[1] vowels and composite shevas. The guttural is not a missing letter and the prefixes, suffixes and, when it is present, the vav consecutive with doubling identify the imperfect.

וַיַּעַשׂ יְהוָה אֱלֹהִים...   The LORD God made... (Gen 3:21)

Some roots are **doubly weak**. The previous example—from עשׂה—is doubly weak. It is both a I-guttural and a III-heʾ.

The vowel pointing on frequently occurring I-ʾaleph imperfects is peculiar:

וַיֹּאמֶר   he said (Gen 1:3, etc.)

וַתֹּאכַל   she ate (Gen 3:6)

When the 1cs prefix is added, you would expect to see two ʾalephs, but one of the ʾalephs is lost:

וָאֹמַר   I said (Gen 20:13)

**Charting Verbs**

A convenient way of presenting the information about a verb form is to chart it. For example, וַיֹּאמֶר would be charted as:

| Root | Stem | Conjugation | PGN | Special Features |
|------|------|-------------|-----|------------------|
| אמר | Qal | Imperfect | 3ms | vav consecutive |

**Interrogative Particle (–הֲ)**

Be careful not to confuse the interrogative particle (–הֲ) with the definite article. Note the different vowel pointing. Hebrew uses the interrogative particle prefixed to a word at the beginning of a question.

הֲלֹא אָנֹכִי יְהוָה   Am I not the LORD? (Exod 4:11)

---

[1] See the discussion of classes of vowels and chart of vowels in Chapter 2.

Some questions are marked by other question words. And some
questions are not marked—the context tells us they are questions.

**Vocabulary**

You may be familiar with many of the verbs in this
vocabulary, because you looked up their root meaning in Chapter
1. The vowel points on the root are from the 3ms form of the
perfect conjugation that you will learn in Chapter 10. Lexicons
normally use it because it has no consonants added to the root.

| | |
|---|---|
| אָכַל | eat, devour |
| אָמַר | say |
| אֵת or אֶת־ | (The sign of the definite direct object. Not translated.) |
| בּוֹא | come in, enter, come, go, go in |
| הֲ־ | (prefixed, interrogative particle) |
| הָיָה | be, become, happen |
| הָלַךְ | go, walk |
| יָדַע | know |
| יָצָא | go out, come out |
| יָשַׁב | sit, remain, dwell, inhabit |
| לָקַח | take |
| מוּת | die |
| נָתַן | give |
| עָשָׂה | do, make |
| רָאָה | see |
| שׁוּב | turn, return |
| שָׁמַע | hear, obey |

## Exercises

1. Read aloud and translate the following. Make several copies of the verb chart worksheets from Appendix A. In this and all future exercises, chart the verbs.

(Ezek 8:10) וָאָבוֹא וָאֶרְאֶה

(Gen 2:15) וַיִּקַּח יְהוָה אֱלֹהִים אֶת־הָאָדָם

(Gen 13:9) הֲלֹא כָל־הָאָרֶץ לְפָנֶיךָ

(Gen 3:13) וַיֹּאמֶר יְהוָה אֱלֹהִים לָאִשָּׁה . . . וַתֹּאמֶר הָאִשָּׁה . . .

(1 Kgs 1:15) וַתָּבֹא בַת־שֶׁבַע² אֶל־הַמֶּלֶךְ

(Gen 26:32) וַיְהִי בַּיּוֹם הַהוּא וַיָּבֹאוּ

(Exod 4:18) וַיֵּלֶךְ מֹשֶׁה וַיָּשָׁב אֶל־יֶתֶר³

---

² "Bathsheba"
³ "Jethro"

2. Read aloud and translate the following and chart the verbs. You will need to use a lexicon to translate a few of the words.

(Gen 3:21) וַיַּעַשׂ יְהוָה אֱלֹהִים לְאָדָם וּלְאִשְׁתּוֹ[4] כָּתְנוֹת

(Gen 3:6) וַתֹּאכַל וַתִּתֵּן גַּם־לְאִישָׁהּ עִמָּהּ וַיֹּאכַל

(Judg 1:4) וַיַּעַל יְהוּדָה וַיִּתֵּן יְהוָה אֶת־הַכְּנַעֲנִי וְהַפְּרִזִּי בְּיָדָם[5]

*Yahweh gave Judah he went up*
*in*
*a*

_____

[4] "and for his wife"

[5] To recognize this word, you may need to identify the prefix and suffix and remove them.

## Chapter 7
## Qal Imperfect, Part II

**Meaning of the Qal**

The Qal stem may have either a dynamic or a stative meaning. A **stative verb** is a verb that describes a state or circumstance, one that is either external and physical, or internal and psychological (or perceptual).

> She was old (*external stative*).

> He was afraid (*internal stative*).

English tends to express them with adjectives and a form of the verb "to be." They also tend to be **intransitive**. An intransitive verb is one whose action does *not* pass over from the subject to an object.

Qal verbs that have a stative meaning tend to have a tsere or a pataḥ under the second root letter instead of a ḥolem. (See the chart in the previous chapter.)

וַיִּזְקַן יְהוֹיָדָע    Jehoida was old (2 Chr 24:15)

**Dynamic[1] verbs** describe a state of activity. The subject puts energy into the action of the verb and the activity may have different phases. Dynamic verbs tend to be **transitive**. Transitive verbs transfer the effects of the verb from a subject to an object.

וַיֹּאכְלוּ עִמּוֹ לֶחֶם    They ate bread with him
(Job 42:11)

---

[1] Other names for dynamic verbs are: fientive (Waltke & O'Connor), voluntaria, *freiwillig* (Haupt) and active (Brockelmann).

Some verbs in Hebrew have both dynamic and stative forms and meanings. Some verbs, such as those expressing emotion or a mental state, have meanings that are partially stative and partially dynamic.

"I was afraid" (ירא Gen 3:10): *stative*

"Do not fear the people of the land" (ירא Num 14:9):
*partially stative, partially dynamic*

## Meaning of the Imperfect

In the last chapter, we saw that the imperfect was often used with a prefixed vav to narrate the past. Scholars debate the meaning of the imperfect. Older Jewish grammarians and some modern scholars understand the imperfect as a present and future tense. In this understanding, the prefixed vav is called a **vav conversive** because it is thought of as converting the imperfect from a present-future to a past tense.

This understanding seems inadequate for at least two reasons. First, it seems unlikely that a tense could be converted in this way. Second, a number of the ways the imperfect is used do not fit into a simple tense system.

Therefore, beginning in the nineteenth-century the view was advanced and eventually came to predominate among scholars that the Hebrew conjugations represented not tense but aspect. In grammar, **aspect** refers to the duration and completion of an action. The imperfect, they suggested, described *an incomplete action*. The context determined whether the action occurred in the past, present or future. The name imperfect comes from this understanding of the conjugation.

According to this theory, the use of the imperfect to narrate the past with a prefixed vav is not because the imperfect is converted, but because it is in a narrative sequence. The imperfect with a prefixed vav continued a narrative sequence that began with a perfect (perfect . . . vav+imperfect . . . vav+imperfect . . .). Since many sequences do not actually begin with a perfect, the perfect verb could be implied. In this understanding, the prefixed vav was called a **vav consecutive** because the vav indicates that the imperfect is consecutive to or depends on the preceding perfect.

Some modern scholars also make use of comparative material from other Semitic languages to explain the historical development of the imperfect. Akkadian and Arabic have a longer, prefix conjugation with a range of meanings similar to the Hebrew imperfect and a shorter, prefix conjugation with a past tense or preterite meaning. With some weak verbs and the Hiphil stem (see Chapter 17), Hebrew uses a shorter form of the imperfect when it is prefixed by a vav in a narrative sequence and a longer form when the imperfect stands alone. Many scholars, therefore, think that Hebrew originally had two prefix conjugations—a longer one (*yaqtulu*) and a shorter one (*yaqtul*). When the language lost its final short vowels around 1100 B.C.E., the two conjugations became almost identical. The earlier conjugation and its preterite meaning are present in Biblical Hebrew as the imperfect with prefixed vav in narrative sequences, and rarely without prefixed vav.

Many Hebrew scholars today hold some combination of the aspect and historical-comparative theories. Hebrew conjugations may communicate a complex interaction of tense, aspect, and other factors such as mood. As it refers to verbs, **mood** has to do with marking whether the speaker thinks that a state or an action is real (factual) or unreal (commands, wishes, possibilities, and the like). English expresses unreal moods by adding words like should and might.

Waltke and O'Connor, in *Biblical Hebrew Syntax*, are typical of contemporary scholars who attempt to synthesize various theories. They suggest the imperfect represents an *incomplete, progressive, repeated, or dependent situation.*

Progressive or repeated situations may be habitual, customary, or proverbial and may best be translated into English with the present tense or phrases such as "used to."

יֹאמְרוּ הַמֹּשְׁלִים    The poets *used to* say (Num 21:27)

Dependent uses often require a modal translation in English (would, should, could, might).

מִי יְהוָה אֲשֶׁר      Who is the LORD that

אֶשְׁמַע בְּקֹלוֹ      I *should* listen to his voice (Exod 5:2)

Certain dependent situations may require "let" or "may" in English.

וְיֵשְׁבוּ בָאָרֶץ      *Let* them live in the land (Gen 34:21)

    The form and meaning of these modal and dependent uses of the imperfect overlap with the form and meaning of the jussive and cohortative, which will be discussed in Chapters 22 and 23.

    The exercises in this and subsequent chapters include a variety of uses of the imperfect so that you will avoid being lulled into a false sense that the imperfect is an English tense and will become sensitive to a range of uses. Questions remain and the above theories need to be tested against the evidence. Each of us may want to test them ourselves by asking what the imperfect means each time we translate it. On the one hand, with a prefixed vav, the imperfect may be translated as a simple past. Even with a prefixed vav, however, be alert that in a few cases the imperfect may refer to an incomplete, progressive, repeated, or dependent situation. On the other hand, when the imperfect stands alone, without a prefixed vav, it probably communicates an incomplete, progressive, repeated, or dependent situation and the tense will need to be determined by the context. Without a prefixed vav, however, be alert that occasionally it may be a remnant of the older, shorter, prefix conjugation and communicate a past tense or preterite meaning.

**Negation**

    The imperfect is negated with לֹא.

לֹא אֹכַל      I will not eat (Gen 24:33)

The second person imperfect with לֹא may express a commandment, legislation, or prohibition ("Do not [ever] . . ." or "You shall not . . .").

לֹא תֹאכַל מִמֶּנּוּ          you shall not eat from it (Gen 3:17)

The second person jussive, which will be discussed in more detail in Chapters 22 and 23, often has the same form as the imperfect. The jussive with אַל expresses urgency ("Stop . . ." or "Don't . . .").

אַל־תִּירָא אַבְרָם          Do not be afraid, Abram
(Gen 15:1)

## The Preposition מִן

The preposition מִן (from, than) has both independent and prefixed forms. The **independent** form is linked to a following word with a maqqeph.

מִן־הָעִיר          from the city

With the **prefixed** form, the nun assimilates into the first letter of the word. Thus the form is –מִ with a dagesh in the first letter.

מִמֶּלֶךְ          from a king

Since the gutturals (ע ח ה א) and resh (ר) do not take doubling, the preposition is – מֵ or – מֶ without a dagesh in the first letter.

מֵעִיר          from a city
מִחוּץ          from outside

Unlike other prefixed prepositions, the definite article does not disappear.

מֵהָעִיר          from the city

The prefixed form is doubled before some suffixed pronouns.

מִמְּךָ          from you

מִמֶּ֫נִּי          from me

Note that the forms with the 3ms suffix and 1cp suffix are identical.

מִמֶּ֫נּוּ          from him

מִמֶּ֫נּוּ          from us

This is because the 3ms pronoun suffix has assimilated into the nun making it look like the 1cp suffix:

מִן + הוּ became מִמֶּנְהוּ* became מִמֶּ֫נּוּ

## Suffixed Pronouns

Both the Qal imperfect and the sign of the definite direct object can take the suffixed pronouns introduced in Chapter 5.

וַיֹּאכְל֫וּהָ          they ate it

The imperfect may undergo vowel changes with the addition of the suffix. They do not change the indicators you have learned so they should not affect your ability to recognize and chart the verbs. However, you may want to be aware of the ways in which the vowels can change.

When the vowel between the second and third root letter is a holem (יִשְׁמֹר) or a tsere (יִתֵּן), it may be reduced to a sheva:

יִשְׁמְרֵ֫נִי          he was watching over me
                  (Job 29:2)

יִתְּנֵ֫נִי          [if] it gives me (Isa 27:4)

Before 2ms and 2mp suffixes, however, the holem may be shortened to qamets hatuph, and the tsere to segol.

| | |
|---|---|
| יִשְׁאָלְךָ | he asks you (Exod 13:14) |
| יִתֶּנְךָ | he will give you (Deut 28:25) |

When the vowel between the second and third root letters is a patah, however, it lengthens to a qamets.

| | |
|---|---|
| וַיִּקָּחֶהָ | he took it (Gen 33:11) |

Note that when the form of the imperfect ends in a consonant, a helping vowel, either tsere or segol may be added. In the above example, a segol has been added.

A greater challenge for recognizing the suffixed pronouns is that nuns may also be added.

| | |
|---|---|
| אֲשִׂימֶנּוּ | I will make him (Gen 21:13) |

The sign of the definite direct object has the form –אֹת, –אוֹת or –אֶת before suffixed pronouns.

| | |
|---|---|
| וַיִּתֵּן אֹתָם אֱלֹהִים | God set them (Gen 1:17) |
| יִפְקֹד אֱלֹהִים אֶתְכֶם | God will visit you (Exod 13:19) |
| וַיַּעַשׂ אוֹתוֹ גִדְעוֹן | Gideon made it (Jdg 8:27) |

The suffixed pronouns on either the imperfect or the sign of the definite direct object function as objects of the verb. There is apparently no difference in meaning. Compare the previous example to this one.

| | |
|---|---|
| וַיַּעֲשֵׂהוּ | He made it (Exod 32:4) |

## Vocabulary

| | |
|---|---|
| אַיִן (אֵין) | there is, there are not |
| אַל | no, not |
| אִם | if, then |
| אֲשֶׁר | that, which, who |
| גַּם | also, indeed |
| הִנֵּה | behold! lo! look! |
| יָד | hand |
| כֹּהֵן | priest |
| לֹא | no, not |
| מִן | from, out of, part of, because of; than |
| עַד | to, unto, as far as (of space); until, while (of time) |
| עִיר | city |
| עָרִים | cities (irregular plural) |
| עַם | people |
| פָּנִים | face (You have already had this word in the vocabulary for Chapter 3 as part of the preposition, לִפְנֵי "before." It does not occur in the singular—פנה.) |

*[handwritten margin note: ר יֵשׁ = there is / are]*

## Exercises

1. Read aloud and translate the following and chart the verbs:

(Gen 1:26) וַיֹּאמֶר אֱלֹהִים נַעֲשֶׂה אָדָם בְּצַלְמֵנוּ[2]

*[handwritten: in our image Adam (man) we gave God he said]*

(Gen 3:6) וַתִּקַּח מִפִּרְיוֹ[3] וַתֹּאכַל וַתִּתֵּן גַּם־לְאִישָׁהּ עִמָּהּ וַיֹּאכַל

*[handwritten: and he ate with her husband also she gave and she ate ✓ she took]*

---

[2] You will need to look up this word in a lexicon. Beware that there is a prefix and a suffix you will need to remove before you can look up the word.

[3] "some of its fruit"

(Isa 33: 20) עֵינֶיךָ תִרְאֶינָה⁴ יְרוּשָׁלַ͏ִם

(Gen 3:3) לֹא תֹאכְלוּ מִמֶּנּוּ וְלֹא תִגְּעוּ⁵ בּוֹ
פֶּן־תְּמֻתוּן⁶

(Exod 24:7) וַיֹּאמְרוּ כֹּל אֲשֶׁר־דִּבֶּר⁷ יְהוָה נַעֲשֶׂה וְנִשְׁמָע

(Gen 17:6) וּמְלָכִים מִמְּךָ יֵצֵאוּ

2. Read aloud and translate the following. You will need to use a lexicon to translate some of the words. Chart the verbs.

(Gen 2:8) וַיָּשֶׂם שָׁם אֶת־הָאָדָם

(Jer 22:12) וְאֶת־הָאָרֶץ הַזֹּאת לֹא־יִרְאֶה עוֹד

(Exod 3:11) וַיֹּאמֶר מֹשֶׁה אֶל־הָאֱלֹהִים מִי אָנֹכִי כִּי אֵלֵךְ
אֶל־פַּרְעֹה

(Exod 32:4) וַיִּקַּח מִיָּדָם וַיָּצַר⁸ אֹתוֹ בַּחֶרֶט
וַיַּעֲשֵׂהוּ עֵגֶל מַסֵּכָה⁹ וַיֹּאמְרוּ אֵלֶּה אֱלֹהֶיךָ יִשְׂרָאֵל

---

⁴ "your eyes"

⁵ Try to figure out the root. One letter is missing. Then look up the meaning in a lexicon.

⁶ Look up פֶּן in a lexicon. תְּמֻתוּן is an exception to the indicator for the imperfect of hollow verbs. The expected qamets under the prefix sometimes reduces to a sheva when a suffix is added. In this case, the suffix is the long form of the imperfect suffix with a nun added. The qamets sometimes reduces with the 2fp or 3fp suffix of the imperfect, although not always.

⁷ "has spoken" (This is a verb form that you have not yet had.)

⁸ One letter is missing, but if you use the indicators, you should be able to find this verb in a lexicon.

⁹ "molten metal" or "image"

(Lev 10:2) וַתֵּצֵא אֵשׁ מִלִּפְנֵי יְהוָה וַתֹּאכַל אוֹתָם
וַיָּמֻתוּ לִפְנֵי יְהוָה׃

## Chapter 8

## Opening the Hebrew Bible

The best Hebrew Bible for most purposes is *Biblia Hebraica Stuttgartensia*, abbreviated *BHS* in biblical studies. When you open this Bible, you will see many marks on the letters, and notes in the margins. Some of the footnotes are from the contemporary scholars who edited *BHS*, but the majority of marks and notes are from Jewish scholars, called **Masoretes**, who worked from the third to the eleventh centuries C.E. There were Western Masoretes centered in Tiberias and Eastern Masoretes centered in Babylonia. The Masoretes developed the vowel points and accents to indicate the traditional pronunciation.

The text of the Hebrew Bible is called the Masoretic Text (MT) because it goes back to a family of texts produced by the Masoretes.

The Western Masoretes eventually became dominant. The text of *BHS* is a copy of the **Leningrad Codex** copied in 1008 C.E. It is one of the best representatives of the Western, Tiberian tradition. A **codex** is an ancient book. This one was in the Russian Public Library in Leningrad (now St. Petersburg).

### Divisions

There are markers of various divisions in the Hebrew Bible that probably go back before the time of the Masoretes.

**Soph Pa-suq**. This looks like a large colon made of diamond shapes ( : ) and indicates the end of a verse. Verses often do not correspond to English sentences.

**Open and Closed Paragraphs**. Originally, an open paragraph was a paragraph that began on a new line after an incomplete or empty line. A closed paragraph began on the same line after a space. By the time of the Leningrad Codex, the Masoretes no longer maintained this distinction. But a פ for **open** and ס for **closed** appears in spaces between verses. In *BHS*, the editors have laid out the paragraphs on the pages in ways that represent their interpretive understanding of the divisions in the text. Their paragraph divisions may or may not agree with the Masoretes.

**Seder and Parashah.** These two symbols appear on the inside margin and are the divisions between liturgical readings or lessons. The **seder** (ס֘) is from the Palestinian tradition and divides the Pentateuch, the first five books of the Bible, into three years of weekly readings. The **parashah** (פרש) is from the Babylonian tradition and divides the Pentateuch into readings for one year. You can see open and closed paragraph markers and a seder on page five of *BHS*.

## Accents

The Masoretic accents serve three functions. First, they show the accented or stressed syllable in a word. Second, they indicate the grouping of words. Third, they are musical. Although their primary function is the third, the first two are the main concern for reading and interpretation.

For reading, it is only necessary to note their location and stress the appropriate vowel in pronunciation. Most accents appear above or below the stressed vowel. For interpretation, the meaning of the accents and what the Masoretes are saying about how to join the words together may be significant. For this reason a list follows of the most frequently occurring and important accents and their meanings.

There are two different systems of accents in the Hebrew Bible—the **accents of the twenty-one books** and the **accents of the three books**. The three books are Psalms, Job, and Proverbs. Their system of accents is slightly different from the rest of the Hebrew Bible, the twenty-one books.

The accents are either **conjunctive** (joining) or **disjunctive** (dividing). The disjunctive accents occur on the last word of a group of related words. For the beginning student it is enough to learn to recognize some of the disjunctive and conjunctive accents. The placement of the accents is illustrated on the letter מ in the following lists.

## A Few Major Disjunctive Accents

| | | |
|---|---|---|
| מֽ | silluq | On the stressed syllable immediately preceding soph pasuq ( ׃ ). |
| מֿ | ʿoleh veyored | Note that this accent has two parts, one on the syllable before the stressed syllable. It divides verses in two in the three books but is not used in the twenty-one books. |
| מֿ | ʾatnaḥ | Divides verses in two in the twenty-one books. In a short verse tiphḥah or zaqeph may play this role. In the three books it divides the second half of the verse or may divide short verses in two. |
| מֿ | reviaʿ | In the three books it may divide in half a short verse without an ʾatnaḥ. It may also divide the first half of a verse with ʾatnaḥ or be the accent immediately before ʿoleh veyored. In the twenty-one books it is a less important accent. |
| מֿ | zaqeph qaton | In the twenty-one books it divides the verse into quarters. Or, in other words, it is the next major division before or after ʾatnaḥ. Not used in the three books. |
| מֿ | zaqeph gadol | While the musical value is different than the previous accent, the use for dividing the verse is the same. |

| | | |
|---|---|---|
| מֵ | tiphḥah | In the twenty-one books, it takes over the function of zaqeph in dividing the verse into quarters when the division comes on the word before ʾatnaḥ or silluq. Looks the same as a conjunctive accent in both the twenty-one and the three books. |
| מֵ | segolta | May replace zaqeph in first half of a verse. Located on the syllable after the stressed syllable (postpositive). |
| מֵ | tsinnor | In the three books the next major disjunctive accent after ʿoleh veyored. Thus, it divides a verse into quarters. Postpositive. In the twenty-one books the disjunctive accent zarqaʾ has the same appearance. |

## A Few Major Conjunctive Accents

| | | |
|---|---|---|
| מֵ | munaḥ | |
| מֵ | mehuppach | Not a conjunctive accent in the three books. |
| מֵ | merekaʾ | |
| מֵ | dargaʾ | Only in the twenty-one books. |
| מֵ | ʾazlaʾ | |
| מֵ | ʿilluy | Only in the three books. |

These are only a few important accents. For in-depth analysis of the accents consult Yeivin, §176–374.

The accents represent the Masoretic understanding of which words belonged together and thus the interpretation of a verse. Commentators sometimes disagree. When you are doing a close reading of a passage, you may want to consider the possibility that different arrangements might make better sense. For example, look at the last verse of the exercises in the previous chapter (Exod 32:4) and you will see the way accents divide the verse into sense units. You can also practice reading the verse using the accents.

## Pause

When a word occurs with a major disjunctive accent such as silluq or ʾatnaḥ, it is **in pause**, because it comes at a break or pause in the verse. This pause often causes vowel changes, usually lengthening. Some typical examples follow:

| Normal | In Pause | Translation |
|--------|----------|-------------|
| דֶּרֶךְ | דָּרֶךְ | road |
| בַּיִת | בָּיִת | house |

## Maqqeph

The maqqeph is a horizontal line that indicates a close connection between two words.

לֹא־מָצָא  he did not find

This connection may result in the first word losing its accent. The loss of the accent often causes a change in the vowel pointing and pronunciation of the first word.

| Without Maqqeph | With Maqqeph | Translation |
|-----------------|--------------|-------------|
| אֵת יְהוָה | אֶת־יְהוָה | The LORD |
| כֹּל בָּשָׂר | כָּל־בָּשָׂר | all flesh |

## Marginal Notes

The notes printed beside the text in *BHS* are the **Masora**. The final Masora is at the end of the Bible. The marginal Masora is in the four margins of a *BHS* page.

The **Masora parva** (Mp) is the notes in the side margins. They contain information that assisted the Masoretes in preserving the text unchanged when making copies. A small circle over a word in the text indicates there is a note in the margin. Small circles between words indicate a note in the margin about the whole phrase. Two circles between two words indicate there are two notes, one referring to the whole phrase, and one referring to part of the phrase. The notes are mostly abbreviations of Aramaic. Dots over the letters indicate they are either abbreviations or numbers. The Latin translations of the words and abbreviations in the margins are on pages L–LV in *BHS*. The English translations are in Scott, *A Simplified Guide to BHS*. Most of the information in the Mp seems trivial to modern readers. Subsequent sections of this chapter discuss some of the more significant notes.

The **Masora magna** (Mm) is the notes at the bottom of the page in *BHS* between the end of the Hebrew text and the text-critical notes. The superscript numbers in the Mp direct you to the appropriate note in the Mm. When the Mp gives the number of occurrences of a word, the Mm gives a list of these occurrences. In early manuscripts, the lists were printed in the upper and lower margins. *BHS* collected these in a separate, multi-volume work and put notes at the bottom of the page indicating the relevant list in this separate work. Unfortunately, only the first volume of the three volumes was ever published.

### "It is Written" and "It is Read"

Where the Masoretes felt the form preserved in the text was unsatisfactory, they placed under the word in the text the vowel points for a more satisfactory reading. The consonants for these vowels were placed in the margin. These may indicate that the Masoretes had other manuscripts whose reading they considered preferable. The form in the consonantal text is called the **Kethiv,** "it is written." The form preferred by the Masoretes is in the margin and is called the **Qere,** "it is read." The note is distinctive because it appears over top of a qoph with a dot (קׄ). For examples, see pages 12 and 13 of *BHS*.

There are some words that are to be read differently throughout the Hebrew Bible so there is no note in the margin. These are called **perpetual Qere**. In your vocabulary and exercises, you have already seen two of the most common examples. The name for God that regularly appears with the vowel points for the Hebrew word for lord is one example. Another perpetual Qere that occurs frequently in the Pentateuch is הּוא. The consonantal text has הוא but הִיא would be a preferable reading.

Although the exercises continue to print selections from *BHS*, from this point forward it would be good to look up the verses in *BHS* and practice using what you have learned in this chapter.

**Exercises**

1. Translate the following verse and note the perpetual Qere. You will need to look up עֵץ in a lexicon.

וַיֹּאמֶר הָאָדָם הָאִשָּׁה אֲשֶׁר נָתַתָּה¹ עִמָּדִי (Gen 3:12)
הוּא נָתְנָה²־לִי מִן־הָעֵץ וָאֹכֵל:

2. In the following passage, each word has two accents. There were two different traditions about how to divide the commandments. The Masoretes included the accents from both traditions. Christian denominations also differ on how they count the Ten Commandments. Use a lexicon to translate this passage. Look up the names and uses of the accents that are in this chapter's tables of conjunctive and disjunctive accents. What is the difference in interpretation represented by the two sets of accents?

לֹא יִהְיֶה־לְךָ אֱלֹהִים אֲחֵרִים עַל־פָּנָיַ: (Deut 5:7–8)
לֹא־תַעֲשֶׂה־לְךָ פֶסֶל ׀

¹ "you put"
² "she gave"

# Chapter 9

## Nouns in Construct

Hebrew does not have a word that corresponds to the English word "of" and, by the biblical period, it no longer had a genitive case ending like Greek. Hebrew uses the construct state to express such relationships between nouns.

### The Construct State

אֶרֶץ לֶחֶם      a land *of* bread (2 Kgs 18:32)

בֵּית דָּוִד      the house *of* David (1 Sam 19:11)

in construct form [ בַּיִת ]

The word that is in the last position—"bread" and "David" in the above examples—is called the **absolute**. It is the absolute because the word in this position does not change its form. It has the dictionary or absolute form. The word (or words) before the last position—"land" and "house" in the above examples—is called the **construct**. The construct may change its form, as is the case with "house" in the second example. Lexicons usually list construct forms.

More than one noun may be in construct.

מִשְׁכַּן בֵּית הָאֱלֹהִים      tabernacle of the house of God
(1 Chr 6:33)

### Definiteness and Indefiniteness

The absolute determines the definiteness or indefiniteness of the whole phrase. The phrase is **indefinite** if the absolute is indefinite as in the first example above. "A" is the article in English that indicates a noun is indefinite.

The whole phrase is **definite** if the absolute is definite. (You may want to review the definition of the definite article on page 27.) The absolute is definite if it has a definite article (the first example below), is a name (the second example), or is joined to a pronoun such as "our" or "his" (the third example).

עֶבֶד הָאֱלֹהִים    *the* servant of *the* God (1 Chr 6:34 ET 49)

מֶלֶךְ יִשְׂרָאֵל    *the* king of Israel (1 Sam 24:15 ET 14 )

יַד־אָבִיו    *the* hand of *his* father (Gen 48:17)

The construct cannot be definite if the absolute is indefinite or vice versa. Such a relationship between two nouns would not be expressed with the construct state in Hebrew but with the preposition lamed.

מִזְמוֹר לְדָוִד      *a* psalm *of* David (Ps 3:1)

This then is another way of saying "of" when the absolute and construct are not either both definite or both indefinite.

Prefixes and the conjunction –וְ may be prefixed to the construct:

בְּאֶרֶץ־כְּנַעַן    in the land of Canaan (Gen 13:12)

וְאֶרֶץ כְּנַעַן    and the land of Canaan (Gen 47:13)

**Indicators of the Construct**

Sometimes only context indicates that a word is in construct. Often, however, the Masoretes indicate that a word is in construct in one or more ways.

A **maqqeph**, the horizontal line in some of the above examples, may join the construct to the following word or words.

The word may have a special construct ending if it is **feminine singular** or **masculine plural**.

מַלְכֵי מִדְיָן    the kings of Midian (Num 31:8)

Study the endings in the following table carefully:

| GN | Absolute | | Construct | |
|---|---|---|---|---|
| ms | מֶ֫לֶךְ | king | מֶ֫לֶךְ | king of |
| fs | מַלְכָּה | queen | מַלְכַּת | queen of |
| mp | מְלָכִים | kings | מַלְכֵי | kings of |
| fp | מְלָכוֹת | queens | מַלְכוֹת | queens of |

For many common nouns, the vowels in the construct differ from the vowels in the absolute form of the noun. בֵּית, for example, is the construct of בַּ֫יִת. The root is usually still recognizable.

The word in construct may have a conjunctive Masoretic accent. The conjunctive accents indicate a close relationship with the following word. They may indicate a construct or some other joining of words.

## The Meaning of the Construct

The meaning of the construct is ambiguous in Hebrew. English phrases with "of" are similarly ambiguous. An example is the phrase "love of God." This may mean "someone's love of God," or "God's love for someone," or "divine love." The word God in the absolute state may be a subject, an object, or an adjective. The interpreter of Biblical Hebrew who is aware of these possible meanings can look for indications in the context of the specific meaning or meanings.

English uses "of" constructions less often than Hebrew uses the construct, so translating every construct relationship with "of" would sound peculiar to an English speaker. It may be helpful to note that, in translating into English, reading the words in reverse order to the Hebrew often produces a translation that sounds more English—"God's house" rather than "the house of God."

## Suffixed Pronouns

Nouns can take suffixed pronouns. They are the ones you have already learned with prepositions. Suffixed pronouns usually express possession in Hebrew: "my house." The suffixes are usually attached to the construct form of the noun.

יְדֵיכֶם          your hands

In addition, the noun may add a helping vowel before the suffixed pronoun.

בְּנוֹתֶיהָ          her daughters

## Finding Nouns in BDB

In order to recognize a word and look it up in BDB, you need to know the three-letter root. To do this, remove markers for gender and number, prepositions, and suffixed pronouns. You may still have more than three letters, because vowel letters, prefixes, or suffixes have been added to create the noun.

Often nouns are created by adding vowels to the root. Sometimes the vowel letters ו and י are inserted.

| Noun | | Root |
|---|---|---|
| מֶלֶךְ | king | מלך |
| נָבִיא | prophet | נבא |
| אוֹיֵב | enemy | איב |

Frequently מ, sometimes ת, and rarely א, ה, and י are prefixed to roots to form nouns.

| Noun | | Root |
|---|---|---|
| מִזְבֵּחַ | altar | זבח |
| תּוֹרָה | law | ירה |
| אֶצְבַּע | finger | צבע |

These may be tricky for beginners because the prefixes are similar to common verb prefixes.

In addition, nouns may add endings to a root.

| Noun | | Root |
|---|---|---|
| מִצְרִי | Egyptian | מִצֹר |
| זִכָּרוֹן | memorial | זכר |
| מַלְכוּת | reign | מלך |

The observant reader may notice that certain vowel patterns and endings are characteristic of certain types of nouns. The ending –ִי in the first example is used for the name of a people or land similar to "-ian" or "-ite" in English. The ending –וֹת in the second example is used to form abstract nouns. The ending –וֹן (or –ֹן) is used for abstract nouns, as in the third example, and for diminutive nouns, שִׁמְשׁוֹן "Samson" = "Little Sun," and adjectives, רִאשׁוֹן "first."

Several suffixes may originally have come from feminine endings but came to be used for abstract nouns. These include –וֹת, –ִית and rarely –וֹת.

| Noun | | Root |
|---|---|---|
| מַלְכוּת | reign | מלך |
| רֵאשִׁית | beginning | ראש |

There are, of course, other ways letters may be added to form nouns, but these are the most common.

The opposite problem in finding a root is having too few letters. After you have removed all the vowels, markers, prefixes, and suffixes from a noun, you may be left with only two letters. BDB may list these in alphabetical order when a three-letter root is uncertain or unknown in Hebrew. Some examples are in the following table.

| Noun | | Root |
|---|---|---|
| בֵּן | son | בן |
| יָד | hand | יד |

In other cases, the noun may have a missing letter. These are often the same letters that are missing in verbs. For example, with a **III-he**ʾ noun the heʾ may be present, replaced by a yod or absent:

| Noun | | Root |
|---|---|---|
| שָׁנָה | year | שנה |
| אָב | father | אבה |
| גּוֹי | people | גוה |

Many commonly occurring two-letter nouns are listed by BDB under **geminate** roots. The name geminate is related to the word Gemini, "twins." Geminate roots have the same last two root letters. While nouns from these roots are common, verbs are rare and therefore are not treated until Chapter 34.

| Noun | | Root |
|---|---|---|
| לֵב | heart | לבב |
| הַר | hill | הרר |
| רַע | evil | רעע |

In some cases, vowel letters may represent root letters and therefore are not removed to find the root. Nouns from **hollow** roots are frequent. In these nouns, the vowel letter is not removed to find the root.

| Noun | | Root |
|---|---|---|
| טוֹב | good | טוב |
| קוֹל | voice | קול |

A few two-letter nouns are from **II-nun** roots.

| Noun | | Root |
|---|---|---|
| אַף | anger | אנף |
| אִשָּׁה | woman | אנש |

Nuns sometimes assimilate in verbs, but not usually in the second position.

Nouns that come from roots listed as **I-yod** (including original **I-vav**) may have a vowel letter after one of the noun prefixes.

| Noun | | Root |
|---|---|---|
| תּוֹרָה | law | ירה |
| מוֹעֵד | appointed time | יעד |
| תּוֹלֵדוֹת | generations | ילד |
| תִּירוֹשׁ | new wine | ירשׁ |

Finally, a noun may, as in the above examples, have more than one of the above vowel letters, prefixes, suffixes, or missing letters.

When a missing letter might make it difficult to locate a noun, BDB often provides a cross reference, as mentioned before. The note on page one of BDB is an example:

אבה v. II. אָב

This means for the word אָב "father" look under the second root
אבה.

Only a few of the most common nouns in the vocabularies
and exercises are formed by adding prefixes or suffixes or have
missing letters. When you have difficulty finding the root of a
noun, you may want to review this summary.

**Vocabulary**

| | |
|---|---|
| אָדוֹן | lord, master |
| אָח | brother |
| אַחַר   אַחֲרֵי | behind, after |
| בַּת | daughter |
| בָּנוֹת | daughters (irregular plural) |
| לֵב   לֵבָב | heart (short and long form) |
| מָה   מֶה   מַה | what? how? |
| נֶפֶשׁ | (f) life, self, being; throat |
| עֶבֶד | servant, slave |
| עַיִן | (f) eye; spring, well |
| עָלָה | go up |
| קָרָא | call |
| שָׁלַח | stretch out, let go, send |
| שָׁם | there |
| שֵׁם | name |
| שָׁנָה | year |

**Exercises**

1. Read aloud and translate the following. Chart the verbs.

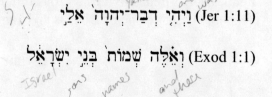

וַיְהִי דְבַר־יְהוָה אֵלַי (Jer 1:11)

וְאֵלֶּה שְׁמוֹת בְּנֵי יִשְׂרָאֵל (Exod 1:1)

(Gen 24:34) וַיֹּאמַר עֶבֶד אַבְרָהָם אָנֹכִי:

(Ps 42:3 ET 2) אָבוֹא וְאֵרָאֶה¹ פְּנֵי אֱלֹהִים:

(1 Kgs 1:20) וְאַתָּה אֲדֹנִי הַמֶּלֶךְ עֵינֵי כָל־יִשְׂרָאֵל עָלֶיךָ

(Ezek 18:4) כָּל־הַנְּפָשׁוֹת לִי הֵנָּה כְּנֶפֶשׁ הָאָב
וּכְנֶפֶשׁ הַבֵּן לִי־הֵנָּה

2. Read aloud and translate the following. You will need to use a lexicon to translate some of the words. Chart the verbs.

(Exod 3:1) וַיָּבֹא אֶל־הַר הָאֱלֹהִים

(Lev 25:5) שְׁנַת שַׁבָּתוֹן יִהְיֶה לָאָרֶץ

(Joel 2:11) כִּי־גָדוֹל יוֹם־יְהוָה

(Gen 2:19) מַה־יִּקְרָא־לוֹ וְכֹל אֲשֶׁר יִקְרָא־לוֹ הָאָדָם
נֶפֶשׁ חַיָּה הוּא שְׁמוֹ:

(2 Sam 2:4) וַיָּבֹאוּ אַנְשֵׁי יְהוּדָה וַיִּמְשְׁחוּ־שָׁם אֶת־דָּוִד
לְמֶלֶךְ עַל־בֵּית יְהוּדָה

---

¹ The vowel points are for a stem which you have not studied yet, but you should be able to recognize the root and translate it adequately.

# Chapter 10
## Qal Perfect, Part I

The second major conjugation in Hebrew is the perfect.

### Perfect Conjugation

The perfect conjugation adds **suffixes** to the end of the stem. The suffixes to the stem indicate the person, gender and number (PGN) of the subject. (Some introductory grammars refer to them as affixes or afformatives to distinguish them from the suffixed pronouns.) The **subject** is the person, place or thing that does the action of the verb. As mentioned above, a separate subject, as is customary in English, is the exception in Hebrew.

The conjugation of the **Qal perfect** is as follows:

| PGN | Form | PGN | Form |
|-----|------|-----|------|
| 3ms | שָׁמַר *shamar* | 3cp | שָׁמְרוּ *shamerv* |
| 3fs | שָׁמְרָה *shamerah* | | |
| 2ms | שָׁמַרְתָּ *shamartah* | 2mp | שְׁמַרְתֶּם *shemar tom* |
| 2fs | שָׁמַרְתְּ *shamar teh* | 2fp | שְׁמַרְתֶּן *shemar ten* |
| 1cs | שָׁמַרְתִּי *shamar ti* | 1cp | שָׁמַרְנוּ *shamar nv* |

Note: the qamets ( ָ ) under the first root letter occurs in most forms and so is a good **indicator** when you see it in reading that you have a Qal perfect.

In the lexicon the vowels of the 3ms form are put on the root. If this form does not have all the letters of the root, then the vowels of the infinitive are used. (The infinitive will be introduced later.)

A number of roots take an i-class or u-class vowel under the middle root letter. Many of these are statives.

English does not distinguish gender (masculine or feminine) in the second person as Hebrew does, so the translation is always "you." English also does not distinguish number in the second person. The translation is "you" whether the number in Hebrew is singular or plural.

In the 3fs and 3cp forms, the sheva could be either silent or vocal and either close the previous syllable or open a new one. Thus the qamets could be translated either as a long *a* or a short *o*. The **meteg**, the small vertical line beside the qamets ( ‚ ), is to indicate that it is a long *a*.

The **suffixes** of the perfect are the same in all stems. Except for a few minor alterations, they remain unchanged on all verbal roots in all stems. They are, therefore, reliable **indicators** when you are reading that the form you are looking at is a perfect. While the system of indicators reduces the need to memorize future conjugations, you should memorize the Qal perfect on the root שמר in the previous table, taking note of the suffixes in the following table which will function as indicators of the perfect in future conjugations:

| PGN | Suffix | PGN | Suffix |
|------|--------------|------|---------|
| 3ms | (none) | 3cp | ‫ו‬– |
| 3fs | ‫ָה‬– | | |
| 2ms | ‫ָתָּ‬– (or ‫תָּה‬–) | 2mp | ‫תֶּם‬– |
| 2fs | ‫תְּ‬– | 2fp | ‫תֶּן‬– |
| 1cs | ‫תִּי‬– | 1cp | ‫נוּ‬– |

## III-he³ verbs

When perfect verbs are formed with III-he³ roots, the he³ can be missing or be represented by a hireq yod. In the development of the Hebrew language III-yod roots became III-he³ roots. The yod reappears or more correctly is retained in first and second person forms of the perfect. Because the root ends with a he³, the 3ms form looks like a 3fs form. This may be why the 3fs form distinguishes itself by adding another feminine marker, the tav. The he³ is missing altogether in the 3cp. With the exception of the 3fs form, therefore, the **indicators** of a III-he³ verb are the same in the perfect as in the imperfect.

| 3ms | עָשָׂה | 3cp | עָשׂוּ |
|-----|--------|-----|--------|
| 3fs | עָשְׂתָה | | |
| 2ms | עָשִׂיתָ¹ | 2mp | עֲשִׂיתֶם² |
| 2fs | עָשִׂית | 2fp | עֲשִׂיתֶן |
| 1cs | עָשִׂיתִי | 1cp | עָשִׂינוּ |

## Vav Consecutive

In Chapter 6 we saw that the normal way to indicate past action was the vav consecutive prefixed to the imperfect (וַיָּקָם "he arose"). Similarly, the normal way to indicate that an action takes place in the future in Hebrew is by prefixing וְ to the perfect. (An alternate form is וּ.) Note, however, that the vowel pointing is the same as for the conjunction –וְ "and." With the perfect it may be translated "and." Often, though, some other word ("so," "then," etc.), or a comma (,), semicolon (;), or capitalization is a better translation in English.

| וְשַׁבְתָּ | You will return (Deut 4:30) |
|------------|------------------------------|

---

¹ The weak dagesh that was present in the tav in the previous tables is no longer present, because the tav now comes after a vowel and a weak dagesh will not follow a vowel.

² The previous tables had a sheva here. Gutturals do not take a vocal sheva. They take a hateph-patah or in few cases a hateph-segol instead. Despite minor changes such as that mentioned in this and in the previous footnote, the perfect is easily recognizable from the suffixes.

# Vocabulary

|  |  |
|---|---|
| גָּדוֹל | great |
| גּוֹי | people, nation |
| דֶּרֶךְ | way, road, journey, custom |
| הַר | mountain |
| טוֹב | good (adj); be good (verb); goodness (noun) |
| כַּאֲשֶׁר | as |
| כֹּה | thus, so |
| כֵּן | right, upright; thus, so |
| מַיִם | water |
| מִצְרַיִם | Egypt (מִצְרִי "Egyptian") |
| נָשָׂא | lift up, bear, carry |
| עָבַר | pass over, transgress |
| עָמַד | stand |
| קוּם | rise, stand |
| רֹאשׁ | head |

# Exercises

1. Read aloud and translate the following and chart the verbs.

וַעֲשִׂיתֶם אֹתָם וִישַׁבְתֶּם עַל־הָאָרֶץ (Lev 25:18)

וְיָשְׁבוּ בָהּ יְהוּדָה וְכָל־עָרָיו (Jer 31:24)

וְאָמַרְתָּ לְבִנְךָ עֲבָדִים הָיִינוּ לְפַרְעֹה בְּמִצְרַיִם (Deut 6:21)

אַתֶּם רְאִיתֶם אֲשֶׁר עָשִׂיתִי לְמִצְרַיִם (Exod 19:4)

(1 Kings 18:12) וְהָיָה אֲנִי אֵלֵךְ מֵאִתָּךְ וְרוּחַ יְהוָה יִשָּׂאֲךָ עַל
אֲשֶׁר לֹא־אֵדַע

(Gen 24:4) כִּי אֶל־אַרְצִי וְאֶל־מוֹלַדְתִּי תֵּלֵךְ וְלָקַחְתָּ אִשָּׁה
לִבְנִי לְיִצְחָק׃

2. Read aloud and translate the following. In order to translate, you will need to look up some words in a lexicon. Chart the verbs.

(1 Sam 19:3) וַאֲנִי אֵצֵא וְעָמַדְתִּי לְיַד־אָבִי בַּשָּׂדֶה אֲשֶׁר
אַתָּה שָׁם וַאֲנִי אֲדַבֵּר בְּךָ אֶל־אָבִי וְרָאִיתִי מָה
וְהִגַּדְתִּי לָךְ׃

(Gen 19:5) וַיִּקְרְאוּ אֶל־לוֹט וַיֹּאמְרוּ לוֹ אַיֵּה הָאֲנָשִׁים
אֲשֶׁר־בָּאוּ אֵלֶיךָ

(Exod 4:15) וְדִבַּרְתָּ אֵלָיו וְשַׂמְתָּ אֶת־הַדְּבָרִים בְּפִיו

(Gen 3:5) וִהְיִיתֶם כֵּאלֹהִים יֹדְעֵי טוֹב וָרָע׃

---

3 "the spirit of"

4 "my kindred"

5 "I will speak"

6 "I will tell" (Perfect of a stem you will learn later.)

7 "you will speak"

8 "knowing" (A conjugation you will learn later.)

# Chapter 11

## Qal Perfect, Part II

### Meaning of the Perfect

The name of the perfect, like the name of the imperfect, is misleading because the English perfect has a much narrower range of meanings than does the Hebrew perfect. For this reason some grammars prefer to use terms that refer to form, such as affix conjugation, or to a more adequate definition of meaning, for example, perfective conjugation.

In the Hebrew verb system, the perfect contrasts with the imperfect. But, as we saw with the imperfect, scholars debate its meaning when it stands alone without a vav. Older Jewish grammarians and some contemporary scholars, who understand the imperfect as a present and future tense, understand the perfect as *a past tense.* But the perfect may need to be translated with a present or future tense depending on the context.

Other Hebrew grammarians, who instead understand the imperfect as describing an incomplete action, understand the perfect as describing *a complete action.* The tense is determined by the context. The name perfect and the description of the perfect in some grammars as a completed action is misleading. This is true in English grammar, but in Hebrew, the action of the verb may still be incomplete from the perspective of the timeframe of the narrative. The name perfective would be grammatically more accurate, but this book retains the name perfect because that is the name most commonly used in lexicons and reference works. The Hebrew perfect, however, describes not a completed action but instead an action viewed as *a complete, whole situation, or event.* Used with a dynamic verb it describes an event, either long or short. In an individual use the emphasis may be on the beginning, middle, entirety, or end of a complete event. Whereas the imperfect represents a progressive, repeated, or dependant situation, the perfect is used when viewing a situation as a whole.

## Hollow Verbs

The vowel pointing of the perfect is the same for both **II-vav** and **II-yod**. Generally there is much overlap and perhaps confusion between the two types of roots.

Some hollow verbs, such as שׁוּב (turn, return) and שִׂים (set, place) have a-class vowels under the first letter:

| | | | |
|---|---|---|---|
| 3ms | שָׁב | 3cp | שָׁבוּ |
| 3fs | שָׁבָה | | |
| 2ms | שַׁבְתָּ | 2mp | שַׁבְתֶּם |
| 2fs | שַׁבְתְּ | 2fp | שַׁבְתֶּן |
| 1cs | שַׁבְתִּי | 1cp | שַׁבְנוּ |

Notice that the stress is on the second-to-last vowel in many of the forms. This is an **indicator** of a hollow verb.

Some other verbs, such as מוּת (die) or בּוֹשׁ (be ashamed) take i-class or u-class vowels in several perfect forms. The remaining forms have the same a-class vowels as in the table above. These are often called **statives** because they describe states of being, (for example, dead or ashamed). A complete table is not necessary, as these forms can be identified in reading by the perfect suffixes, by having only two letters, and in many cases by having the accent on the second-to-last vowel.

## The Root נתן

This frequently occurring verb is the *only* III-nun verb that shows assimilation of the final nun before suffixes beginning with tav ת.

| | |
|---|---|
| זָקַנְתִּי | I am old |
| נָתַתִּי | I have given |
| נְתַתֶּם | you (mp) have given |

## Suffixed Pronouns

The perfect takes the same suffixed pronouns you have seen on prepositions, nouns, and the imperfect. The endings and vowels of the perfect show some changes with the addition of suffixed pronouns. As a reference, the following table summarizes the forms of the perfect before pronoun suffixes.

| | | | |
|---|---|---|---|
| 3ms | –שָׁמַר | 3cp | –שָׁמְרוּ |
| 3fs | –שָׁמְרַת  –שְׁמָרַת | | |
| 2ms | –שְׁמַרְתָּ | 2mp | –שְׁמַרְתּוּ |
| 2fs | –שְׁמַרְתִּי | 2fp | –שְׁמַרְתּוּ |
| 1cs | –שְׁמַרְתִּי | 1cp | –שְׁמַרְנוּ |

Note that these forms are difficult to identify in reading because the qamets, normally an indicator of the perfect, is reduced to a sheva and many of the endings of the perfect are changed. Moreover, the endings in this table are often written defectively. Thus the 2fs suffix –תִּי is frequently written –תְּ and the 2mp suffix –תּוּ is frequently –תְּ.

The suffixed pronouns function as an object of the verb. As we saw with suffixed pronouns on the imperfect, they can be suffixed either to the end of the verb or the sign of the definite direct object, with no apparent difference in meaning.

| | |
|---|---|
| שְׁמַרְתָּהּ | you kept her |
| שָׁמַרְתָּ אוֹתָהּ | you kept her |

## Vocabulary

| | |
|---|---|
| אֶלֶף | thousand; tribe, clan |
| חֶרֶב | sword |
| יָלַד | bring forth, bear |
| מִזְבֵּחַ | altar |
| מִי | who |

| | |
|---|---|
| מָצָא | find[1] |
| מִשְׁפָּט | judgment, custom, justice |
| נָפַל | fall |
| עוֹד | yet, still, again |
| עוֹלָם עֹלָם | long time; forever |
| עַתָּה | now |
| פֶּה | mouth (כְּפִי, לְפִי "according to") |
| צָבָא | service in war; host, army |
| רַע | evil (ms noun, adj) |
| רָעָה | evil (fs noun) |
| שִׂים | set, place, put |

**Exercises**

1. Read aloud and translate the following. Chart the verbs.

(Gen 19:29) הֶעָרִ֕ים אֲשֶׁר־יָשַׁ֥ב בָּהֵ֖ן לֽוֹט׃

(Dan 10:12) וַאֲנִי־בָ֖אתִי בִּדְבָרֶֽיךָ׃

(Deut 34:10) וְלֹא־קָ֨ם נָבִ֥יא ע֛וֹד בְּיִשְׂרָאֵ֖ל כְּמֹשֶׁ֑ה אֲשֶׁר֙ יְדָע֣וֹ
יְהוָ֔ה פָּנִ֖ים אֶל־פָּנִֽים׃

(Exod 4:15) וְאָנֹכִ֗י אֶֽהְיֶה֙ עִם־פִּ֨יךָ֙ וְעִם־פִּ֔יהוּ וְהוֹרֵיתִ֣י[2] אֶתְכֶ֔ם
אֵ֖ת אֲשֶׁ֥ר תַּעֲשֽׂוּן׃

(Ps 47:9 ET 8) מָלַ֣ךְ[3] אֱ֭לֹהִים עַל־גּוֹיִ֑ם

---

[1] In the Hiphil stem, which will be discussed later, מצא can mean "present."

[2] "I will teach"

[3] Although you have not had this verb in the vocabularies, you should be able to figure out its meaning from the noun of the same root.

(2 Kgs 23:25) וְכָמֹהוּ⁴ לֹא־הָיָה לְפָנָיו מֶלֶךְ אֲשֶׁר־שָׁב
אֶל־יְהוָה בְּכָל־לְבָבוֹ וּבְכָל־נַפְשׁוֹ וּבְכָל־מְאֹדוֹ⁵ כְּכֹל
תּוֹרַת⁶ מֹשֶׁה וְאַחֲרָיו לֹא־קָם כָּמֹהוּ:

(Ezek 37:25) וְיָשְׁבוּ עַל־הָאָרֶץ אֲשֶׁר נָתַתִּי לְעַבְדִּי לְיַעֲקֹב אֲשֶׁר
יָשְׁבוּ־בָהּ אֲבוֹתֵיכֶם וְיָשְׁבוּ עָלֶיהָ הֵמָּה וּבְנֵיהֶם וּבְנֵי בְנֵיהֶם
עַד־עוֹלָם וְדָוִד עַבְדִּי נָשִׂיא⁷ לָהֶם לְעוֹלָם:

2. Read aloud and translate the following and chart the verbs.
You will need to look up some of the words in a lexicon.

(Gen 13:12) אַבְרָם יָשַׁב בְּאֶרֶץ־כְּנָעַן וְלוֹט יָשַׁב בְּעָרֵי הַכִּכָּר

(Deut 4:44) וְזֹאת הַתּוֹרָה אֲשֶׁר־שָׂם מֹשֶׁה לִפְנֵי בְּנֵי יִשְׂרָאֵל:

(Exod 20:22) וַיֹּאמֶר יְהוָה אֶל־מֹשֶׁה כֹּה תֹאמַר אֶל־בְּנֵי יִשְׂרָאֵל
אַתֶּם רְאִיתֶם כִּי מִן־הַשָּׁמַיִם דִּבַּרְתִּי⁸ עִמָּכֶם:

(Isa 9:1 ET 2) רָאוּ אוֹר גָּדוֹל

(Gen 3:20) וַיִּקְרָא הָאָדָם שֵׁם אִשְׁתּוֹ חַוָּה כִּי הִוא הָיְתָה
אֵם כָּל־חָי⁹:

3. Discuss the meaning of the perfect in the above exercises.

---

⁴ "like him"

⁵ "his strength"

⁶ "the law of"

⁷ "a prince"

⁸ Although you have not had this stem, you should be able to
recognize the root and translate.

⁹ "living"

4. What is the meaning of חַוָּה in Genesis 3:20 above and how does it contribute to the meaning of the passage?

# Chapter 12

## Textual Criticism

The Masoretic Text (MT) of 1 Samuel 13:1 literally reads: "Saul was *one year* old when he began to reign; and he reigned *two years* over Israel." Scribes copied ancient manuscripts, including the Bible, by hand. Even though great care was taken in copying, errors crept in over time. Various types of errors or differences occur even in modern, printed Hebrew Bibles. Textual criticism tries to identify and correct these errors. As in the example above, establishing the text is often a necessary first step in translation.

Several qualifications are necessary to the traditional aim of textual criticism. First, in practice, the boundary between textual criticism and higher criticism is blurred. Textual criticism or lower criticism deals with changes during transmission (copying and recopying). Higher criticism deals with changes during writing and editing. The writer or editors, however, may have made errors or, as in the case of Jeremiah, may have written more than one text. Considering these qualifications, the aim of textual criticism is to establish the original or traditional text.

The following sections are a step-by-step guide to using the footnotes in *BHS* for textual criticism. The first section, "Reading *BHS*' Footnotes," explains how to read the footnotes in *BHS* dealing with textual criticism. The second section, "Causes of Textual Corruption," shows how choosing between the different readings or making corrections requires knowledge of the scribes and the types of errors they made. The final section, "Choosing between Readings," contains guidelines for choosing the original reading.

## Reading *BHS*'s Footnotes

The **text-critical apparatus** is another name for these footnotes. A small raised letter beside a Hebrew word indicates a **text-critical note**. When two of the same raised letters appear in a verse, this indicates a note referring to all the words between the two raised letters.

In *BHS,* the notes are at the bottom of the page below the Masora Magna. In the case of 1 Samuel 13:1 there is a small, raised *a* before the first Hebrew word. Appearing at the bottom of the page, on the third line of text-critical notes, is **Cp 13,1** (in boldface type), which is the abbreviation for Chapter 13, verse 1. A series of abbreviations follow. A key to the abbreviations, "Sigla et Compendia Apparatuum," appears in the beginning of *BHS. An English Key* translated by H. P. Rüger is available from United Bible Societies and is reprinted in *A Simplified Guide to BHS\** by Scott.

In the footnotes, the editors of *BHS* list different readings of the text in manuscripts or versions that they consider significant. In the above example, the **text** is 1 Samuel. **Manuscripts** are Hebrew copies of 1 Samuel. (The word manuscript may also refer to individual copies in Hebrew or other ancient languages.) **Versions** are ancient translations of 1 Samuel into other languages, such as Greek and Syriac. The text-critical notes for 1 Samuel 13:1, for example, have the abbreviation ⅏ for the Septuagint, an ancient Greek version of the Bible, and ⅏ for the Peshitta, the Syriac version. The small raised letters after ⅏ in the first note ("a") indicate individual copies or manuscripts of the Septuagint.

An appendix at the back of this book lists BHS' abbreviations, signs, and symbols that appear in the exercises.

The testimony of versions must be carefully evaluated. **Retroversion** refers to the process of reconstructing the Hebrew manuscript that a version translated. Some versions or parts of versions are very free translations characterized by many additions. Because they so often add interpretations, we cannot safely figure out the Hebrew that lies behind their translation. Their witness is of little use for textual criticism. Even fairly literal translations may be attempting to understand or interpret a difficult passage, rather than witnessing to a different Hebrew text. In 1 Samuel 13, for example, the translators of the Septuagint and Peshitta may have made additions or changes to create a translation that made sense. The translation therefore would not be an authentic witness to a Hebrew manuscript different from the MT.

## Causes of Textual Corruption

In order to work backward from several readings to the original it is necessary to understand how errors occur. One guideline of textual criticism points out that the shorter reading is preferable. Scribes were more likely to add rather than omit something. Thus, a shorter reading is more likely to be the original.

Different types of textual corruption are additions that make the text longer, changes that do not alter the length of the text, and omissions that make the text shorter.

**Additions.** A scribe may unintentionally add to a text, for example, by inserting words like אֵת for correctness or clarity, or כֹּל for emphasis. Scribes might also add standard phrases like "servant of the LORD" or phrases remembered from other parts of the passage they are translating. There may also be mechanical reasons for additions.

**Dittography** means "writing again." A scribe accidentally writes a letter, several letters, a word, or many words twice. The MT of Leviticus 20:10 writes the same group of words twice:

> A man who commits adultery with the wife of *a man who commits adultery with the wife of* his neighbor should be put to death . . .

This sounds rather peculiar. The note in *BHS* tells us that some copies of the Septuagint do not have the italicized words above. It suggests deleting these words because they were added by dittography.

**Glosses** are notes that a scribe may write in the margins or between the lines to explain difficult words. Another scribe may accidentally copy the gloss into the line.

**Changes.** Several types of changes do not change the length of the text. A scribe may confuse one letter for another. You may already have had trouble with this in your reading and writing. A list of commonly confused letters follows:

| | | |
|---|---|---|
| בּ | and | כּ |
| ד | and | ר[1] |
| ה | and | ח |
| ה | and | ת |
| ו | and | י |
| ע | and | צ |
| כ | and | נ |

The square letters *BHS* uses were taken over for writing Hebrew from the closely related language Aramaic. Confusion of similar letters may date back before the introduction of Aramaic square letters to Old Hebrew scripts. The NJPS translates Ezekiel 3:12: "Then a spirit carried me away, and behind me I heard a great roaring sound: '*Blessed* is the Presence of the LORD, in His place,' with the sound of the wings of the creatures beating against one another, and the sound of the wheels beside them—a great roaring sound." (Italics mine.) The meaning and syntax are awkward. If an ancient scribe confused the Old Hebrew kaph in בָּרוּךְ "blessed" with the similar Old Hebrew mem, then the original would have been בְּרוּם "when rose up." Thus the NJPS suggests this emendation in a footnote, and the NRSV translates: "Then the spirit lifted me up, and as the glory of the LORD rose from its place, I heard behind me the sound of loud rumbling."

---

[1] See Genesis 22:13, footnote a.

Below is a list of letters easily confused in various Old Hebrew scripts:

| | | |
|---|---|---|
| י | and | ה |
| א | and | ת |
| כ | and | ב |
| ע | and | ד |
| ב | and | ר |
| ה | and | ח |
| מ | and | ב |

Also common in writing is the **transposition** of two letters. The order of two letters is reversed in writing. The use of consonants to indicate vowels in Hebrew also makes it possible for a vowel to be confused with a consonant.

**Omissions.** As with all text-critical principles, "the shorter reading is preferable" is only a guideline. The longer reading may be original, especially when we understand the reason for leaving something out.

**Haplography** or "single writing" is one kind of omission error. Haplography occurs when two identical or similar letters, groups of letters, or words are copied only once by mistake.

A second type of omission is **parablepsis**, meaning "oversight," whereby a scribe overlooks or misses a section of the manuscript being copied. The most common cause of such an oversight is **homoioteleuton** or "similar ending." When words in close proximity have similar or identical endings, the eye of the scribe may pass from one to the other, leaving out the words in between. In *BHS*, the editors printed Joshua 21:36–37 in small letters. The footnote at the beginning of the verse tells us that these verses are not in many Hebrew manuscripts and versions, including the Leningrad Codex, but are present in many other Hebrew manuscripts and versions. The error occurred when a scribe copied the end of verse 35, found the same words: "with its pasture lands—four towns," at the end of verse 37, and began copying verse 38, thereby leaving out verse 36.

**Homoioarkton,** meaning "similar beginning," is a less common type of oversight. Two words or phrases with similar beginnings cause an omission.

Occasionally a scribe might change a text, intentionally or unintentionally, for reasons of style or theology. For example, scribes might change a rare word for a more common word (see Gen 22:12, note a; Gen 22:23, note b) or might modify a passage to make it conform to their understanding (see Gen 22:2, note a).

**Harmonizations** occur when a scribe changes a passage to make it consistent with a similar passage elsewhere in the Bible.

## Choosing between Readings

External criteria are less reliable than internal criteria for choosing the original reading. External criteria are the manuscripts and versions that witness to different readings.

**External Criteria.** In textual criticism, as in a court of law, some witnesses are more reliable than others. Judging a witness' reliability is a complex issue that involves extensive knowledge of that witness. Although one might think an older manuscript would be closer to the original, poor copies can be made at an early date and careful copies later. Thus, reliability is more important than age.

For more detailed discussions of witnesses and their reliability, consult the bibliography. According to Würthwein, however, the relative reliability of the witnesses can be ranked in descending order for beginners. Würthwein's ranking is in the table on the next page. Those at the top are generally considered more reliable than those at the bottom. In the right column are the symbols (or **sigla**) used in the text-critical apparatus of *BHS* to indicate these manuscripts and versions.

| | |
|---|---|
| Masoretic Text | 𝔐 |
| Samaritan Pentateuch | 𝔪 |
| Septuagint | 𝔊 |
| Aquila | α |
| Symmachus | σ |
| Theodotian | 0 |
| Syriac | 𝔖 |
| Targums | 𝔗 |
| Vulgate | 𝔙 |
| Old Latin | 𝔏 |
| Sahidic | Sa |
| Ethiopic | 𝔞 |
| Arabic | 𝔞 |
| Armenian | Arm |

A reading with witnesses from several families and geographical areas is preferable. **Families** are groups of manuscripts and versions that have similar additions, deletions, and so on. The Masoretic Text, the Samaritan Pentateuch, and the Septuagint represent the three types of families.

Witnesses should be weighed, not counted. One reliable witness outweighs three unreliable witnesses. Nevertheless, even the most reliable tradition may have erroneous readings and unreliable witnesses may preserve an original reading. Internal criteria, therefore, are more important for choosing the original reading than external criteria.

**Internal Criteria.** The basic principle of textual criticism is "Which is most likely to have changed into the other?" This gives rise to the two basic and most important guidelines for choosing a reading: (1) *the more difficult reading is to be preferred,* and (2) *the shorter reading is to be preferred.*

The beginning student can learn to read the footnotes in *BHS* and use these two principles. A difficult reading here does not mean so problematic that it is unintelligible or impossible to understand. The preferable reading is the one that is an unusual, poetic use of the language. A scribe would probably change words in such a reading to make it more understandable to most readers. Likewise, a shorter reading is not preferable when you can show a reason like haplography (a very common error) that would make the text shorter.

**Emendation** is proposing an original reading that is not witnessed to by the manuscripts or versions. When it is evident that none of the witnesses has the original reading, emendation may be necessary. Textual critics have developed controls for making emendations. A person proposing an emendation should be able to show how the emendation gave rise to all the other readings (through haplography, dittography, or other causes). The emendation should also fit the context of the biblical book.

Although these abstract rules can make textual criticism sound like an objective science, the application of these rules is subjective and textual criticism is more of an art than a science.

**Exercises**

In order to practice using the text-critical notes in *BHS*, read the text-critical notes on the passages below. They are all passages you have already translated in previous chapters. The text-critical notes, which would be at the bottom of the page in *BHS*, are in parentheses after the text. The abbreviations of *BHS* used in this textbook are in Appendix E.

Chapter 3

שְׁמוּאֵל עִם־ᵈיְהוָה: ס (1 Sam 2:21)
(ᵈ pc Mss את, 𝕼 לפני cf 𝕲𝕾𝕮.)

אֱלֹהִים ªאֶת־הָאָדָםª עַל־הָאָרֶץ (2 Chr 6:18)
(ª⁻ª > 1 R 8,27)

כִּי מֶלֶךְª כָּל־הָאָרֶץ אֱלֹהִים (Ps 47:8 ET 7)
(ª mlt Mss + עַל)

(Gen 2:4) בְּיֹום עֲשֹׂות יְהוָֽה אֱלֹהִים ᶜאֶרֶץ וְשָׁמָֽיִם ᶜ:
( שָׁמַיִם וָאֶרֶץ ᶜ⁻ᶜ ‎𝔊 ‎𝔐𝔰 )

## Chapter 5

(Deut 34:4) וַיֹּאמֶר יְהוָה אֵלָיו ᵇ זֹאת הָאָרֶץ אֲשֶׁר ²נִשְׁבַּעְתִּי
לְאַבְרָהָם לְיִצְחָק וּֽלְיַעֲקֹב
(לאבתיך + ‎𝔐𝔰 ‎ᵃ ‖ ᵇ למשה = ‎𝔊 πρὸς Μωυσην ᵃ)

(Jer 30:4) וְאֵלֶּה הַדְּבָרִים אֲשֶׁר דִּבֶּר³ יְהוָה אֶל־יִשְׂרָאֵל
ᵃוְאֶל־יְהוּדָֽה: (ᵃ⁻ᵃ add)

## Chapter 6

(Exod 4:18) וַיֵּלֶךְ מֹשֶׁה וַיָּשָׁב ׀ אֶל־יֶתֶר ᵃ
(ᵃ Ms ‎𝔐𝔰𝔊𝔖ℭ'ᵛ יִתְרֹו, ‎𝔊 Ιοθορ)

## Chapter 7

(Gen 3:6) וַתִּקַּח מִפִּרְיֹו⁴ וַתֹּאכַל וַתִּתֵּן גַּם־לְאִישָׁהּ עִמָּהּ
וַיֹּאכַֽל ᵇ:
(ᵇ ‎𝔊 ‎𝔐𝔰 ‎כלו־)

## Chapter 9

(Ps 42:3 ET 2) אָבֹוא ᵇוְאֵרָאֶהᵇ פְּנֵי ᶜ אֱלֹהִים:
(ᵇ pc Mss ‎𝔖ℭ וְאֶרְאֶה ‖ ᶜ ‎𝔖 + suff 2 sg)

(Exod 3:1) וַיָּבֹא אֶל־הַר הָאֱלֹהִים ᵃ חֹרֵֽבָה⁶:
(ᵃ > ‎𝔊*)

## Chapter 10

(Lev 25:18) וַעֲשִׂיתֶם אֹתָם ᶜ וִישַׁבְתֶּם עַל־הָאָרֶץ
(אני יהוה + ℭ ᶜ)

(Exod 19:4) אַתֶּם רְאִיתֶם אֲשֶׁר עָשִׂיתִי לְמִצְרָיִם ᵃ
(בְּמִ ‎ℭᴹˢ mlt Mss ᵃ)

---

² "I promised"

³ "spoke"

⁴ "some of its fruit"

⁵ The vowel points are for a stem that you have not studied yet, but you should be able to recognize the root and translate adequately.

⁶ "Horeb"

(Gen 24:4) כִּי[a] אֶל־אַרְצִי וְאֶל־מוֹלַדְתִּי[7] תֵּלֵךְ וְלָקַחְתָּ
אִשָּׁה לִבְנִי לְיִצְחָק:
([a] 𝔊 Seb mlt Mss 𝔐 כִּי־אִם)

## Chapter 11

(Ps 47:9 ET 8) מָלַךְ[8] אֱלֹהִים עַל־[a]גּוֹיִם
([a] 2 Mss 𝔊^RAal + כָּל־)

---

[7] "my kindred"

[8] Although you have not had this verb in the vocabularies, you should
be able to figure out its meaning from the noun of the same root.

# Chapter 13

## Adjectives

Adjectives are words that modify a noun by limiting, defining, or qualifying it. In the phrase "a wise woman," for example, "wise" is the adjective. In English adjectives sometimes end with -able, -ous, -er, or -est and are recognized by their position in the sentence, whether or not they have these endings. An English speaker identifies "wise" as an adjective because it comes between the article "a" and the noun "woman."

### Gender and Number

Hebrew uses endings, similar to those for nouns, in order to denote the gender and number of adjectives.

| ms | גָּדוֹל | mp | גְּדוֹלִים |
|----|---------|----|-----------|
| fs | גְּדוֹלָה | fp | גְּדוֹלוֹת |

As with endings added to nouns, the vowels of the adjective may change when the endings are added.

### Uses of the Adjective

The **attributive** adjective attributes something to a noun. It agrees with the noun in gender, number, and definiteness. A noun is definite if it has a definite article, is a name, or has a suffixed pronoun. An attributive adjective usually follows the noun it modifies and is definite if it has a definite article.

גּוֹי גָּדוֹל      a great nation (Gen 12:2)

הַיָּם הַגָּדוֹל      the great sea (Num 34:6)

| | |
|---|---|
| אִשׁוֹ הַגְּדוֹלָה | his great fire (Deut 4:36) |
| יָמִים רַבִּים | many days (Gen 21:34) |

Several adjectives may modify one noun. When demonstratives (Chapter 5) appear in a series of adjectives, they come last in the series.

| | |
|---|---|
| לָעִיר הַגְּדוֹלָה הַזֹּאת | to this great city (Jer 22:8) |

The **predicate adjective** functions as a verb. A predicate is a verb and its modifiers. In English translation, a form of the verb "to be" is necessary. The predicate adjective agrees in gender and number with the noun it modifies, but does not have an article. It usually comes before the noun.

| | |
|---|---|
| טוֹבָה הָאָרֶץ | The land is good (Deut 1:25) |
| רַבִּים עַתָּה עַם הָאָרֶץ | the people of the land are now many (Exod 5:5) |

Often an adjective is the **absolute** with a noun(s) in construct.

| | |
|---|---|
| בֵּית גָּדוֹל | a great house (2 Kings 25:9) |

Adjectives may also be used as **nouns**.

| | |
|---|---|
| הָרָשָׁע | the guilty (Deut 25:1) |

**Vocabulary**

| | |
|---|---|
| אֹהֶל | tent |
| אוֹ | or |
| אֵשׁ | fire |
| בֵּין בֵּין | interval (noun); between (prep) |
| בָּנָה | build |

| | |
|---|---|
| בָּרַךְ | bless |
| דָּם | blood |
| קֹדֶשׁ | holy |
| קוֹל | voice, sound |
| רַב | much, many; captain, chief |
| שַׂר | official, leader, prince |
| שָׁמַיִם | heavens, sky |
| שָׁמַר | keep, watch, guard |
| תָּוֶךְ | midst, middle |
| בְּתוֹךְ | in the midst, middle; into, among, through |
| תַּחַת | beneath, under, instead of (prep) |

**Exercises**

1. In this and all future exercises, some of the text-critical notes from *BHS* will be included in parentheses. Read these notes by looking up the meaning of the abbreviations in Appendix E (or in Ruger's *Guide* or Scott). Be prepared to discuss what text you would translate and why. Begin, as usual, by reading the exercises aloud, translating the Hebrew, and charting the verbs.

וְאֶעֶשְׂךָ לְגוֹי גָּדוֹל (Gen 12:2)

וְאַנְשֵׁי־קֹדֶשׁ תִּהְיוּן לִי (Exod 22:30)

לֹא־יֹאכַל ᵃכִּי־קֹדֶשׁ הֵם: (Exod 29:33)
(ᵃ 𝕲[ᴰ] + ἀπ' αὐτῶν "from them" [𝕲ᴮ -τοῦ "it"])

וַיֵּשֶׁב־שָׁם יִרְמְיָהוּ יָמִים רַבִּים: (Jer 37:16)

(Joel 4:17 ET 3:17) וִידַעְתֶּ֗ם כִּ֣י אֲנִ֤י יְהוָה֙ אֱלֹ֣הֵיכֶ֔ם
שֹׁכֵן֙ בְּצִיּ֣וֹן הַר־קָדְשִׁ֔י וְהָיְתָ֥ה יְרוּשָׁלַ֖͏ִם
קֹ֑דֶשׁ וְזָרִ֥ים לֹא־יַעַבְרוּ־בָ֖הּ עֽוֹד׃

(Jer 16:10) וְהָיָ֗ה כִּ֤י תַגִּיד֙ לָעָ֣ם הַזֶּ֔ה אֵ֥ת כָּל־הַדְּבָרִ֖ים
הָאֵ֑לֶּה וְאָמְר֣וּ אֵלֶ֗יךָ עַל־מֶה֩ דִבֶּ֨ר יְהוָ֤ה עָלֵ֙ינוּ֙
אֵ֣ת כָּל־הָרָעָ֥ה הַגְּדוֹלָ֖ה הַזֹּ֑את

(Num 5:17) וְלָקַ֧ח הַכֹּהֵ֛ן מַ֥יִם קְדֹשִׁ֖ים

2. Read aloud and translate the following. You will need to
look up some words in a lexicon. Chart the verbs.

(Ps 95:3) כִּ֤י אֵ֣ל גָּד֣וֹל יְהוָ֑ה וּמֶ֥לֶךְ[a] גָּד֜֗וֹל
עַל־כָּל־אֱלֹהִֽים׃    ([a] pc Mss ⅁ מ׳)

(2 Kgs 22:8) וַיֹּ֣אמֶר חִלְקִיָּ֣הוּ הַכֹּהֵ֣ן הַגָּדוֹל֘ עַל־[a]שָׁפָ֗ן
הַסֹּפֵר֒ סֵ֤פֶר הַתּוֹרָה֙ מָצָ֣אתִי בְּבֵ֣ית יְהוָ֔ה וַיִּתֵּ֨ן
חִלְקִיָּ֧ה אֶת־הַסֵּ֛פֶר אֶל־שָׁפָ֖ן וַיִּקְרָאֵֽהוּ׃    ([a] = אֶל, sic mlt Mss cf ⅁)

---

[1] An infinitive construct meaning "dwell."
[2] "strangers"
[3] "you will tell"
[4] "spoke" (Piel perfect)

# Chapter 14

## Numbers

There are two main series of numbers in Hebrew: cardinal and ordinal. **Cardinal** numbers express amount (one, two, three, and so on). **Ordinal** numbers express order in a series (first, second, third, and so on).

## Cardinal Numbers

|  | Masculine | | Feminine | |
|---|---|---|---|---|
|  | Absolute | Construct | Absolute | Construct |
| one | אֶחָד | אַחַד | אַחַת | אַחַת |
| two | שְׁנַיִם | שְׁנֵי | שְׁתַּיִם | שְׁתֵּי |
| three | שָׁלֹשׁ | שְׁלֹשׁ | שְׁלֹשָׁה | שְׁלֹשֶׁת |
| four | אַרְבַּע | אַרְבַּע | אַרְבָּעָה | אַרְבַּעַת |
| five | חָמֵשׁ | חֲמֵשׁ | חֲמִשָּׁה | חֲמֵשֶׁת |
| six | שֵׁשׁ | שֵׁשׁ | שִׁשָּׁה | שֵׁשֶׁת |
| seven | שֶׁבַע | שְׁבַע | שִׁבְעָה | שִׁבְעַת |
| eight | שְׁמֹנֶה | שְׁמֹנֶה | שְׁמֹנָה | שְׁמֹנַת |
| nine | תֵּשַׁע | תְּשַׁע | תִּשְׁעָה | תִּשְׁעַת |
| ten | עֶשֶׂר | עֶשֶׂר | עֲשָׂרָה | עֲשֶׂרֶת |
| teen | עָשָׂר | | עֶשְׂרֵה | |

The cardinal numbers **one** and **two** agree in gender with the nouns they modify. When used like an adjective, one usually comes after the noun, but two can come either before or after the

noun. Both can also be used like nouns, in which case they are
often in construct, with a following noun in the absolute position.

| אֶל־מָקוֹם אֶחָד | to one place (Gen 1:9) |
| שְׁתֵּי נָשִׁים | two wives (Gen 4:19) |

The cardinal numbers **three** through **ten** take a form that is
opposite in gender to the noun they modify. They often do not
agree in definiteness. They may be in construct before the noun, or
in the absolute form either before or after the noun.

| שְׁלֹשָׁה בָנִים | three sons (Gen 6:10) |
| שִׁבְעַת יָמִים | seven days (Gen 8:10) |

The **teens**, eleven through nineteen, have the numeral ten
with a unit either before or after. Ten agrees in gender, while the
units follow their own rules of agreement (one, two) or opposition
(three to ten). The combination usually comes before the noun.

| שְׁתֵּים עֶשְׂרֵה שָׁנָה | twelve years (Gen 14:4) |
| חֲמֵשׁ עֶשְׂרֵה שָׁנָה | fifteen years (2 Kgs 14:17) |

The addition of a masculine plural ending to ten forms the
number **twenty**. The **other tens** (30, 40, and so on) add masculine
plural endings to the masculine numbers from three to nine.

| הָעֶשְׂרִים | the twenty (Gen 18:31) |
| וּשְׁלֹשִׁים אַמָּה | and thirty cubits (Gen 6:15) |

The combination of tens and other numbers may come before
or after the noun. The tens are always masculine plural and the
units follow their own rules of agreement or opposition.

| עֶשְׂרִים וּשְׁתַּיִם שָׁנָה | twenty-two years (Judg 10:3) |

## Ordinal Numbers

| | Masculine | Feminine |
|---|---|---|
| First | רִאשׁוֹן | רִאשׁוֹנָה |
| Second | שֵׁנִי | שֵׁנִית |
| Third | שְׁלִישִׁי | שְׁלִישִׁית    שְׁלִישִׁיָּה |
| Fourth | רְבִיעִי | רְבִיעִית |
| Fifth | חֲמִישִׁי | חֲמִישִׁית |
| Sixth | שִׁשִּׁי | שִׁשִּׁית |
| Seventh | שְׁבִיעִי | שְׁבִיעִית |
| Eighth | שְׁמִינִי | שְׁמִינִית |
| Ninth | תְּשִׁיעִי | תְּשִׁיעִית |
| Tenth | עֲשִׂירִי | עֲשִׂירִית    עֲשִׂירִיָּה |

## Vocabulary

The following list includes numbers from one to ten and numbers that occur more than one hundred times.

| | |
|---|---|
| אֶחָד | one (m) |
| אַחַת | one (f) |
| רִאשׁוֹן | first (ordinal number) |
| שְׁנַיִם | two (m) |
| שְׁתַּיִם | two (f) |
| שֵׁנִי | second (ordinal number) |
| שָׁלוֹשׁ שָׁלֹשׁ | three (m) |
| שְׁלֹשָׁה | three (f) |
| שְׁלֹשִׁים | thirty |
| שְׁלִישִׁי | third (ordinal number) |
| אַרְבַּע | four (m) |
| אַרְבָּעָה | four (f) |
| אַרְבָּעִים | forty |

| | |
|---|---|
| חָמֵשׁ | five (m) |
| חֲמִשָּׁה | five (f) |
| חֲמִשִּׁים | fifty |
| שֵׁשׁ | six (m) |
| שִׁשָּׁה | six (f) |
| שֶׁבַע | seven (m) |
| שִׁבְעָה | seven (f) |
| שְׁמֹנֶה | eight (m) |
| שְׁמֹנָה | eight (f) |
| תֵּשַׁע | nine (m) |
| תִּשְׁעָה | nine (f) |
| עֶשֶׂר    עָשָׂר | ten (m) (עָשָׂר in numbers 11–19) |
| עֲשָׂרָה    עֶשְׂרֵה | ten (f) (עֶשְׂרֵה in numbers 11–19) |
| עֶשְׂרִים | twenty |
| מֵאָה | hundred |
| זָהָב | gold |
| חַי | alive, living (adj) |
| חַיִּים | life, lifetime (noun) |
| יָם | sea |
| יָרֵא | fear, be afraid |
| יָרַד | go down |

## Exercises

1. Read aloud and translate the following and chart the verbs.

(Deut 6:4) שְׁמַע[1] יִשְׂרָאֵל יְהוָה אֱלֹהֵינוּ יְהוָה ׀ אֶחָד׃

---

[1] "Hear!" or "Listen!" (a Qal imperative). You will study the Qal imperative in Chapter 22.

*years · seven · to you · not · said · famine · in your land*

(2 Sam 24:13) וַיֹּאמֶר לוֹ הֲתָבוֹא לְךָ[a] שֶׁבַע[b] שָׁנִים ׀
רָעָב[2] ׀ בְּאַרְצֶךָ

($^a$ > pc Mss ǁ $^b$ 𝔊 τρία "three" ex 1 Chron 21,12)

(Exod 34:28) וַיְהִי־שָׁם[a] עִם־יְהוָֹה[b] אַרְבָּעִים יוֹם
($^a$ 𝔊 + Μωυσῆς "Moses" ǁ $^b$ לִפְנֵי 𝔊 мṡ)

(Exod 15:27) וַיָּבֹאוּ אֵילִמָה[3] וְשָׁם[a] שְׁתֵּים עֶשְׂרֵה עֵינֹת מַיִם
($^a$ мṡ𝔊$^{314}$ Philo 𝔗$^J$ וּבְאֵילִם)

(Neh 11:18) כָּל־הַלְוִיִּם בְּעִיר הַקֹּדֶשׁ מָאתַיִם[4]
שְׁמֹנִים וְאַרְבָּעָה:

(2 Sam 2:11) וַיְהִי מִסְפַּר[5] הַיָּמִים אֲשֶׁר הָיָה דָוִד מֶלֶךְ
בְּחֶבְרוֹן עַל־בֵּית יְהוּדָה שֶׁבַע שָׁנִים וְשִׁשָּׁה חֳדָשִׁים[6]:

2. Read aloud and translate the following. You will need to use a lexicon to translate some of the words. Chart the verbs.

(Hag 1:1) בִּשְׁנַת שְׁתַּיִם לְדָרְיָוֶשׁ הַמֶּלֶךְ בַּחֹדֶשׁ הַשִּׁשִּׁי בְּיוֹם אֶחָד
לַחֹדֶשׁ הָיָה דְבַר־יְהוָה בְּיַד־חַגַּי הַנָּבִיא אֶל־זְרֻבָּבֶל בֶּן־שְׁאַלְתִּיאֵל
פַּחַת יְהוּדָה וְאֶל־יְהוֹשֻׁעַ בֶּן־יְהוֹצָדָק הַכֹּהֵן הַגָּדוֹל

(Ezek 3:19) וְלֹא־שָׁב מֵרִשְׁעוֹ[a] וּמִדַּרְכּוֹ הָרְשָׁעָה[7]
($^{a–a}$ add cf 33,9)

---

[2] "famine"

[3] אֵלִם is a place name (full spelling: אֵילִים). In Chapter 21 you will learn the meaning of the ־ָה on the end. Its sense here is "to אֵלִם."

[4] This is the dual form of מֵאָה: "two hundred."

[5] "the number of"

[6] "months"

[7] "from his wickedness"

(1 Kgs 18:4) וַיִּקַּח עֹבַדְיָהוּ מֵאָה נְבִאִים

(Gen 31:41) זֶה־לִּי עֶשְׂרִים שָׁנָה בְּבֵיתֶךָ עֲבַדְתִּיךָ אַרְבַּע־עֶשְׂרֵה
שָׁנָה בִּשְׁתֵּי בְנֹתֶיךָ וְשֵׁשׁ שָׁנִים בְּצֹאנֶךָ

# Chapter 15
## Verb Stems

The Qal is the simplest of several verb stems. Hebrew adds consonants and vowels to the three-letter root of the verb in order to express different meanings. Traditionally, the root פָּעַל is used to name the stems other than Qal. The 3 ms perfect form of the stem with this root is essentially the name of the stem. The following table lists the name in Hebrew and English. The **indicators** of the stem for the perfect and imperfect are placed on the root שׁמר.

When you are reading Hebrew, if you still cannot make sense of a form, remember that lexicons list and identify the forms of a verb. (Because פָּעַל is a II-guttural you may notice some differences between the stem and indicators columns in the table of indicators below.)

| Stem | Name | Indicators | Comments |
|---|---|---|---|
| | Qal *a/o vowels* | שָׁמַר<br>יִשְׁמֹר | Lack of additions identifies Qal. Qamets under first letter identifies the perfect. Prefixes indicate the imperfect. |
| נִפְעַל | Niphal | נִשְׁמַר<br>יִשָּׁמֵר | Nun indicates Niphal perfect. Dagesh in first letter and qamets under it indicate Niphal imperfect. |
| פִּעֵל | Piel *common vowel pattern* | שִׁמֵּר<br>יְשַׁמֵּר | Doubling of middle letter indicates a Piel. A hireq under first letter indicates the perfect. Sheva under the prefix indicates the imperfect. |

| | | | |
|---|---|---|---|
| פֻּעַל | Pual | שֻׁמַּר<br>יְשֻׁמַּר | Qibbuts or another u-class vowel under first letter and doubling of middle letter indicate Pual. |
| הִפְעִיל | Hiphil | הִשְׁמִיר<br>יַשְׁמִר | "Dot vowel" under middle letter indicates Hiphil.[1] Prefixed he° indicates the perfect. Pataḥ under prefix indicates the imperfect. |
| הָפְעַל | Hophal | הָשְׁמַר<br>יָשְׁמַר | U-class vowel under prefixes indicates Hophal. Prefixed he° indicates the perfect. U-class vowel is under prefix of the imperfect. |
| הִתְפַּעֵל | Hitpael | הִתְשַׁמֵּר<br>יִתְשַׁמֵּר | Inserted tav and doubling of middle letter indicates stem. Prefixed he° indicates the perfect. Prefix, as usual, indicates the imperfect |

## Meaning of the Stems[2]

Central to understanding the different meanings of the Hebrew stems are the differences between the top three stems in the examples in the table on the next page: Qal, Piel, and Hiphil.

1. The **Qal** is the *simple action* expressed by the verbal root, "walk" in the example.

2. The **Piel** *brings about the state* expressed by the verbal root, "walking" in the example. An *object* of the verb tends to be a "passive" *secondary subject*. The state tends to be *habitual* or *ongoing*.

3. The **Hiphil** actively *causes the event* expressed by the verbal root. The *object* of the verb is caused to take part in the action, to be "active" as a *secondary subject*, and the event tends to be *occasional* or *one-time*.

4. The **other stems** are the *passive* or *reflexive* (or sometimes *middle*) counterparts of these three stems, as the table indicates.

---

[1] "Dot vowels:" hireq, tsere, or segol.

[2] The description and table is adapted from Waltke and O'Connor, *IBHS*, p. 358 § 21.2.2n.

Normally a verb would occur only in the stems appropriate to its meaning. The use of "walk" as an example for all the stems below is for the sake of illustration and thus is somewhat forced and unnatural.

| | | Voice of Secondary Subject | | |
|---|---|---|---|---|
| | | None | Passive | Active |
| **Voice** | Active | Qal — She walked | Piel — She was walking the people | Hiphil — She caused the people to walk |
| **of** | Passive | Niphal — She was walked | Pual — She was being walked by the people | Hophal — She was caused by the people to walk |
| **Subject** | Reflexive | Niphal — She walked herself | Hitpael — She made herself walk | Hiphil — She caused herself to walk |

*(handwritten annotations: "reflexive / vascillating / back and forth")*

These differences are difficult to conceive and express in English. As a result, lexicons, grammars, and translations have tended to miss these nuances.

**Vocabulary**

| | |
|---|---|
| בָּקַשׁ*[3] | (Pi) seek (בַּקֵּשׁ) |
| דָּבַר* | (Pi) speak (דִּבֵּר) |

---

[3] The asterisk indicates a hypothetical form. A Qal form of the root is listed, as is customary, but this form never appears in the Hebrew Bible. Some people choose to memorize the forms of these roots in the stems in which they occur rather than in the hypothetical Qal form.

| | |
|---|---|
| יָשַׁע\* | (Ni) be saved; (Hi) save |
| כּוּן\* | (Ni) be firm, established; (Hi) prepare |
| כְּלִי | vessel, utensil |
| כֶּסֶף | silver *(money)* |
| מִלְחָמָה | war, battle |
| מָלַךְ | reign, be king |
| מָקוֹם | place |
| נְאֻם | utterance, declaration |
| נָגַד\* | (Hi) make known, report, tell |
| נָכָה\* | (Ni) be hit; (Hi) smite; kill |
| נָצַל\* | (Ni) be delivered; (Hi) snatch away |
| סוּר | turn aside; (Hi) take away, remove |
| צָוָה\* | (Pi) command (צִוָּה) |

## Exercises

1. Read aloud and translate the following. Identify the new verb stems in each of the following using the chart of **indicators**. Be prepared to discuss how the new stems express the activity or passivity of primary and secondary subjects (objects), and whether a one-time event or ongoing state is in view. Keep in mind the rules for missing and weak letters that you learned in Chapter 6.

וַיַּרְא⁴ כִּי אֵין אִישׁ (Exod 2:12)

וַיַּךְ⁵ אֶת־הַמִּצְרִי

---

⁴ Note: III-heʾ Qal and Hiphil verbs sometimes have the same form when the heʾ is missing. The context then determines the verb stem.

⁵ From a word in the vocabulary. Only the middle root letter appears here.

(Gen 28:1) וַיִּקְרָא יִצְחָק אֶל־יַעֲקֹב וַיְבָרֶךְ אֹתוֹ וַיְצַוֵּהוּ וַיֹּאמֶר
לוֹ לֹא־תִקַּח אִשָּׁה מִבְּנוֹת כְּנָעַן:

*construct*

(1 Sam 30:31) וְלַאֲשֶׁר בְּחֶבְרוֹן וּלְכָל־הַמְּקֹמוֹת
אֲשֶׁר־הִתְהַלֶּךְ־שָׁם דָּוִד הוּא וַאֲנָשָׁיו:

*Hitp*

✗ (Exod 20:2) אָנֹכִי יְהוָה אֱלֹהֶיךָ אֲשֶׁר הוֹצֵאתִיךָ[6] מֵאֶרֶץ מִצְרַיִם
מִבֵּית עֲבָדִים:

*Hiph perf. I brought you out*

(Jer 45:5) וְאַתָּה תְּבַקֶּשׁ־לְךָ גְדֹלוֹת אַל־תְּבַקֵּשׁ

2. Read aloud and translate the following. You will need to
use a lexicon to translate some of the words. Chart the verbs.

(Isa 43:12) אָנֹכִי הִגַּדְתִּי וְהוֹשַׁעְתִּי[7]
וְהִשְׁמַעְתִּי וְאֵין בָּכֶם זָר[8] וְאַתֶּם
עֵדַי[9] נְאֻם־יְהוָה[a] וַאֲנִי־אֵל:

([a] frt huc tr :)

---

[6] Listed in lexicons under יצא rather than וצא. This will be explained
in subsequent chapters on Hiphil imperfect and perfect verbs.

[7] Listed in lexicons under ישע rather than ושע. See the previous
footnote.

[8] "strange (god)"

[9] "my witnesses"

(Gen 28:15) וְהִנֵּה אָנֹכִי עִמָּךְ וּשְׁמַרְתִּיךָ בְּכֹל אֲשֶׁר־תֵּלֵךְ
וַהֲשִׁבֹתִיךָ אֶל־הָאֲדָמָה הַזֹּאת כִּי לֹא אֶעֱזָבְךָ עַד אֲשֶׁר
אִם־עָשִׂיתִי אֵת אֲשֶׁר־דִּבַּרְתִּי לָךְ:

(Deut 8:10) וְאָכַלְתָּ וְשָׂבָעְתָּ וּבֵרַכְתָּ אֶת־יְהוָה אֱלֹהֶיךָ
עַל־[a]הָאָרֶץ הַטֹּבָה אֲשֶׁר נָתַן־לָךְ:
([a] pc Mss אל)

# Chapter 16

## Translation

Many people are unaware of the considerable difficulties involved in translating the Hebrew Bible. The New Jewish Publication Society Translation (NJPS) acknowledges these difficulties with such notes as: "Meaning of Hebrew uncertain." These notes may refer to a word, several words, a chapter, such as Psalm 68, or many parts of the book of Job.

Some of these difficulties are treated in other chapters of this book. Chapter 12, Textual Criticism, discusses which Hebrew text to translate, and how to identify and correct errors that have crept in through centuries of copying and recopying. The meaning of individual words, especially if they only occur once or twice in the Hebrew Bible, is one of the topics in Chapter 4, Word Studies. The meaning of grammar and the process of understanding the ancient writings of a different culture appear in other chapters (and many other books on exegesis). After determining the text and meaning in Hebrew, there are many issues involved in how to translate that meaning into another language.

The present chapter discusses different **theories of translation**, supported by examples from the resulting modern translations. The two poles on the spectrum are **literal** translation (also called text-oriented translation or formal correspondence) and **idiomatic** translation (dynamic equivalence or audience-oriented translation).

### Literal Translation

Many biblical students think the best translation is the most literal one. Each term in Hebrew should be translated word-by-word with corresponding terms in the translation language. This is called **text-oriented** because the meaning is in the text and it is important to reproduce that text as faithfully as possible in another language. This is also called **formal correspondence** because the form in Hebrew (A B C) corresponds to the form in the translation language (A B C).

This type of biblical translation has a long history in the West. Jerome is well known for recognizing that translation should be "not word-for-word, but sense-for-sense," but less well-known for qualifying this by saying, "except for Holy Scripture where even the word order is sacred." The Septuagint, Jerome's Vulgate, and modern English translations, such as the King James Version (KJV), the American Standard Version (ASB), the Revised Standard Version (RSV), and the New Jewish Publication Society (NJPS) translation are literal translations. The NJPS even holds that there should be a one-to-one correspondence between Hebrew and English words; one Hebrew word should be translated with one English word as often as possible. This tradition of translation, especially the KJV, influenced the work of many of the first missionary translators in the two-thirds (non-Western) world.

Literal translation, however, may create peculiar, awkward, or even misleading translations. English and Hebrew words have different ranges of meaning. Thus, the Hebrew word בְּרִית can be between God and a person (NJPS translates "covenant" in Genesis 15:18), between two persons (NJPS translates "pact" in Genesis 21:27), and between two rulers (NJPS translates "treaty" in 1 Kings 5:26 ET 5:12). Word order is different in Hebrew than in some other languages, so early on the rabbis decided it was acceptable for the Septuagint to reverse the Hebrew word order and translate "In the beginning God created" so that careless readers would not mistake "in the beginning" for the creator of God. The translation of every vav with "and" also makes these translations sound childish to English readers. Most of these translations recognize the need to be idiomatic sometimes in order to avoid misunderstanding. As the chair of the NRSV translation committee, Bruce Metzger said, they translate "as literally as possible, as idiomatically as necessary."

## Idiomatic Translation

This leads to the second major type of translation—idiomatic translation. An **idiom** is an expression, such as "kick the bucket," or a style that is peculiar to one language. Idioms can be meaningless, misleading, or peculiar if translated word for word into another language. Idiomatic translations attempt to understand the meaning of one language's idioms and express the meaning in the idioms that are the special genius of the translation language. Idiomatic translations aim to have the same effect on the recipients of the translation as on the original recipients. According to Eugene Nida, this includes trying to produce the same feelings and actions in the audience.[1] Because of this willingness to change the text to produce the same effect on the audience, this type of translation is called **audience-oriented** and described as **dynamic equivalence**.

Examples of this type of translation are Today's English Version (TEV) and the Common English Version (CEV), produced by the American Bible Society, and the New English Bible (NEB) and its successor the Revised English Bible (REB). Since the TEV focuses on expressing meaning clearly, it influences many current translation projects in the third world.

The medium, however, is the message. The form influences the meaning. We expect something different from poetry than from a narrative. Many passages in the Hebrew Bible were meant to be memorized and sung; therefore, they employ poetic and memorable constructions. As a result, some commend two recent literal translations of Genesis (by Mary Phil Korsak and Everett Fox) for bringing out the culture and literary structure of the stories. Harvey Minkoff jokes that if the trend to accessibility continues, we may end up with translations that sound like George Orwell's parody of Ecclesiastes 9:11 in the language of Government bureaucrats:

> Objective consideration of contemporary phenomena compels the conclusion that success or failure in competitive activities exhibits no tendency to be commensurate with innate capacity,

---

[1] Nida and Taylor, 24.

but that a considerable element of the unpredictable must invariably be taken into account.

## Audience and Purpose

The **audience** and how they will use the Bible are also important considerations in translation. Consider the **type of language**. Is it the language of the literate or uneducated? The TEV uses "common English," understood by most speakers of the language. Translations, such as the KJV, RSV, and NEB, though more literate and less understandable, are often said to have greater majesty and beauty.

Part of the wide appeal of the KJV and RSV is that they retain archaic language that is not common, contemporary English and seemingly more suitable for Scripture. The NEB retains the archaic "thou" and "thy" in addressing God, even though Hebrew has no such expression, since the translators felt their audience was not ready for "you" in addressing God.

Related to the type and level of language are the issues of slang and vulgar language. Keep in mind that what is vulgar at one time period, or in one particular culture, may not be in another time or culture. In the KJV of 1 Samuel 25:22, David vows to kill anyone from Nabal's family "that *pisseth* against the wall" (italics added). Since the writing of the KJV, most modern translations avoid this type of language, now considered vulgar in English. The Hebrew Bible normally uses the root שכב (lie with) for sexual intercourse. However, four times (Deut 28:28–30; Isa 13:16; Jer 3:1–2; Zech 14:2) the Hebrew Bible uses the root for sexual intercourse, שגל. Scholars disagree about whether this was vulgar in Hebrew, but it is clear that these passages intended to shock the readers. Most English translations prefer to reduce the shock.

## Gender

One aspect of English that is changing is the use of references to **gender**. Many native speakers now recognize that "man" and "he" did not include women. They will therefore choose more inclusive language such as "humanity" and "she and he" or "they." Israelite culture was also patriarchal and Hebrew therefore uses similar exclusive language. As English usage becomes more inclusive, however, translating with exclusive language may create meanings that would not have been so strong for the original hearers.

Thus, several recent translations in English make **inclusive language** their goal. The NRSV uses inclusive human language. Exactly what "inclusive language" meant varied over the years the translation committee met, and varied between committees translating different books. The *Inclusive Language Lectionary* uses more extensive inclusive language and imagery for both humanity and God.

## Scripture

Most of the writers of the Bible did not know that what they were writing would become scripture. As the Hebrew Bible is the scripture of church and synagogue, Jews and Christians through the centuries have felt justified in removing vulgar language in translation. The function of the Hebrew Bible as scripture is also one of the reasons for inclusive translations.

Many translations are meant to be read in church or synagogue. The RSV of Psalm 50:9 reads: "I will accept no bull from your house." Most translations for church reading try to avoid such unintentional misunderstandings, associations, and vulgarisms. Therefore, the NRSV translates: "I will accept no ox from your house."

## Translators

The translators and how they are organized also affect the translation. Translations by an individual often bear the peculiarities of that one translator. For that reason, and due to the enormous amount of work involved, committees do many contemporary translations. In addition, many translations use individuals or committees as stylists, who identify idioms created by literal translation that do not sound natural or appropriate to native speakers of the language. Some translations done by expatriates are unpopular with local people because they sound peculiar. More natural sounding translations will start to appear in the third world as native speakers receive the education and training to do their own translations.

The theology and social status of the translators may intentionally or unintentionally affect the translation. The slightly archaic and more difficult language of translations, such as the NEB and NRSV, is produced and used by a literate elite. American evangelical scholars produced the NIV. The worst example, The Living Bible, is not a translation. It is a compilation from the various English versions by one individual who regularly expanded the Bible with his own fundamentalist theological bias and anti-Semitic statements (Matt 12:45; 16:4; Luke 17:25; John 1:17; Gal 4:3; 5:1).

Whatever one decides about these and many other translation issues, making two translations is a good practice for exegesis. The first is a literal translation that brings out the literary structure of the Hebrew. (Chapter 28, Hebrew Narrative, discusses this type of literal translation.) The second is a more idiomatic translation that attempts to communicate the results of the exegesis.

**Exercises**

1. The NIV translates Psalm 103:1 as "Praise the LORD, O my soul." The NRSV translated it as "Bless the LORD, O my soul." Why is the translation different?

2. In Psalm 1:1 the word אַשְׁרֵי is translated "blessed" by the NIV and "happy" by others such as the NRSV, TEV, and NJPS. What do you think would be the best translation and why?

3. The description of God as אֶרֶךְ אַפַּיִם is common in the Hebrew Bible.[2] What does this idiom say literally? What does it mean?

---

[2] Exod 34:6; Num 14:18; Neh 9:17; Ps 86:15; 103:8; 145:8; Prov 14:29; 16:32; Joel 2:13; Jonah 4:2; Nah 1:3.

# Chapter 17

## Hiphil Imperfect

The second most common stem in Hebrew is the Hiphil. A "dot vowel"—hireq ( . ), tsere ( .. ) or segol ( .. )—under the middle root letter is a consistent **indicator** of the Hiphil stem. (Verbs in stems other than Hiphil, however, may have a dot vowel under the middle root letter.)

### Form of the Hiphil Imperfect

The **indicator** of the Hiphil imperfect is a pataḥ ( _ ) under the imperfect prefix.

יַשְׁמִיר

With a vav consecutive, the form is shortened.

וַיַּשְׁמֵר

or

וַיַּשְׁמֶר

With **III-gutturals** (ע ח ה), because they prefer a-class vowels before them, a pataḥ may replace the dot vowel.

וַיַּשְׁלַח

**III-heʾ**. The heʾ may be present, absent, or replaced by a tav or yod. When the final heʾ disappears, then the dot vowel may be under the first root letter or absent altogether.

וַיֶּגֶל
וַיַּגְלוּ

Note that in the first example the expected pataḥ under the yod has changed to a segol under the influence of the segol under the gimel. The Qal imperfect of this root has a ḥireq under the yod.

Some forms could be either Qal or Hiphil. For example,

$$\text{וַיַּעַל from עלה}$$

The final heᵓ is lost in both Qal and Hiphil. In the above example, the pataḥ may be a sign of the Hiphil. On the other hand, because gutturals prefer a-class vowels underneath and before them, it could be a Qal. The reader must use the meaning in context to determine the stem.

**I-nun** assimilates.

$$\text{יַגִּיד from נגד}$$

**I-vav.** Although now usually listed in lexicons as I-yod, original I-vav remains in the Hiphil.

$$\text{יוֹשִׁיב from ישׁב}$$

הלך behaves like a I-vav.

$$\text{יוֹלִיךְ}$$

**II-vav or yod** are the same in the Hiphil. A qamets under the prefix is an indicator of a II-vav or yod root (as in Qal), and the first root letter, rather than the second, has a dot vowel.

$$\text{יָקִים from קום}$$

**Meaning of the Hiphil**

The differences of meaning between Qal, Piel, and Hiphil are important to understanding the Hebrew stems. Older grammars called the Piel intensive and the Hiphil causative. But this did not bring out the difference between the two stems because many Piels also seemed causative. (Moreover, both Piel and Hiphil had similar factitive and denominative uses.) According to Ernst Jenni, the difference is that, whereas Piel indicates bringing about a state, Hiphil indicates *causing an event*. In other words, Piel tends to be action that is habitual or ongoing; Hiphil tends to be *action that occurs only once or a few times.* Piel tends to have a passive object; Hiphil tends to have an object that takes part as a second subject in the action.

Verbs that are intransitive in Qal tend to be transitive in Hiphil. Transitive verbs take an object or objects. Intransitive verbs do not take an object. When a verb is transitive in Qal, it tends to take two objects in the Hiphil.

## Vocabulary

| | |
|---|---|
| אֹיֵב אוֹיֵב | enemy |
| אַף | nose, nostril; anger |
| בְּרִית | covenant |
| בָּשָׂר | flesh |
| חֹדֶשׁ | new moon, month |
| חָזַק | be(come) strong; (Hi) seize, grasp |
| חַטָּאת | sin, sin-offering |
| חָיָה | live, be (stay) alive |
| כָּרַת | cut off, fell, exterminate; make (a covenant) |
| נָבִיא | prophet |
| עָנָה | answer |
| עֵץ | tree(s) (often collective) |
| רוּחַ | spirit, wind |
| שָׂדֶה שָׂדַי | field |
| שַׁעַר | gate |

## Exercises

1. Read aloud, translate, and chart the verbs in the following verses. Discuss the meaning of the Hiphil verbs. By now you

should be able to use a lexicon or be ready to learn to use one. For that reason, exercises will no longer be separated. You will need to use a lexicon to look up some words in many exercises.

(Gen 3:21) וַיַּעַשׂ יְהוָה אֱלֹהִים לְאָדָם[a] וּלְאִשְׁתּוֹ כָּתְנוֹת
עוֹר וַיַּלְבִּשֵׁם: ([a] cf 17[a])[1]

(Exod 3:6) וַיֹּאמֶר אָנֹכִי אֱלֹהֵי אָבִיךָ[a] אֱלֹהֵי אַבְרָהָם
אֱלֹהֵי[b] יִצְחָק וֵאלֹהֵי יַעֲקֹב וַיַּסְתֵּר מֹשֶׁה פָּנָיו כִּי יָרֵא
([a] ＊𝕲[58.72] et Act 7,32 Just אֲבֹתֶיךָ ‖
[b] pc Mss ＊𝕲 וֵאלֹהֵי cf 15[a].16[b] 4,5[b])

(Exod 3:11) וַיֹּאמֶר מֹשֶׁה אֶל־הָאֱלֹהִים מִי אָנֹכִי כִּי אֵלֵךְ
אֶל־פַּרְעֹה וְכִי אוֹצִיא אֶת־בְּנֵי יִשְׂרָאֵל מִמִּצְרָיִם:

(Deut 6:2) יַאֲרִכֻן יָמֶיךָ:

(Ruth 3:16) וַתָּבוֹא אֶל־חֲמוֹתָהּ וַתֹּאמֶר מִי־אַתְּ בִּתִּי
וַתַּגֶּד־לָהּ אֵת כָּל־אֲשֶׁר עָשָׂה־לָהּ הָאִישׁ

(Gen 2:15) וַיִּקַּח יְהוָה אֱלֹהִים אֶת־הָאָדָם וַיַּנִּחֵהוּ
בְגַן־עֵדֶן

(Gen 2:19) [2]וַיִּצֶר יְהוָה אֱלֹהִים[a] מִן־הָאֲדָמָה[b] כָּל־חַיַּת
הַשָּׂדֶה וְאֵת כָּל־עוֹף הַשָּׁמַיִם וַיָּבֵא אֶל־הָאָדָם
([a] ＊𝕲 + עוֹד ‖ [b] ins c ＊𝕲 אֶת)

(Gen 2:21) וַיַּפֵּל יְהוָה אֱלֹהִים׀ תַּרְדֵּמָה עַל־הָאָדָם

---

[1] Footnote 17[a] (on וּלְאָדָם in Gen 3:17) reads: וּלְ וְלַ .
[2] You may have difficulty charting this verb unless you recognize that the vowel under the yod is written defectively.

(Gen 2:22) וַיִּבֶן יְהֹוָה אֱלֹהִים ׀ אֶת־הַצֵּלָע אֲשֶׁר־לָקַח מִן־הָאָדָם
לְאִשָּׁה וַיְבִאֶהָ אֶל־הָאָדָם:

(Isa 42:6) אֲנִי יְהֹוָה קְרָאתִיךָ בְצֶדֶק וְאַחְזֵק[a] בְּיָדֶךָ
([a] 1 ' ך cf 𝔖𝔙)

(Gen 2:9) וַיַּצְמַח יְהֹוָה אֱלֹהִים מִן־הָאֲדָמָה כָּל־עֵץ נֶחְמָד[3]
לְמַרְאֶה וְטוֹב לְמַאֲכָל וְעֵץ הַחַיִּים בְּתוֹךְ הַגָּן וְעֵץ הַדַּעַת
טוֹב וָרָע:

---

[3] "desirable"

# Chapter 18

## Piel Imperfect

The third most frequent stem in Hebrew is the Piel. The **stem indicator** is the strong dagesh (doubling) in the middle root letter.

דבּר

The gutturals (ע ח ה א) and resh (ר) do not double when they are the middle root letter. Occasionally, doubling is lost when a suffixed pronoun is added, or in the imperfect of III-he᾽ roots with vav consecutive.

| | | |
|---|---|---|
| II-guttural or II-resh: | וַיְבָרֶךְ | he blessed |
| Sheva under middle root letter: | בִּקְשָׁה[1] | she sought |
| Suffixed pronoun: | וּתְהַלְלֶךָ | that she may praise you |
| III-he᾽ with vav consecutive: | וַיְצַו | he commanded |

When the doubling is missing as in the examples above, the indicators of the Piel imperfect and Piel perfect are all the more important to recognize the stem. The indicators for the Piel imperfect are in the next subsection and the indicators for the Piel perfect are in Chapter 21.

---

[1] This is a Piel *perfect*, which will be discussed in Chapter 21.

**Form of the Piel Imperfect**

The Piel imperfect also has the same prefixes and suffixes as the Qal imperfect. The **indicator** of the Piel imperfect is a sheva under the imperfect prefix.

יְדַבֵּר       תְּדַבֵּר       אֲדַבֵּר       נְדַבֵּר

Notice that the 1cs prefix is a guttural, which prefers composite shevas.

Verbs in stems other than Piel may have a sheva under the prefix of the imperfect. For example, III-heʾ Qal verbs with vav consecutive may have a sheva under the prefix.

וַיְהִי־אוֹ

      And there was light (Gen 3:1)

The simple meaning in this context and the fact that היה does not appear in the Piel identify this as a Qal.

Verbs with suffixed pronouns may also have a sheva under the prefix of the Qal imperfect.

וַיְבִאֶהָ

      he brought her (Gen 2:22)

In this case, however, the dot vowel under the bet and the meaning in context identify the stem as Hiphil.

**Meaning of the Piel**

Older grammars called the Piel intensive. The designation intensive was appealing because the doubling of the middle root letter seemed intensive, so form and meaning seemed to correspond. But few if any verbs could be shown to have a more intensive meaning in the Piel than in the Qal. Ernst Jenni proposed a better way to understand the Piel: Piel indicates *bringing about a state*. Hebrew uses the Piel when the subject is putting the object into the state or condition corresponding to the meaning of the verb root. The object thus takes part in the action as a passive, secondary subject. Being a state, *the action tends to be habitual or ongoing*.

This general meaning can be further divided into factitive, denominative, and frequentative. (The Piel forms below are those of the Piel perfect, discussed in Chapter 21).

**Factitive.** According to Webster's Dictionary a factitive verb is one that expresses the idea of making, calling, or thinking something to be of a certain character.

| Qal | | Piel | |
|---|---|---|---|
| צָדַק | be just, righteous | צִדֵּק | declare just |

**Denominative** verbs are formed from nouns. Generally, it is thought that they are formed from nouns because the noun forms appear earlier and more frequently than the verb forms.

| Noun | | Piel | |
|---|---|---|---|
| דָּבָר | word | דִּבֶּר | speak (make or declare a word) |

A subgroup of denominative verbs is **privative**, which indicate taking something away from or injuring the noun.

| Noun | | Piel | |
|---|---|---|---|
| חַטָּאת | sin | חִטֵּא | free from sin |

**Frequentative.** These are also called iterative or pluralic, indicating multiple or repeated action.

| Qal | | Piel | |
|---|---|---|---|
| הָלַךְ | walk | הִלֵּךְ | walk around |

The reason why some verbs use Piel is unclear because either they do not occur in Qal, or when they do occur in both Qal and Piel, there is no apparent difference in meaning.

## Vocabulary

| | |
|---|---|
| אֶבֶן | stone (f) |
| אֲדָמָה | ground |
| לֶחֶם | bread |
| מְאֹד | force, might (noun); <u>very</u>, <u>exceedingly</u> (adv) |
| מִדְבָּר | pasturage, wilderness, steppe |
| מִשְׁפָּחָה | family; clan |
| סָבִיב | circuit (noun); all around, round about, surrounding (adv) |
| עָבַד | serve |
| עֹלָה | burnt offering |
| עֵת | time |
| פְּלִשְׁתִּי | Philistine (פְּלֶשֶׁת "Philistia") |
| פָּקַד | visit; number; appoint; miss; take care of; muster |
| צֹאן | flock |
| קָרַב | draw near |
| שְׁלֹמֹה | Solomon |

## Exercises

1. Read aloud and translate the following. Chart the verbs.
Discuss the meaning of the Piel verbs.

וַיְבָרֶךְ אֹתָם אֱלֹהִים (Gen 1:28)

וַיְצַו יְהוָה אֱלֹהִים עַל־הָאָדָם ... (Gen 2:16)
מִכֹּל עֵץ־הַגָּן ... תֹּאכֵל:

וַיְבָרֶךְ אֱלֹהִים אֶת־יוֹם הַשְּׁבִיעִי וַיְקַדֵּשׁ אֹתוֹ (Gen 2:3)

(Num 6:24) יְבָרֶכְךָ יְהוָה וְיִשְׁמְרֶךָ:

(Exod 3:20) וְשָׁלַחְתִּי אֶת־יָדִי וְהִכֵּיתִי אֶת־מִצְרַיִם בְּכֹל
נִפְלְאֹתַי[2] אֲשֶׁר אֶעֱשֶׂה בְּקִרְבּוֹ וְאַחֲרֵי־כֵן יְשַׁלַּח אֶתְכֶם:

(1 Kgs 1:2) וַיֹּאמְרוּ לוֹ[a] עֲבָדָיו יְבַקְשׁוּ לַאדֹנִי[b] הַמֶּלֶךְ
נַעֲרָה בְתוּלָה וְעָמְדָה לִפְנֵי הַמֶּלֶךְ וּתְהִי־לוֹ
סֹכֶנֶת[3] וְשָׁכְבָה בְחֵיקֶךָ[c]

( [a] > 𝕲* ‖ [b] 𝕲ᴮ𝕯 suff 1 pl ‖ [c] 𝕲* μετ' αὐτοῦ "with him," 𝕯ᴹˢˢ *in sinu suo*)

(Exod 2:17) וַיָּבֹאוּ הָרֹעִים וַיְגָרְשׁוּם וַיָּקָם מֹשֶׁה וַיּוֹשִׁעָן
וַיַּשְׁקְ אֶת־צֹאנָם:

(Deut 5:11) לֹא תִשָּׂא אֶת־שֵׁם־יְהוָה אֱלֹהֶיךָ לַשָּׁוְא כִּי לֹא יְנַקֶּה
יְהוָה אֵת[a] אֲשֶׁר־יִשָּׂא[b] אֶת־שְׁמוֹ לַשָּׁוְא[b]:

( [a] 𝕼𝕮ᴶ + כָּ]ל[וֹ, 1 𝕸 ut Ex 20,7 ‖ [b–b] > 𝕼)

(Deut 5:24) וַתֹּאמְרוּ[a] הֵן הֶרְאָנוּ יְהוָה אֱלֹהֵינוּ אֶת־כְּבֹדוֹ
וְאֶת־גָּדְלוֹ[b] וְאֶת־קֹלוֹ שָׁמַעְנוּ מִתּוֹךְ הָאֵשׁ הַיּוֹם הַזֶּה רָאִינוּ
כִּי־יְדַבֵּר אֱלֹהִים[c] אֶת־הָאָדָם וָחָי:

( [a] cf 𝕼 יהוה ‖ [b–b] > 𝕲⁻ᴸᴼ ‖ [c] 𝕼 ואתם ת 𝕼ᵃ)

2. Begin a word study by reading the entry in your lexicon
for ברך and noting the possible meanings. Prepare for a discussion
of the meaning of the word.

---

[2] "my wonders"
[3] "one serving"

# Chapter 19

## Hiphil Perfect

### Form of the Hiphil Perfect

The **indicator** of the Hiphil **stem,** as mentioned in Chapter 17, is a dot vowel—ḥireq ( ), tsere ( ) or segol ( )—under the middle root letter. The **indicator** of the Hiphil **perfect** is a prefixed heʾ (–הַ). The vowel pointing is usually –הִ and sometimes –הַ, –הֶ or –הָ.[1] This heʾ may derive from the heʾ of the pronouns (הִיא הוּא) and represent the "second subject" mentioned in Chapter 17.

הִגְדִּיל

The dot vowel occurs only in third-person forms in the perfect. It is still a helpful indicator because third-person forms are the most commonly occurring.

**I-nun.** When the first root letter is a nun (נ), it assimilates into the second root letter.

*הִנְגִּיד < הִגִּיד

**I-vav.** Although listed as I-yod in lexicons, the original vav remains in the Hiphil perfect.

ישׁב from הוֹשִׁיב

---

[1] This heʾ could be easily confused with the interrogative heʾ or the definite article, especially since the pointing of the last example is the same as that of the interrogative heʾ.

The verb הָלַךְ acts like a I-vav in the Hiphil.

$$\text{הוֹלִיךְ}$$

A few I-vav verbs, usually with צ as the middle root letter, show assimilation of yod into the second root letter like a I-nun verb.

הִצִּיתוּ from יצת

**II-vav or yod**. Both II-vav and II-yod have the same form in the Hiphil perfect, with a ḥireq yod between the first and third root letters.

הֵקִים from קוּם
הֵשִׂים from שִׂים

The forms may have a ḥireq or tsere without the yod. For unknown reasons a ḥolem or ḥolem-vav sometimes appears before perfect suffixes beginning with a consonant.

*phonetic ḥolem-vav*

הֲבִיאוֹתָ from בוא

**III-heʾ**. As elsewhere the heʾ may be present, absent, or replaced by a tav or yod.

| PGN | גלה |
|-----|-----|
| 3ms | הִגְלָה |
| 3fs | הִגְלְתָה |
| 2ms | הִגְלִיתָ |
| 3cp | הִגְלוּ |

I-guttural, III-guttural, III-heʾ, and I-yod all have minor vowel changes in keeping with the character of these letters, but the indicators and all the letters of the roots are still visible.

## Vocabulary

| | | |
|---|---|---|
| — | אֵל | God, god |
| — | אַמָּה | forearm, cubit |
| — | גְּבוּל | boundary, territory |
| — | זָכַר | remember |
| — | זֶרַע | seed, descendant |
| — | חָטָא | miss (a mark), sin *(vb.)* |
| — | חַיִל | strength; wealth; army |
| — | חֶסֶד | loyalty, faithfulness |
| — | יְהוֹשׁוּעַ | Joshua (short form: יֵשׁוּעַ) |
| — | יָרַשׁ | subdue, possess, dispossess; tread |
| — | כָּתַב | write |
| — | לַיְלָה   לֵיל | night |
| — | לְמַעַן | for the sake of, on account of (prep); in order that (conj) |
| — | מוֹעֵד | appointed place or time; season |
| — | מַטֶּה | rod, staff; tribe |

## Exercises

1. Read aloud and translate the following. Chart the verbs. Discuss the meaning of the Hiphil verbs.

(Mic 6:8) הִגִּיד לְךָ אָדָם מַה־טּוֹב

(Josh 12:1) וְאֵלֶּה ׀ מַלְכֵי הָאָרֶץ אֲשֶׁר הִכּוּ בְנֵי־יִשְׂרָאֵל
וַיִּרְשׁוּ אֶת־אַרְצָם

(Num 17:6 ET 16:41) אַתֶּם הֲמִתֶּם אֶת־עַם יְהוָה:

(Amos 2:10) וְאָנֹכִי הֶעֱלֵיתִי אֶתְכֶם מֵאֶרֶץ מִצְרַיִם וָאוֹלֵךְ אֶתְכֶם
בַּמִּדְבָּר אַרְבָּעִים שָׁנָה

(Gen 3:11) וַיֹּאמֶר מִי הִגִּיד לְךָ כִּי עֵירֹם אָתָּה

(Gen 3:13) וַיֹּאמֶר יְהוָה אֱלֹהִים לָאִשָּׁה מַה־זֹּאת עָשִׂית וַתֹּאמֶר
הָאִשָּׁה הַנָּחָשׁ הִשִּׁיאַנִי וָאֹכֵל:

(Deut 11:23) וְהוֹרִישׁ יְהוָה אֶת־כָּל־הַגּוֹיִם הָאֵלֶּה מִלִּפְנֵיכֶם[a]
וִירִשְׁתֶּם גּוֹיִם גְּדֹלִים וַעֲצֻמִים מִכֶּם[b]:
(מִמְּךָ שׁׁ[b] ‖ יָד שׁׁ[a])

(Isa 36:20) מִי בְּכָל־אֱלֹהֵי הָאֲרָצוֹת הָאֵלֶּה אֲשֶׁר־הִצִּילוּ
אֶת־אַרְצָם מִיָּדִי כִּי־יַצִּיל יְהוָה אֶת־יְרוּשָׁלִַם מִיָּדִי:

(Exod 16:5) וְהָיָה בַּיּוֹם הַשִּׁשִּׁי וְהֵכִינוּ אֵת אֲשֶׁר־יָבִיאוּ וְהָיָה
מִשְׁנֶה עַל אֲשֶׁר־יִלְקְטוּ יוֹם׀ יוֹם[2]:

(Judg 2:18) וְכִי־הֵקִים יְהוָה׀ לָהֶם שֹׁפְטִים[3] וְהָיָה יְהוָה
עִם־הַשֹּׁפֵט וְהוֹשִׁיעָם מִיַּד אֹיְבֵיהֶם כֹּל יְמֵי הַשּׁוֹפֵט

(Ezek 37:6) וְנָתַתִּי עֲלֵיכֶם גִּדִים וְהַעֲלֵתִי עֲלֵיכֶם בָּשָׂר וְקָרַמְתִּי
עֲלֵיכֶם עוֹר וְנָתַתִּי בָכֶם רוּחַ[a] וִחְיִיתֶם וִידַעְתֶּם כִּי־אֲנִי יְהוָה:
([a] 𝔊 + μου "my," 1𝔐)

---

[2] This is a Hebrew idiom. Look up the meaning in a lexicon.
[3] "judges"

# Chapter 20

## Authors and Editors

When we read a newspaper article, we make judgments about the perspective and reliability of the writer. Historians make similar judgments about their historical sources (including newspapers) when they write histories. The idea that the Bible could and should be read like any other book revolutionized biblical studies. Biblical scholars began to question the Bible, just as historians and literary critics did: Who wrote this? When did they write it? What was their perspective?

Ancient authors lived in traditional, communal societies where the individual and therefore individual authorship were not as important as in the modern world. The community's oral and written traditions were copied and handed down from generation to generation. Modern historians are interested in identifying these authors and their sources in order to understand more precisely their historical context and perspective.

### Source Criticism

The method for identifying and analyzing sources in biblical studies is called source criticism. In a few cases, biblical writers indicate their sources. When the book of 2 Chronicles refers to the "Book of the Kings of Israel and Judah,"[1] it may be referring to the biblical books of Samuel and Kings. In other cases, long lost books are mentioned. The "Book of the Wars of the LORD" is quoted in Numbers 21:14. Joshua 10:13 and 2 Samuel 1:18 refer to the "Book of Jashar" and 1 Kings 11:41 refers to the "Book of the Acts of Solomon." The books of Kings often state that more information can be found in the "Book of the Annals of the Kings

---

[1] 2 Chr 16:11; 25:26; 28:26; 32:32.

of Israel"[2] or the "Book of the Annals of the Kings of Judah."[3] We can only speculate about what was in these books.

Over vast expanses of the Hebrew Bible, the writers do not identify themselves or their sources. However, sources can still be identified by the following evidence:

- Stories told twice in slightly different ways or repetitions within one story (doublets);
- Shifts in vocabulary and style;
- Differences in theology and ideology;
- Evidence of different historical contexts;
- Disruptions in the logical or narrative flow.

In the history of biblical studies, evidence of sources was first discovered in the Pentateuch. Two stories of creation in Genesis 1:1–2:4a and 2:4b–3:24 create a disruption in logical or narrative flow, especially because the order of creation is different in the second account. They also show differences in theology, vocabulary, and style. Note this often cited difference in vocabulary: Genesis 1:1–2:4a refers to אֱלֹהִים "God," whereas Genesis 1:1–2:4a refers to יְהוָה אֱלֹהִים "LORD God." Biblical scholars call the source of the first story P for the Priestly writer. The source of the second story is called J because German scholars first discovered the sources and J is the first letter of the transliteration into German of the proper name of God (יְהוָה).

These sources seem to continue beyond the creation stories, as the same differences in vocabulary, style, and theology appear on the same sides of doublets throughout the Pentateuch. For example, in the story of Noah, אֱלֹהִים "God" commands Noah to take two of every kind of animal into the ark (Gen 6:19–22), whereas יְהוָה "the LORD" tells Noah to take seven pairs of all clean animals and a pair of unclean animals (7:1–3).

---

[2] 1 Kgs 14:19; 15:31; 16:5, 14, 20, 27; 22:39; 2 Kgs 1:18; 10:34; 13:8, 12; 14:15, 28; 15:11, 15, 21, 26, 31.

[3] 1 Kgs 14:29; 15:7, 23; 22:45; 2 Kgs 8:23; 12:19; 14:18; 15:6, 36; 16:19; 20:20; 21:17, 25; 23:28; 24:5.

This source theory is often referred to as **JEDP**, after the names of the sources, or as the **Documentary Hypothesis**. J and P are the most prominent sources in the first four books of the Pentateuch. D is largely identical to the book of Deuteronomy. E is less frequent and sometimes difficult to distinguish. Although aspects of the hypothesis continue to be hotly debated, the existence of the sources is widely accepted by biblical scholars, because no one has presented a more persuasive explanation of the evidence.

A beginning student cannot assess the theory by reading the entire Pentateuch in Hebrew, but will rely partly on the identification, dating, and description of the sources in critical introductions, commentaries, and Bible dictionaries. However, knowledge of Hebrew does allow the student to examine the vocabulary and style of a particular passage. The student can also find out when scholars date the source and think about its ideology and message within its context. For example, the first creation story (Gen 1:1–2:4a) is commonly assigned to the priestly source written in the exilic or post-exilic period. A student studying a passage in Genesis 1 could therefore compare the passage to creation stories from Mesopotamia[4] that Israel would have been exposed to in exile, and consider how the passage reflects and reacts to those stories and the situation of the exile.

In this chapter's exercises, you can compare the reasons given for the Sabbath commandment by P and D. You may want to look at examples of sources that you have already translated. In the previous chapter, Genesis 3:11 and 3:13 were from the J source. Deuteronomy 11:23 was from D. The reading from Exodus 16:5 reflected the priestly (P) writers' interest in Sabbath, rituals, and time. In the examples in subsequent chapters, you can observe their Hebrew vocabulary and style, and reflect on their theology and ideology in historical context.

---

[4] Several Mesopotamian creation stories are translated in James Pritchard, ed., *Ancient Near Eastern Texts Relating to the Old Testament* (3d ed.; Princeton: Princeton University Press, 1969).

**Redaction Criticism**

Continuing study of the literature of the Hebrew Bible revealed that not only were there different sources, but these were selected and arranged by editors in order to present a certain perspective or interpretation. In some cases, the editors also inserted passages with their own interpretations of the sources. These editors in biblical studies are often called **redactors** and the method for identifying redactors is called redaction criticism.

Editorial activity is easiest to identify when we have two different accounts of the same material. An example would be the repetition of laws in P and D. Deuteronomy means "second law." Another example is the history of Israel in Joshua through Kings and the parallel history in Chronicles.

Even if we do not have two accounts of the same material, we still may be able to distinguish the work of one or more editors. Editorial activity, often speeches or prayers, is most evident in the introduction and conclusion, and at the transitional or bridging passages. In these passages, the hand of an editor is evident, when passages are not self-contained stories and therefore cannot be told on their own. Editors orient the reader to the meaning of the longer work using language and idioms that typically appear in these introductory, transitional, and concluding passages.

The theology and style of Deuteronomy influenced the editors of the books from Joshua to 2 Kings that tell Israel's story from entry into the land to exile. These books are therefore referred to as the **Deuteronomistic History** (DH) and the editor or editors as the **Deuteronomist** (Dtr) or Deuteronomists. Deuteronomistic style and theology helps us identify these editors' additions. They placed Deuteronomy at the beginning of their history and organized their source materials into four historical periods: the time of Moses, the entry into the land under Joshua, the judges, and the reigns of kings. They inserted their own compositions throughout, especially at transitions between periods of history. Sometimes these are speeches or prayers by prominent figures, for example, speeches by Joshua that introduce (Joshua 1) and conclude (Joshua 23) the entry into the land. Samuel's speech in 1 Samuel 12 makes a transition between the period of the judges and the beginning of the monarchy. Nathan's oracle in 2 Samuel 7 introduces the promise to David and the building of the temple. Solomon's prayer in 1 Kings 8 concludes the first period of the monarchy and marks the completion of the temple. In other places, Dtr speaks through the voice of the narrator (Josh 12; Judg 2:11–22; 2 Kgs 17:7–18, 20–23).

Martin Noth, the biblical scholar who first recognized the Deuteronomistic History as a unified work, thought an exilic editor created it to show how the exile was punishment for Israel and Judah's long history of unfaithfulness. Other scholars thought this was too simple and negative a message for such a long work. Gerhard von Rad and Hans Walter Wolff pointed to the promise to David and the pattern of apostasy, punishment, return (שׁוּב), and deliverance. (The reading from Judges 2:18 in the previous chapter is an example of the last part of this Deuteronomistic pattern.) Although the exile was the punishment for a long history of unfaithfulness and injustice, God would be merciful and deliver, if the people returned to God.

Rudolph Smend and Frank Moore Cross detected more than one edition of the Deuteronomistic History. Josiah seemed to fulfill the hope for a king such as David. Then, when he dies in battle, the Deuteronomistic History quickly ends. Cross suggested the first edition was produced around the time of Josiah. Dtr 1 blamed the fall of the northern kingdom of Israel on the many northern kings who "walked in the way of Jeroboam," causing Israel to sin.[5] Dtr 1 wrote to encourage the people to support Josiah's religious reforms based on the book of Deuteronomy and hoped for restoration under this king "like David." When Josiah's sudden death in battle dashed these hopes, the Deuteronomistic History came to an abrupt end. An exilic redactor (Dtr 2) blamed the exile on the sins of Manasseh, which could not be overcome even by Josiah (2 Kgs 21:10-25), and added a brief conclusion. According to Cross, Dtr 2 inserted passages that predict the exile and say restoration is

[5] 1 Kgs 15:26, 30, 34; 16:2, 19, 26, 31; 22:52; 2 Kgs 3:3; 10:29; 13:2, 6, 11; 14:24; 15:9, 18, 24, 28.

possible if the people return to God.[6] Cross' theory of two editions, one of them pre-exilic, is more widely accepted in North America than in Europe. Recently several scholars have shifted their attention to uncovering the sources used by Dtr that appear to contain prophetic and anti-monarchical strains.

Although scholars do not always agree about exactly how the Deuteronomistic History was edited and the message of the editors, this discussion can help us appreciate the historical meaning of this great work.

## Hebrew Style

After reading many writings of a particular English novelist, poet, or journalist, we come to recognize recurring themes, perspectives, and a typical writing style. The same is true for ancient Hebrew writers and editors. Knowledge of Hebrew gives you the ability to investigate and appreciate the style of different sources, authors, and editors.

In order to discover whether certain Hebrew words or idioms are typical of an author or source, the use of a concordance is essential. The new computerized concordances can help you search quickly for a particular word, form, or phrase from the Bible. If it occurs almost exclusively in the writing of one author or source, it is probably typical of his or her style.

Deuteronomy has one of the most distinctive manners of expression, including the frequent use and mixing of singular and plural second person verbs and pronouns. Deuteronomy wants to address the people as a whole as well as each individual. Also typical is the use of הַיּוֹם "today." Although this is a common expression throughout the Bible, a concordance search reveals that it is quite frequent in Deuteronomy. Deuteronomy wants to make the observance of the teachings present "today:" "The LORD did not make this covenant with our ancestors, but with us, we who are here today (הַיּוֹם), all of us who are alive" (Deut 5:3).

Deuteronomy 6:4 is important in both the Jewish and Christian traditions, and many consider it to be central to the

---

[6] See, for example, 1 Kgs 8:46-53.

theology of Deuteronomy. Deuteronomy preaches one people, and the worship of one God, in one place. In Chapter 27, you will read a selection from Deuteronomy 6.

**Exercises**

1. Read the different reasons given for the Sabbath in the two versions of the Ten Commandments:

(Exod 20:11) כִּי שֵׁשֶׁת־יָמִים֩ עָשָׂ֨ה יְהוָ֜ה אֶת־הַשָּׁמַ֣יִם
וְאֶת־הָאָ֗רֶץ אֶת־הַיָּם֙ וְאֶת־כָּל־אֲשֶׁר־בָּ֔ם וַיָּ֖נַח בַּיּ֣וֹם הַשְּׁבִיעִ֑י
(וְאֵת ט Ms 𝔊𝔖ℭ᷍ℭ᷍ mlt Mss ᵃ)

(Deut 5:15) וְזָכַרְתָּ֞ כִּי־עֶ֣בֶד הָיִ֣יתָ ׀ בְּאֶ֣רֶץ מִצְרַ֗יִם וַיֹּצִֽאֲךָ֩
יְהוָ֨ה אֱלֹהֶ֤יךָ מִשָּׁם֙ בְּיָ֤ד חֲזָקָה֙ וּבִזְרֹ֣עַ נְטוּיָ֔ה עַל־כֵּ֗ן צִוְּךָ֙
יְהוָ֣ה אֱלֹהֶ֔יךָ לַעֲשׂ֖וֹת אֶת־י֥וֹם הַשַּׁבָּֽתᵃ׃ ס
(וּלְקַדְּשֽׁוֹ = καὶ ἁγιάζειν αὐτήν + 𝔊ᴼ ᵃ cf Ex 20, 11)

2. Read the verses from Deuteronomy below, the Deuteronomistic History, and the Chronicler. Note the similarities and differences in vocabulary, style, and theology. (You have already read the second passage, 2 Kings 23:25 in the exercises for Chapter 11.)

(Deut 6:5–6) וְאָהַבְתָּ֔ אֵ֥ת יְהוָ֖ה אֱלֹהֶ֑יךָ בְּכָל־לְבָבְךָ֥ וּבְכָל־נַפְשְׁךָ֖
וּבְכָל־מְאֹדֶֽךָ׃ וְהָי֞וּ הַדְּבָרִ֣ים הָאֵ֗לֶּה אֲשֶׁ֨ר אָנֹכִ֧י מְצַוְּךָ֛ הַיּ֖וֹם
עַל־לְבָבֶֽךָ׃

(2 Kgs 23:25) וְכָמֹ֩הוּ֩ לֹֽא־הָיָ֨ה לְפָנָ֜יו מֶ֗לֶךְ אֲשֶׁר־שָׁ֣ב
אֶל־יְהוָ֗ה בְּכָל־לְבָבוֹ֙ וּבְכָל־נַפְשׁוֹ֙ וּבְכָל־מְאֹד֔וֹ
כְּכֹל᷍ᵃ תּוֹרַ֣ת מֹשֶׁ֑ה וְאַחֲרָ֕יו לֹֽא־קָ֥ם כָּמֹֽהוּ׃
(וּבְכֹל nonn Mss, בְּכֹל Seb nonn Mss ᵃ)

(2 Chr 35:26–27) וְיֶתֶר דִּבְרֵי יֹאשִׁיָּהוּ וַחֲסָדָיו כַּכָּתוּב[a] כַּכָּתוּב[7] בְּתוֹרַת
יְהוָה: וּדְבָרָיו[a] הָרִאשֹׁנִים וְהָאַחֲרֹנִים הִנָּם כְּתוּבִים[8]

( **26** [a] 𝔊 καὶ ἡ ἐλπὶς αὐτοῦ "and his hope")

---

[7] "as written." A Qal passive particle. See Chapter 25.
[8] "are written." See previous footnote.

# Chapter 21

## Piel Perfect

### Form of the Piel Perfect

The perfect in the Piel is easily identifiable because it has the same suffixes as the Qal perfect. The **indicator** of the Piel **perfect** is the ḥireq under the first root letter.

דִּבֶּר

As mentioned in Chapter 18 (Piel imperfect), the **indicator** of the Piel **stem** is the doubling of the middle root letter.

When the middle root letter is a guttural (א ה ח ע) or resh (ר), these letters cannot take a dagesh (doubling). In some cases, there is "compensation" by lengthening the previous vowel. The **indicator** of the Piel in these roots is a tsere under the first root letter.

בֵּרֵך

You can think of this as a "traveling dagesh" because it moves from the middle root letter under the first root letter to change a ḥireq into a tsere.

### Locative he⁾

Nouns, names, and adverbs sometimes suffix a qamets he⁾ (הָ־) to indicate direction toward the noun or just emphasize the location. Other books call it a he⁾ *locale* or directive he⁾. In reading you can tell the difference between this he⁾ and most other qamets-he⁾ endings (הָ־), especially the feminine singular ending that takes a Masoretic accent. Although the locative he⁾ comes at the end of a word where you would expect an accent, it does not take an accent.

The addition of the locative heʾ may change slightly the vowels of the word.

*if w/ a*
*mapiq = her hand*

אַרְצָה כְּנַעַן      *toward the land* of Canaan (Gen 11:31)

וְהִנֵּה סֻלָּם מֻצָּב      there was a ladder standing
אַרְצָה      *on the earth* (Gen 28:12)

## Vocabulary

| | |
|---|---|
| אָהֵב | love, like |
| אֵם | mother |
| אָסַף | gather, take in |
| אָרוֹן | ark, chest |
| בֶּגֶד | garment |
| בֹּקֶר | morning |
| יָסַף | add |
| מָלֵא | be full; (Pi) fill, fulfill |
| מַעֲשֶׂה | work |
| נַחֲלָה | inheritance |
| נַעַר | boy, youth |
| עָוֹן | transgression, iniquity (the vav is pronounced as a consonant) |
| קֶרֶב | inward part, midst |
| בְּקֶרֶב | in the midst (of), among |
| רָבָה | be(come) numerous, be great; (Hi) multiply, make many |
| רֶגֶל | foot |

**Exercises**

1. Read aloud, translate, and chart the verbs in the following passages. Discuss the meaning of the Piel verbs.

(Deut 6:7) וְשִׁנַּנְתָּם לְבָנֶיךָ וְדִבַּרְתָּ בָּם

(Exod 20:11) כִּי שֵׁשֶׁת־יָמִים עָשָׂה יְהוָה אֶת־הַשָּׁמַיִם וְאֶת־הָאָרֶץ
אֶת־הַיָּם וְאֶת־כָּל־אֲשֶׁר־בָּם וַיָּנַח בַּיּוֹם הַשְּׁבִיעִי עַל־כֵּן בֵּרַךְ
יְהוָה אֶת־יוֹם הַשַּׁבָּת וַיְקַדְּשֵׁהוּ:
(ª mlt Mss 𝔊𝔖ℭᴹˢℭᴾᴅ וְאֶת ‖ ᵇ Pap Nash 𝔊𝔖 הַשְּׁבִיעִי ‖ ᶜ Pap Nash שִׁיֵ–)

(1 Kgs 8:24) אֲשֶׁר שָׁמַרְתָּ לְעַבְדְּךָ דָּוִד אָבִי ªאֵת אֲשֶׁר־דִּבַּרְתָּ לֹוֹ ªⁱ
וַתְּדַבֵּר בְּפִיךָ וּבְיָדְךָ מִלֵּאתָ כַּיּוֹם הַזֶּה:
(ª⁻ª > 𝔊* ‖ ᵇ 𝔊𝔖ᴅ pl)

2. From now on, you will be assigned passages to read from *BHS*. Use these to practice both your Hebrew and exegetical skills. For example, in order to translate, you will need to read the text-critical notes in *BHS*. You may want to do word studies on certain words, or you might discuss the evidence of sources or editors.

Read aloud and translate Genesis 2:7–9 using the following notes. Chart the verbs, as usual.

<u>Verse 7</u>

בְּאַפָּיו — The first letter is a preposition, and the last a suffixed pronoun. BDB gives you help finding the root. Under I. אַף (in small print) it says "v. sub אנף." That is the root.

<u>Verse 9</u>

נֶחְמָד — "Pleasant." This is a Niphal participle. You will study the Niphal and participles in later chapters.

הַדַּעַת — BDB will help you find the root.

# Chapter 22

## Conjugations of Will, Part I

The imperfect and perfect conjugations are **declarative**. They make a simple declaration or assertion such as, "Pharaoh said to Moses." Hebrew also has three **volitional** conjugations. The term volitional is from the Latin verb "to wish." Speakers using these conjugations attempt to impose their will on someone or something. The three volitional conjugations are the **jussive**, **imperative**, and **cohortative**. Originally separate forms, now they work together to make up one volitional class.

| Person | Conjugation | Translation (sample verb: עָבַד) |
|--------|-------------|----------------------------------|
| third | jussive | *Let* him/her/them work. <br> *May* he/she/they work. |
| second | imperative | Work! |
| first | cohortative | *May* I/we work. <br> I/We *might/can* work. <br> *Let* me/us work. |

*urging*

The terms jussive and imperative are from Latin verbs meaning "to order" and "to command." In Hebrew, these conjugations may be used for commands, and also advice, permission, requests, wishes, and so on. In other words, the degree to which the speaker exerts his or her will varies. Often the social status of the speaker relative to the hearer determines whether these forms are used as commands or requests.

This table serves as a guideline only because there is some confusion either in the Masoretic tradition or in our understanding. It is important to note that the jussive and cohortative often have the same form as the imperfect. Perfects may also be used alongside imperatives in prayers. The infinitive absolute (which we will study later) can also be used as an imperative.

The volitional conjugations in this chapter are based on the Qal stem. Hiphil and Piel conjugations expressing will are dealt with in the next chapter.

**Qal Jussive**

Some verbs have a short and long form of the imperfect. The short form is used with vav consecutive and is similar or identical to the jussive.

| Conjugation | Example (verb: הָיָה) | Translation |
|---|---|---|
| Imperfect | וּבֵית־אֵל יִהְיֶה לְאָוֶן׃ | Bethel shall become nothing (Amos 5:5) |
| Short Imperfect | וַיְהִי־אוֹר | There was light (Gen 1:3) |
| Jussive | יְהִי אוֹר | Let there be light (Gen 1:3) |

Most verbs, however, do not have a short form of the imperfect. In that case, the forms of the imperfect and the jussive are the same. For these verbs, context indicates whether the form is an imperfect or a jussive.

In earlier forms of the language, there were short forms in all three persons but, by the time of Biblical Hebrew, the jussive occurred only in the second and third person. The second person jussive occurs with negation and is covered in Chapter 23.

The jussive forms of III-heʾ and II-vav or II-yod (hollow) verbs have missing letters. These forms are usually slightly different from the imperfect with vav consecutive.

The final heʾ is missing for jussive forms of **III-heʾ** verbs.

| Root | Jussive | Translation |
|---|---|---|
| עלה | יַעַל | Let him go up; May he go up |
| היה | יְהִי | Let it be; May it be(come), happen |
| שתה | יֵשְׁתְּ | Let him drink; May he drink |

The middle vav and yod is missing for the jussive forms of **hollow** verbs.

| Root | Jussive | Translation |
|------|---------|-------------|
| מוּת | יָמֹת | Let him die; May he die |
| שׁוּב | יָשֹׁב | Let him return; May he return |
| שִׂים | יָשֵׂם | Let him place; May he place |

## Qal Imperative

The imperative is similar to the form of the imperfect with the prefixes removed. Since this results in two vocal shevas in a row in the 2fs and 2mp forms, which Hebrew cannot tolerate, the first sheva turns into a hireq. (This is the rule of sheva.) The **indicator** of the imperative is a sheva or hireq under the first root letter.

| PGN | Imperfect | Imperative |
|------|-----------|------------|
| 2ms | תִּשְׁמֹר | שְׁמֹר |
| 2fs | תִּשְׁמְרִי | שִׁמְרִי |
| 2mp | תִּשְׁמְרוּ | שִׁמְרוּ |
| 2fp | תִּשְׁמֹרְנָה | שְׁמֹרְנָה |

**I-gutturals** take a composite sheva (usually hateph patah but with I-ʾalephs, hateph segol) instead of a simple sheva in the 2ms and 2fp forms:

| Root | Imperative | Translation |
|------|-----------|-------------|
| אכל | אֱכֹל | Eat! (2ms) |
| חגר | חֲגֹרְנָה | Put on! (2fp) |

Similarly, the 2fs and 2mp forms of **II-guttural verbs** take a composite sheva under the second root letter and the corresponding short vowel under the first root letter.

| Root | Imperative | Translation |
|------|-----------|-------------|
| שָׁאַל | שַׁאֲלִי | Ask! (2fs) |
| זעק | זַעֲקוּ | Cry! (2mp) |

**I-nun** verbs may or may not have the first nun. When they lose the first nun, they are also without the indicators of the imperative. לְקַח behaves like a I-nun, possibly because לְקַח "take" was closely associated with נתן "give" in the spoken language.

| PGN | With nun | נתן | לקח |
|-----|----------|-----|-----|
| 2ms | נְפֹל | תֵּן | קַח |
| 2fs | נְפְלִי | תְּנִי | קְחִי |
| 2mp | נְפְלוּ | תְּנוּ | קְחוּ |
| 2fp | נְפֹלְנָה | תֵּנָּה | not attested |

**I-vav** verbs are without indicators of the imperative because they lose their first root letter. As usual, הלך behaves like a I-vav verb.

| PGN | ישׁב | ידע | הלך |
|-----|------|-----|-----|
| 2ms | שֵׁב | דַּע | לֵךְ |
| 2fs | שְׁבִי | דְּעִי | לְכִי |
| 2mp | שְׁבוּ | דְּעוּ | לְכוּ |
| 2fp | שֵׁבְנָה | דַּעְנָה | לֵכְנָה |

As in the imperfect, **III-heʾ** may be present, replaced by a yod, or absent. The forms for the verbs בָּנָה (build) and הָיָה (be, become) are:

| PGN | בנה | היה |
|-----|-----|-----|
| 2ms | בְּנֵה | הֱיֵה |
| 2fs | בְּנִי | הֱיִי |
| 2mp | בְּנוּ | הֱיוּ |
| 2fp | בְּנֶינָה | הֱיֶינָה |

**Hollow** verbs have all root letters represented, but are missing the normal indicators.

| PGN | קום | בוא | שׂים |
|-----|-----|-----|------|
| 2ms | קוּם | בּוֹא | שִׂים |
| 2fs | קוּמִי | בּוֹאִי | שִׂימִי |
| 2mp | קוּמוּ | בּוֹאוּ | שִׂימוּ |
| 2fp | קֹמְנָה | בֹּאנָה | שֵׂמְנָה |

When joined by a maqqeph to another word or particle, the vowel pointing of the imperative changes. For example:

$$שְׁמֹר becomes שְׁמָר־לְךָ$$

The sheva under the first root letter still identifies this form as an imperative.

The lack of a pronoun identifies an imperative in English. Note that in Hebrew, however, a suffixed pronoun on lamed is idiomatic, as in the previous example.

**Qal Cohortative**

The cohortative is similar to the first person imperfect forms with הָ- on the end:

אֶשְׁמְרָה        נִשְׁמְרָה

The **indicators** for missing letters follow the same rules as for the imperfect: doubling indicates an assimilated nun; a tsere under an ʾaleph or nun prefix indicates I-vav; a qamets under the prefix indicates a hollow verb.

**III-heʾ verbs** do not add the הָ- ending. They use the imperfect forms.

**I-yod** cohortative forms are missing a root letter. The tsere ( ֵ ) is the same **indicator** as in the imperfect for the missing I-yod.

| Root | Form | Translation |
|------|------|-------------|
| יֹשֵׁב | אֵשְׁבָה | Let me live; May I live |
|  | נֵשְׁבָה | Let us live; May we live |

**Vocbulary**

| | |
|---|---|
| בַּעַל | owner, husband, lord; Baal |
| כָּבוֹד | abundance, honor, glory |
| כָּלָה | cease, come to an end, finish, complete |
| מַחֲנֶה | camp, army |
| מַלְאָךְ | messenger |
| מִנְחָה | gift; offering |
| נָטָה | turn, stretch out |
| עָזַב | leave, abandon |
| צַדִּיק | righteous, just (adj) |
| רָשָׁע | guilty, wicked (one) (adj) (f: רְשָׁעָה) |

| | |
|---|---|
| שָׁכַב | lie down; have sexual intercourse |
| שָׁלוֹם | peace, health |
| שָׁפַט | judge, enter into controversy; (Ni) plead |
| שָׁתָה | drink (verb) |
| תּוֹרָה | teaching, law |

## Exercises

1. Read aloud and translate the following. Chart the verbs.

(Num 6.24–26) יְבָרֶכְךָ יְהוָה וְיִשְׁמְרֶךָ: ס

יָאֵר[a] יְהוָה ׀ פָּנָיו אֵלֶיךָ וִיחֻנֶּךָּ:[b][1] ס

יִשָּׂא יְהוָה ׀ פָּנָיו אֵלֶיךָ וְיָשֵׂם לְךָ שָׁלוֹם: ס

(25[a] 𝔐 יאיר ‖ [b] 𝔖 *wnhjk* = וִיחַיֶּךָ)

(Exod 7:19–20) וַיֹּאמֶר יְהוָה אֶל־מֹשֶׁה אֱמֹר אֶל־אַהֲרֹן קַח מַטְּךָ

וּנְטֵה־יָדְךָ עַל־מֵימֵי מִצְרַיִם עַל[a]־נַהֲרֹתָם ׀ עַל[b]־יְאֹרֵיהֶם

וְעַל־אַגְמֵיהֶם וְעַל כָּל־מִקְוֵה מֵימֵיהֶם וְיִהְיוּ־דָם[c] וְהָיָה דָם

בְּכָל־אֶרֶץ מִצְרַיִם וּבָעֵצִים וּבָאֲבָנִים: וַיַּעֲשׂוּ־כֵן מֹשֶׁה וְאַהֲרֹן

כַּאֲשֶׁר ׀ צִוָּה יְהוָה וַיָּרֶם בַּמַּטֶּה[a] וַיַּךְ אֶת־הַמַּיִם אֲשֶׁר

בַּיְאֹר לְעֵינֵי פַרְעֹה וּלְעֵינֵי עֲבָדָיו וַיֵּהָפְכוּ כָּל־הַמַּיִם אֲשֶׁר־בַּיְאֹר לְדָם:

(19[a] 𝔊𝔙 pr cop ‖ [b] mlt Mss 𝔪𝔊𝔖𝔙 ‖ [c-c] 𝔪 וְהָיָה הַדָּם ‖ וְעַל 𝔪

20[a] 𝔪𝔊 בְּמַטֵּהוּ cf 𝔖)

---

[1] "and be gracious to you"

2. Read and translate Genesis 1:26–31 using the following notes. You have already translated two verses of this passage in Chapter 20. Chart the verbs.

## Verse 26

כִּדְמוּתֵנוּ      Listed under the root דמה. III-heʾ nouns (like verbs) can lose the final heʾ with the addition of a suffix.

הָרֹמֵשׂ      "that creeps"—רֹמֵשׂ is a ms Qal participle (with the article הָ) complementing the ms collective noun רֶמֶשׂ just before it. Qal participles are the subject of Chapter 25.

## Verse 28

וְכִבְשֻׁהָ      This may be easier to identify spelled out in full, with the parts separated: וְ כִבְשׁוּ הָ

הָרֹמֶשֶׂת      The fs Qal participle form (with the article הָ) of the verb root רמשׂ. It can be translated like הָרֹמֵשׂ in verse 26.

## Verse 29

זֹרֵעַ      Literally: "seeding" (that is, "yielding" or "producing"). This is a ms Qal participle.

## Verse 31

שִׁשִּׁי      This is an ordinal number.

# Chapter 23

## Conjugations of Will, Part II

### Negation

In the **third person**, Hebrew uses אַל and the jussive, or sometimes לֹא, in order to express negative volition ("Let it not ..."). אַל and לֹא normally come immediately before the verb, but may come before some other word or combination of words for emphasis.

In the **second person**, Hebrew uses either אַל and the jussive, or לֹא and the imperfect, to express negative commands. The first indicates urgency ("Stop..." or "Don't..."), whereas the second indicates prohibition or legislation ("Do not [ever]..." or "You shall not..."). Remember that for many verbs the form of the jussive and imperfect are the same. In such cases, the context, and which of the two negative particles is used, will indicate whether it is a jussive or an imperfect.

In the **first person**, Hebrew uses the cohortative with אַל in order to express negative will or desire ("Let us not..." or "May I not...").

This table summarizes the expression of **negative volition** in Hebrew:

| Person | Conjugation | Negative | Translation |
|--------|-------------|----------|-------------|
| Third | Jussive | אַל | Let him/her/it not . . . |
| Second | Jussive | אַל | Stop . . . or: Don't . . . |
| | Imperfect | לֹא | Do not (ever) . . .<br>You shall not . . . |
| First | Cohortative | אַל | Let us/me not . . . |

## Long Imperative Forms

Imperatives may also take a הָ֫ ending, in which case the vowel pointing is often unusual:

| Root | Imperative | Long Imperative | Translation |
|---|---|---|---|
| שׁמר | שְׁמֹר | שָׁמְרָה | Keep! |
| ישׁב | שֵׁב | שְׁבָה | Sit! |
| נתן | תֵּן | תְּנָה | Give! |

## Piel and Hiphil Conjugations Expressing Will

The forms of the **Piel jussive** are the same as the forms of the Piel imperfect.

As in the Qal, the **Piel imperative** has the same form as the imperfect without the prefix. When the doubling of a middle root letter indicates a verb form is a Piel, a *pataḥ* ( _ ) under the first root letter is the **indicator** of an imperative. When the middle root letter is a guttural (which cannot be doubled), then the pataḥ may, or may not, be lengthened to a qamets ( ָ ).

| Piel Imperative | | | | |
|---|---|---|---|---|
| Root: | דבר | מאן | מהר | גלה |
| 2ms | דַּבֵּר | מָאֵן | מַהֵר | גַּלֵּה |
| 2fs | דַּבְּרִי | מָאֲנִי | מַהֲרִי | גַּלִּי |
| 2mp | דַּבְּרוּ | מָאֲנוּ | מַהֲרוּ | גַּלּוּ |
| 2fp | דַּבֵּרְנָה | מָאֵנָּה | מַהֵרְנָה | גַּלֶּינָה |

The **Piel cohortative**, like the Qal cohortative, has a qamets he᾿ suffix (הָ֫ ). Otherwise the indicators and missing letters are the same as those of the Piel imperfect.

The **Hiphil jussive** has the same form as the short form of the Hiphil imperfect with vav consecutive. (All Hiphil verbal roots have a short form of the imperfect, unlike other stems where only some roots have short forms of the imperfect.) The **indicators** are the same as for the imperfect—a dot vowel under the middle root letter and a pataḥ under the prefix. In the Hiphil, the short form usually has a tsere or segol as a dot vowel rather than a hireq yod. III-gutturals may have a pataḥ rather than a dot vowel, because gutturals prefer a-class vowels. The missing letters are the same as for the imperfect.

| Root | Imperfect | With Vav Consec. | Jussive |
|---|---|---|---|
| | יַשְׁמִיד | וַיַּשְׁמֵד | יַשְׁמֵד |
| I-nun | יַגִּיד | וַיַּגֵּד | יַגֵּד |
| III-guttural | יַשְׁלִיחַ | וַיַּשְׁלַח | יַשְׁלַח |
| III-heʾ | יַעֲלֶה | וַיַּעַל | יַעַל |

As in other stems, the imperfect and imperative forms are closely related. In the **Hiphil imperative**, however, the heʾ prefix is present. The **indicator** of the Hiphil imperative, therefore, is a heʾ prefix, usually with a pataḥ under it (–הַ). The indicator of the Hiphil stem is a dot vowel under the middle root letter.

| Hiphil Imperative | |
|---|---|
| 2ms | הַשְׁמֵר |
| 2fs | הַשְׁמִירִי |
| 2mp | הַשְׁמִירוּ |
| 2fp | הַשְׁמֵרְנָה |

The missing letters are the same as in the Hiphil imperfect.

The **Hiphil cohortative**, like the Qal cohortative, has a qamets heʾ ending (ה–). The indicators and missing letters are the same as for the Hiphil imperfect.

**The Particle נָא**

Frequently attached to the jussive, imperative, and cohortative—or nearby words—is the particle נָא. The traditional understanding is that it expresses a request or prayer and therefore is translated as "please." Lambdin, however, thinks it means that a request is a "logical consequence" of a preceding statement or situation (p. 170), and therefore prefers not to translate it.

## Narrative Sequences

In the sequence

**imperative + ו + perfect,**

the perfect continues the imperative and should be translated as an imperative. Observe the following example and its translation:

שְׁמַע בְּקוֹלָם *Listen (imperative)* to their voice
וְהִמְלַכְתָּ לָהֶם מֶלֶךְ *and make (perfect)* a king reign
over them (1 Sam 8:22)

But any of the following similar sequences are **purpose** or **result clauses**:

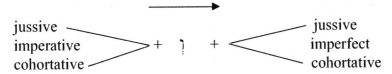

jussive                        jussive
imperative   +   ו   +   imperfect
cohortative                  cohortative

Here is an example:

אָסֻרָה־נָּא וְאֶרְאֶה    Let me turn aside (*cohortative*)
                              so *that* I may see (*imperfect*) . . .
                              (Exod 3:3)

(Another purpose or result clause not covered in the above summary is: jussive + ו + imperative.) Because these sequences are purpose or result clauses, the ו will be translated "that" or "so that."

## Disjunctive –וְ

When a vav is prefixed to anything other than a finite verb, it disrupts the narrative sequence. In previous chapters, you have

learned about the vav prefixed to finite verbs. A vav consecutive
(–ַו ) prefixed to an imperfect narrates the past. A vav (–ְו ) prefixed
to the perfect narrates the future. In this chapter, you learned that a
vav (–ְו ) prefixed to a volitional conjugation could introduce a
purpose or result clause. A vav conjunction (–ְו ) prefixed to
anything other than a finite verb, such as a noun, is disjunctive or
parenthetical.

   A **disjunctive** vav sometimes introduces a contrast and may
be translated "but."

| | |
|---|---|
| וּלְאָדָם לֹא־מָצָא | *But* for Adam was not found a |
| עֵזֶר כְּנֶגְדּוֹ: | helper equal to him (Gen 2:20) |

In addition, a disjunctive vav may introduce a new episode in a
narrative and be translated "now."

| | |
|---|---|
| וְהָאָדָם יָדַע אֶת־חַוָּה | *Now* the man knew Eve, |
| אִשְׁתּוֹ וַתַּהַר | his wife, and she conceived |
| | (Gen 4:1) |

A **parenthetical** vav may be circumstantial, explanatory, or
relative. When it is circumstantial, the vav can be translated
"while," "when," "with," or "since."

| | |
|---|---|
| הָיְתָה־לִּי עֶדְנָה | Shall I have pleasure, |
| וַאדֹנִי זָקֵן | *when* my husband is old? |
| | (Gen 18:12) |

An explanatory vav can be translated "namely" or "that is."

| | |
|---|---|
| וַיָּשֶׂם יְהוָה אֵת חֶרֶב | The LORD set the sword of |
| אִישׁ בְּרֵעֵהוּ | each man against his neighbor, |
| וּבְכָל־הַמַּחֲנֶה | *that is*, against the whole army |
| | (Judg 7:22) |

These are just a few examples of the disjunctive and parenthetical uses and translations of the vav conjunction. Lexicons list the full range of uses and possible translations.

## Vocabulary

| | |
|---|---|
| אָבַד | perish; (Pi) destroy; (Hi) exterminate |
| אֹזֶן | ear |
| בְּהֵמָה | cattle, animals |
| בָּקָר | cows (coll), herd(s), cattle |
| גָּלָה | uncover, reveal; depart, go into captivity |
| זָקֵן | old (adj); old man, elder (n) |
| חָצֵר | permanent settlement, court, enclosure |
| יָכֹל | be able (stative) |
| כַּף | hand, palm |
| לָכֵן | therefore (adv) |
| מִצְוָה | commandment |
| נָא | (particle of request) |
| סֵפֶר | scroll, inscription |
| רוּם | be(come) high, exalted |
| רֵעַ | friend, fellow, companion |

## Exercises

1. Read aloud and translate the following. Chart the verbs.

(Ps 34:15 ET 14) סוּר מֵרָע וַעֲשֵׂה־טוֹב בַּקֵּשׁ שָׁלוֹם

(Exod 3:3) וַיֹּאמֶר מֹשֶׁה אָסֻרָה־נָּא וְאֶרְאֶה אֶת־הַמַּרְאֶה הַגָּדֹל הַזֶּה

(Exod 3:10) וְעַתָּה לְכָה וְאֶשְׁלָחֲךָ אֶל־פַּרְעֹה וְהוֹצֵא[a] אֶת־עַמִּי
בְּנֵי־יִשְׂרָאֵל מִמִּצְרָיִם: (–אֶת ﬡ𝕲𝕾[a])

(Exod 20:2–3) אָנֹכִי יְהוָה אֱלֹהֶיךָ אֲשֶׁר הוֹצֵאתִיךָ מֵאֶרֶץ מִצְרַיִם
מִבֵּית עֲבָדִים: לֹא יִהְיֶה־לְךָ[a] אֱלֹהִים אֲחֵרִים[a] עַל־פָּנָ[a]ַ:
(3[a–a] 𝕲[𝕾ℭℭ[JP]] πλὴν ἐμοῦ "except me")

(Exod 34:9) וַיֹּאמֶר אִם־נָא מָצָאתִי חֵן בְּעֵינֶיךָ אֲדֹנָי[a] יֵלֶךְ־נָא
אֲדֹנָי[b] בְּקִרְבֵּנוּ
([a] > 𝕲 ‖ [b] 𝕲* ὁ κύριός μου "my Lord")

(Gen 22:5) וַיֹּאמֶר אַבְרָהָם אֶל־נְעָרָיו שְׁבוּ־לָכֶם פֹּה עִם־הַחֲמוֹר
וַאֲנִי וְהַנַּעַר נֵלְכָה עַד־כֹּה ... וְנָשׁוּבָה אֲלֵיכֶם:

(Isa 43:12) אָנֹכִי הִגַּדְתִּי וְהוֹשַׁעְתִּי וְהִשְׁמַעְתִּי וְאֵין בָּכֶם זָר
וְאַתֶּם עֵדַי נְאֻם־יְהוָה[a] וַאֲנִי־אֵל:
([a] frt huc tr : .)

(Judg 13:9) וַיִּשְׁמַע הָאֱלֹהִים[a] בְּקוֹל מָנוֹחַ וַיָּבֹא[b] מַלְאַךְ הָאֱלֹהִים[c]
עוֹד אֶל־הָאִשָּׁה וְהִיא יוֹשֶׁבֶת[1] בַּשָּׂדֶה וּמָנוֹחַ אִישָׁהּ אֵין עִמָּהּ:
([a] 𝕲[58.72](ℭ𝕾𝔇) κύριος "Lord" ‖ [b] Ms וַיֵּרָא ‖
[c] 𝕲[61](𝕾) κυρίου "from [the] Lord")

---

[1] "was sitting" This is a particple. Participles with be discussed in Chapters 25 and 26.

# Chapter 24

## Genre and Tradition

Every culture has conventional ways of communicating for specific situations. Over time, for particular occasions and life experiences, people develop appropriate, conventional ways of expressing themselves. We know what to say, and how to say it, on certain occasions, such as marriages, funerals, and religious services. We write a love letter differently than a paper for school. And we expect those with whom we communicate to recognize these differences and react to our communications accordingly, otherwise mistakes could be humorous or embarrassing. These conventional ways of speaking or writing can be referred to as genres or forms.

### Genre or Form Criticism

In biblical studies, the identification and analysis of typical ways of writing and speaking is called **genre criticism** or **form criticism**. The pioneer of this type of analysis in biblical studies was Hermann Gunkel. He wanted to get beyond the written sources back to the oral traditions and life experiences of the people. The typical setting, situation, or life experience he called *Sitz im Leben*, in German. The *Sitz im Leben* or "setting in life" is not one historical occasion, but a repeated situation, such as a harvest or a funeral.

Gunkel identified genres according to their form (grammar and vocabulary), content (mood and thoughts), and setting in life. Hebrew grammar and vocabulary are, therefore, important in identifying genres.

Unlike Gunkel, contemporary literary theory is less interested in the history behind a text, but nonetheless continues to be interested in its genre. **Genre** may be more broadly defined to

include mood, setting, function, speaker, and content. The well-
known literary critic, Northrop Frye, notes that "the point of
criticism by genres is not so much to classify as to clarify"[1] by
bringing out all kinds of traditions, similarities, and literary
relationships to which we might otherwise be blind. How a
particular passage is similar to, and different from, the norm is
significant for comprehending meaning.

**Law**

There are two genres of **law** in the Pentateuch.

Some laws are **conditional** and they introduce the main
regulation with כִּי "when" and various different conditions (or
cases) with אִם "if."

| | |
|---|---|
| כִּי תִקְנֶה עֶבֶד עִבְרִי | **When** you buy a Hebrew slave, |
| שֵׁשׁ שָׁנִים יַעֲבֹד | he shall serve six years, |
| וּבַשְּׁבִעָת יֵצֵא | and in the seventh he shall go out |
| לַחָפְשִׁי חִנָּם: | free, for nothing. |
| אִם־בְּגַפּוֹ יָבֹא | **If** he comes in single, |
| בְּגַפּוֹ יֵצֵא | he shall go out single; |
| אִם־בַּעַל אִשָּׁה הוּא | **if** he is married, |
| וְיָצְאָה אִשְׁתּוֹ עִמּוֹ: | then his wife shall go out with him. (Exod 21:2-3). |

The other genre is **absolute laws**.

| | |
|---|---|
| לֹא תִּרְצָח: | You shall not murder! (Exod 20:13) |

The two types have a different form and content and may
have a different social setting. The first type tends to deal with

---

[1] Northrop Frye, *Anatomy of Criticism* (Princeton: Princeton
University Press, 1957), 247–248.

secular affairs in the land. The second type tends to deal with relationships between God and human beings.

## Prophets

Prophetic messages are the speeches of messengers. They use the language of non-prophetic messengers in the Hebrew Bible and the Ancient Near East. Jacob, for instance, sends messengers ahead to meet Esau and instructs them to say:

כֹּה אָמַר עַבְדְּךָ יַעֲקֹב

Thus says your servant Jacob (Gen 32:5 ET 4)

The character of prophecy as a message from God is evident in the common phrase, "thus says the LORD" (כֹּה אָמַר יְהוָה).

The most prominent prophetic messages are **announcements of judgment** and **announcements of salvation**.

Announcements of judgment have three parts. Amos 7:16–17 can serve as an example:

| | | |
|---|---|---|
| 1. *Reasons* or *Accusation* | וְעַתָּה שְׁמַע | Now hear |
| | דְּבַר־יְהוָה | the word of the LORD. |
| | אַתָּה אֹמֵר² לֹא | You say, "Do not |
| | תִנָּבֵא³ עַל־יִשְׂרָאֵל | prophesy against Israel, |
| | וְלֹא תַטִּיף | and do not preach |
| | עַל־בֵּית יִשְׂחָק⁴: | against the house of Isaac." |
| 2. *Therefore, messenger formula* | לָכֵן כֹּה־אָמַר | Therefore, thus said |
| | יְהוָה | the LORD |

---

² A Qal participle, which will be treated in the next chapter.

³ A Niphal verb.

⁴ An alternate spelling of "Isaac." (There are two root words for "laugh": צחק and שׂחק. The story of Isaac in Genesis contains a play on the word "laugh.")

3. *Judgment*  ... וְיִשְׂרָאֵל גָּלֹה[5]   "... Israel shall surely
יִגְלֶה מֵעַל   go into exile away from
אַדְמָתוֹ:   its land."

Compare other examples in 1 Kings 21:1–19; 2 Kings 1:3–4; Isaiah 8:5–8; 22:8b–14; 28:7–13; 29:13–14; 30:12–14, 15–17; Micah 3:9–12.

**Writings**

The *Kethuvim* ("Writings") of the Hebrew Bible include the books of Psalms and Proverbs, as well as ten other works.

The two major genres of the book of Psalms are **hymns** and **laments**. The typical form of a hymn is a call to praise, in the imperative, followed by the reasons for praise, often introduced by כִּי "for." Claus Westermann notes that the reasons for praise are often in two parts—God's majesty and God's goodness or grace. The following example is from Psalm 100:

| | | |
|---|---|---|
| *Imperative call* | ... הָרִיעוּ | *Make* a joyful noise ... |
| *to praise* | ... עִבְדוּ אֶת־יְהוָה | *Worship* the LORD ... |
| *God's majesty* | ... יְהוָה | ... the LORD is God ... |
| | ... הוּא אֱלֹהִים | |
| *Imperative call* | ... בֹּאוּ | *Enter* ... |
| *to praise* | ... הוֹדוּ | *Give thanks* ... |
| | ... בָּרְכוּ | *Bless* ... |
| *God's* | כִּי־טוֹב יְהוָה | *For* the LORD is good; |
| *goodness* | ... לְעוֹלָם חַסְדּוֹ | eternal is his loyalty ... |

Compare also Psalms 95, 145, 148, 150.

---

[5] This is an infinitive absolute. It emphasizes the verb. Chapter 29 will discuss the infinitive absolute.

Genres by their nature are flexible and adaptable to mixing and use in new combinations. The word הוֹי "woe," for example, is often used in **laments** for the dead.

| | |
|---|---|
| ⁶וַיַּנַּח אֶת־נִבְלָתוֹ | He put to rest his body |
| בְּקִבְרוֹ | in his grave |
| וַיִּסְפְּדוּ עָלָיו | and they mourned over him, |
| הוֹי אָחִי: | "Woe, my brother." (1 Kgs 13:30) |

To announce God's judgment on Israel the prophets use the genre of lament for the dead. Because of its sins, Israel is "dead."

| | |
|---|---|
| לָכֵן כֹּה־אָמַר יְהוָה | Therefore, thus says the LORD, |
| אֱלֹהֵי צְבָאוֹת אֲדֹנָי | God of hosts, my Lord: |
| בְּכָל־רְחֹבוֹת מִסְפֵּד⁷ | In all the open places wailing, |
| וּבְכָל־חוּצוֹת יֹאמְרוּ | and in all the streets they will say, |
| הוֹ־הוֹ | "Woe, woe." (Amos 5:16a) |

Creativity in the mixing of genres contributes power to prophetic preaching.

**Tradition**

Traditions are closely related to genres. Traditions are handed down from generation to generation in certain settings in life and genres. A humorous example from our culture is the sports interview. Traditions about being a good sport and team player are repeated over and over using the same words. In Israel some proverbs may have been used to hand down wisdom traditions in the context of scribal schools.

Traditions have elements of continuity, community, and change. By their nature, traditions are handed down from one generation to the next. To be traditions they must have continuous,

---

⁶ This verb is doubly weak and the vowel pointing is unusual. It is a Hiphil from נוח.

⁷ This is a Piel participle. Chapters 25 and 26 introduce participles.

identifiable form and content. Normally, this is related to the genres in which they are typically expressed. If they did not have identifiable form and content through the generations, they would be better described as recurring themes, motifs, or the like.

Traditions are the property of a community that maintains and passes them on to the next generation. For example, a family might keep stories about their ancestors, a town might keep stories about the naming of important places, priests might keep stories about Aaron and Levi, and the royal court might keep stories about the divine right of kings. Recurring themes, motifs, and the like, differ from traditions in that they are not the property of a particular community and do not have a continuous form and content.

Although traditions must have continuity from generation to generation, they must also be fluid. They must be flexible enough to allow them to adapt to changing needs and remain relevant and living. A tradition can be written down, but it must retain in writing the flexibility of oral traditions.

In biblical studies, tradition critics and historians are interested in identifying traditions, their community, their typical and unique uses, and the way they change and adapt to new situations in the life of the community. Knowledge of Hebrew is important for identifying the form and content of traditions.

**Exercise**

Read aloud and translate Micah 6:1–5 with the assistance of the notes that follow. Micah makes use of a genre that was not discussed above. Verses 1–5 are the first part. Read verses 6–8 in English. Without consulting the scholarly literature, what do you think the genre is? What parts can you distinguish? What traditions are associated with this genre? What is its setting in life? Why does Micah make use of this genre?

Verse 1

אֹמֵר        "is saying" This form is a participle. They will be discussed in the next chapter.

רִיב

The Qal imperative 2ms and the ms noun have the same form. One appears in this verse and the other in the next verse.

## Verse 2

וְהָאֵתָנִים

This word is listed under יתן in BDB.

יִתְוַכַּח

"He will argue." This is a Hitpael stem that will be discussed in Chapter 31.

## Verse 5

דַּעַת

"to know" An infinitive construct which will be discussed in Chapter 27.

# Chapter 25

## Participles, Part I

So far we have studied only **finite verbs,** which are verb forms limited or qualified with respect to person, gender, number, and aspect (duration or completeness of action). **Infinite verbs** are not limited or qualified. The distinction is only relative in Hebrew because the participle (see Chapters 25 and 26) can be marked for gender and number whereas the infinitive (Chapter 27) can be marked with suffixed pronouns.

### Qal Participle

The name **participle** refers to its participation in the characteristics of both a noun and a verb, as seen in the examples below.

The participle takes endings for gender and number like those of the adjective and noun. The feminine singular ending, however, is more often הֶ֫‑ than הָ‑ . The **indicator** of the **Qal participle** is a holem between the first and second root letters. The spelling may be full or defective.

| ms | שֹׁמֵר | mp | שֹׁמְרִים |
|----|--------|----|-----------|
| fs | שֹׁמֶ֫רֶת | fp | שֹׁמְרוֹת |
|    | שֹׁמְרָה |    |           |

When they act like nouns, participles can be in construct, thus taking construct endings—the same construct endings as for nouns (see Chapter 9).

There are also much less frequently occurring **stative participles** of the form שָׁמֵר (see Chapter 7 on stative verbs), as

זָקֵן → to be old

well as **passive participles** of the form שָׁמוּר. They take the same endings as the active participle in the above table.

... אֲהֻבַת רֵעַ ...     ... *who is beloved by* (*passive participle*)

a companion ... (Hosea 3:1)

The gutturals cause some changes to the above patterns, but only in the III-heʾ and hollow verbs are there missing letters.

**III-heʾ verbs** other than the ms lose the final heʾ. Notice therefore that the only difference between the ms and fs form is the vowel pointing.

| III-ה | | | |
|---|---|---|---|
| ms | גֹּלֶה | mp | גֹּלִים |
| fs | גֹּלָה | fp | גֹּלוֹת |

*lose ה in pl.*

**Hollow verbs** have the following form:

| Hollow | | | |
|---|---|---|---|
| ms | קָם | mp | קָמִים |
| fs | קָמָה | fp | קָמוֹת |

As in the perfect, hollow verbs can take a-class (as in the example above), u-class or i-class vowels. The ms and fs participles have the same forms as the Qal perfect 3ms and 3fs. When you come across one of these ambiguous forms, it is probably a participle if:

1. It is parallel to another participle;
2. It appears with an independent pronoun or a suffixed pronoun (because the pronoun is included in the perfect);
3. It has a definite article (because the perfect cannot take a definite article).

## Use and Meaning of Participles

The participle can function as a **verb**. As verbs, participles express ongoing activity or being. The context indicates whether they should be translated as past, present, or future.

| | |
|---|---|
| אָנָה אַתָּה הֹלֵךְ | Where are you *going*? (Zech 2:6) |
| וְרִבְקָה אֹהֶבֶת אֶת־יַעֲקֹב | but Rebekah *loved* Jacob (Gen 25:28) |

The participle may be used like an attributive or predicate adjective. As an **attributive adjective** it agrees with the noun it qualifies in gender, number, and definiteness.

| | |
|---|---|
| יְהוָה כְּאֵשׁ אֹכֶלֶת | The LORD is like a *devouring* fire (Exod 24:17) |

As a **predicate adjective**, the participle is often translated by the English relative pronoun "who."

| | |
|---|---|
| מַלְאָכִים הַבָּאִים יְרוּשָׁלַ͏ִם | the messengers *who have come* to Jerusalem (Jer 27:3) |

Like an adjective, a participle can function as a **noun**.

| | |
|---|---|
| בִּימֵי שְׁפֹט הַשֹּׁפְטִים | in the days *the judges* were judging (Ruth 1:1) |

A participle may take **suffixes**.

| | |
|---|---|
| ... הֲלֹא־בַבֶּטֶן עֹשֵׂנִי | Did not *the one who made me* in the womb ... ? (Job 31:15) |

---

[1] This form is an infinitive construct, which you will learn in Chapter 27.

The suffix is typically the object of the verbal action (as in the above example), but may also be the subject.

Like an adjective or noun, a participle can be in **construct**.

בָּאֵי שַׁעַר־עִירוֹ      *the ones who were entering*
                   the gate of his city (Gen 23:10)

Participles may be charted in the following manner (using אֲהֻבַת from Hosea 3:1 as an example):

| Root | Stem | Conjugation | PGN | Special Features |
|------|------|-------------|-----|------------------|
| אהב | Qal | passive participle | fs cstr | |

## Vocabulary

| | |
|---|---|
| אַחֵר | another |
| אַיִל | ram |
| אַךְ | only; surely (adv) |
| בָּחַר | choose |
| בִּין | understand, perceive |
| גִּבּוֹר | warrior, mighty man |
| דּוֹר | generation, lifetime, life-span |
| דָּרַשׁ | seek |
| הָרַג | kill |
| זֶבַח | sacrifice (noun) |
| חוּץ | place outside the house, street (noun); outside, without (prep, adv) |
| שָׂפָה | lip; shore |
| שֵׁבֶט | rod, staff; tribe |
| *שָׁבַע | (Ni, Hi) swear |
| שֶׁמֶן | oil |

## Exercises

1. Read aloud and translate the following. Chart the verbs.

(Exod 3:5) שַׁל־נְעָלֶ֙יךָ֙ מֵעַ֣ל רַגְלֶ֔יךָ כִּ֣י הַמָּק֗וֹם אֲשֶׁ֤ר אַתָּה֙ עוֹמֵ֣ד
עָלָ֔יו אַדְמַת־קֹ֖דֶשׁ הֽוּא׃

(Exod 3:13) וַיֹּ֨אמֶר מֹשֶׁ֜ה אֶל־הָֽאֱלֹהִ֗ים הִנֵּ֨ה אָנֹכִ֣י בָא֮ אֶל־בְּנֵ֣י
יִשְׂרָאֵל֒ וְאָמַרְתִּ֣י לָהֶ֔ם אֱלֹהֵ֥י אֲבוֹתֵיכֶ֖ם שְׁלָחַ֣נִי אֲלֵיכֶ֑ם
וְאָֽמְרוּ־לִ֣י מַה־שְּׁמ֔וֹ מָ֥ה אֹמַ֖ר אֲלֵהֶֽם׃

(Lev 25:2) דַּבֵּ֞ר אֶל־בְּנֵ֤י יִשְׂרָאֵל֙ וְאָמַרְתָּ֣ אֲלֵהֶ֔ם כִּ֤י תָבֹ֙אוּ֙
אֶל־הָאָ֔רֶץ אֲשֶׁ֥ר אֲנִ֖י נֹתֵ֣ן לָכֶ֑ם וְשָׁבְתָ֣ה הָאָ֔רֶץ שַׁבָּ֖ת לַֽיהוָֽה׃

(Exod 21:2–3) כִּ֤י תִקְנֶה֙ עֶ֣בֶד עִבְרִ֔י שֵׁ֥שׁ שָׁנִ֖ים יַעֲבֹ֑ד וּבַ֨שְּׁבִעִ֔ת
יֵצֵ֥א לַֽחָפְשִׁ֖י חִנָּֽם׃ אִם־בְּגַפּ֥וֹ[a] יָבֹ֖א בְּגַפּ֣וֹ[a] יֵצֵ֑א אִם־[b]בַּ֤עַל אִשָּׁה֙
ה֔וּא וְיָצְאָ֥ה אִשְׁתּ֖וֹ עִמּֽוֹ׃
(3[a] 𝔊𝔖𝔍 pr cop) ‖ [b] בגפיו 𝔴

(Exod 20:12–15) כַּבֵּ֥ד אֶת־אָבִ֖יךָ וְאֶת־אִמֶּ֑ךָ[a] לְמַ֙עַן֙ יַאֲרִכ֣וּן יָמֶ֔יךָ
עַ֚ל הָֽאֲדָמָ֔ה[b] אֲשֶׁר־יְהוָ֥ה אֱלֹהֶ֖יךָ נֹתֵ֥ן לָֽךְ׃ ס [a]לֹ֥֖א תִּרְצָֽח׃ ס
לֹ֣֖א תִּנְאָֽ֑ף׃ ס לֹ֣֖א תִּגְנֹֽ֔ב׃ ס
(12[a] Pap Nash 𝔊 + ‖ [b] 𝔊 + τῆς ἀγαθῆς "the good" ‖ ייטב לך ולמען
13[a] 𝔊* ordinat 14.15.13 et Pap Nash Philo [De Decalogo 12]
Lc 18,20 Rm 13,9 ordinat 14.13.15)

# Chapter 26

## Participles, Part II

### Hiphil Participle

The **indicator** of the Hiphil participle is a prefixed mem with a pataḥ under it: – מַ.

| ms | מַשְׁמִיר | mp | מַשְׁמִירִים |
|----|----------|-----|--------------|
| fs | מַשְׁמֶרֶת | fp | מַשְׁמִירוֹת |

The **indicator** is different for **I-vav**, **I-yod**, and **hollow** verbs.

| Root | ms participle |
|------|---------------|
| יָשֹׁב (original I-vav) | מוֹשִׁיב |
| יָטֹב (I-yod) | מֵיטִיב |
| קוֹם (hollow) | מֵקִים |

In the other forms of the hollow verbs, adding the suffixes causes the reduction of the vowel under the prefix to – מְ.

מְקִימִים (mp) מְקִימָה (fs) מְקִימוֹת (fp)

The – מְ looks like the indicator of a Piel participle (see below), but the ḥireq yod distinguishes a Hiphil from a Piel participle.

### Piel Participle

The **indicator** of the Piel participle is a prefixed mem with a sheva under it: – מְ. The indicator of the Piel stem continues to be the doubling of the middle root letter. The participle has a pataḥ under the first root letter, as do the imperative and imperfect.

| Piel Participle | | | |
|---|---|---|---|
| ms | מְשַׁמֵּר | mp | מְשַׁמְּרִים |
| fs | מְשַׁמֶּרֶת | fp | מְשַׁמְּרוֹת |

When the middle root letter is a guttural or has a sheva under it, the dagesh in the middle root letter may be missing. The heʾ is missing on III-heʾ verbs in the same way as in the Qal.

## Vocabulary

| | |
|---|---|
| אַשּׁוּר | Assyria; Assyrian |
| הָלַל* | (Pi) praise; (Hitp) boast |
| חָכְמָה | experience, wisdom |
| טָמֵא | be unclean (stative) |
| כָּנָף | wing |
| לָחַם | (Ni) fight |
| לָמָה לָמֶּה | why? |
| מְלָאכָה | work |
| נוּס | flee |
| סָפַר | write, count, number; (Pi) recount, report, enumerate |
| פֶּתַח | gate, opening, entrance |
| קָדַשׁ | be holy; (Pi) consecrate |
| רוּץ | run |
| רָעָה | feed, graze, tend (cattle) |
| רַק | only (adv) |
| שָׁאַל | ask (for), demand |
| שָׁחַת | (Ni) be corrupt, spoiled; (Pi) spoil, ruin; (Hi) destroy |

**Exercises**

1. Read aloud and translate the following. Chart the verbs.

(Isa 40:9) עַל הַר־גָּבֹהַ<sup>a</sup> עֲלִי־לָךְ מְבַשֶּׂרֶת צִיּוֹן הָרִימִי בַכֹּחַ קוֹלֵךְ מְבַשֶּׂרֶת יְרוּשָׁלָ͏ִם הָרִימִי אַל־תִּירָאִי אִמְרִי לְעָרֵי יְהוּדָה הִנֵּה אֱלֹהֵיכֶם:

(<sup>a</sup> sic L, mlt Mss Edd ה–)

(Isa 49:11) וְשַׂמְתִּי כָל־הָרַי לַדָּרֶךְ וּמְסִלֹּתַי יְרֻמוּן':

(Ps 19:2 ET 1) הַשָּׁמַיִם מְסַפְּרִים כְּבוֹד־אֵל וּמַעֲשֵׂה<sup>a</sup> יָדָיו מַגִּיד הָרָקִיעַ: (–שׁי עשׂ' 𝔖 ,מ' σ'עשׂ' 𝔖 pc Mss 𝔗 <sup>a</sup>)

(Jer 31:8) הִנְנִי מֵבִיא אוֹתָם מֵאֶרֶץ צָפוֹן וְקִבַּצְתִּים מִיַּרְכְּתֵי־אָרֶץ <sup>a</sup>בָּם עִוֵּר וּפִסֵּחַ<sup>a</sup> הָרָה וְיֹלֶדֶת יַחְדָּו קָהָל גָּדוֹל יָשׁוּבוּ הֵנָּה<sup>b</sup>:

(9 et cj c הֵנָּה <sup>b</sup> ‖ בְּמוֹעֵד פֶּסַח = 𝔊 ἐν ἑορτῇ φασεκ <sup>a–a</sup>)

2. Read aloud and translate Exodus 3:1–7 using the following notes. Chart the verbs.

| | | |
|---|---|---|
| Verse 2 | וַיֵּרָא | Niphal: "appeared" |
| | אֻכָּל | Pual: "consumed" |
| Verse 4 | לִרְאוֹת | "to see" (infinitive construct) |
| Verse 7 | רָאֹה | "surely" (infinitive absolute) |

---

<sup>1</sup> The sheva under the prefix looks like the indicator of the Piel imperfect, but the middle root letter is not doubled.

# Chapter 27
## Infinitive Construct

In addition to the participle, Hebrew has two other infinitive forms: the infinitive absolute and the infinitive construct. Whereas the participle focuses on the action or situation of the subject or object of the verb, the infinitive focuses on the verb's action or situation. Some grammarians object to the name infinitive construct because it sounds like it is a construct form of the infinitive absolute. The two infinitives, in fact, have different origins. One is not the construct of the other.

### Form of the Qal Infinitive Construct

The **indicator** of the Qal infinitive construct is a sheva under the first root letter. The form of the infinitive construct is:

שְׁמֹר

*[handwritten note: same as imv. ms]*

The form and indicator of the Qal infinitive construct are the same as the ms imperative. The context will distinguish the two verb types.

Before most suffixes, the form of the infinitive construct is:

שָׁמְר-

*[handwritten note: qamets hatuph]*

Before 2ms and 2mp suffixes, or when attached by a maqqeph to a following word, the form of the infinitive construct is:

שָׁמָר-

The qamets in the previous examples is a qamets ḥatuph, pronounced "o." Sometimes the infinitive construct before suffixes has ḥireq or pataḥ instead of qamets.

$$שָׁמְר-$$
$$שָׁמַר-$$

Several types of verb roots have missing letters. **III-he³** roots take an וֹת– ending:

$$בְּנוֹת$$
$$עֲשׂוֹת$$
$$הֱיוֹת$$

**I-vav** verbs lose the vav and add a tav ending. As usual, הלך acts like a I-vav.

| Root | Infinitive Construct | | With Suffixes | |
|------|------|------|------|------|
| יָשַׁב | שֶׁבֶת | to dwell | שִׁבְתִּי | my dwelling |
| יָצָא | צֵאת | to go out | צֵאתִי | my going out |
| יָדַע | דַּעַת | to know | דַּעְתִּי | my knowing |
| הָלַךְ | לֶכֶת | to walk | לֶכְתִּי | my walking |

**I-nun** verbs may retain their nun and be regular or lose their nun and add a tav like I-vav verbs. Some verbs show forms both with and without nun. לקח, as one would expect, loses its first root letter like a I-nun.

| Root | Infinitive Construct | | |
|------|------|------|------|
| | With nun | Without nun | |
| נטע | נְטֹעַ | טַעַת | to plant |
| נתן | נְתֹן | תֵּת | to give |
| לקח | | קַחַת | to take |

Notice that the final nun of נתן also may assimilate.

The forms of infinitives construct of **hollow** verbs are:

| Infinitive Construct | Translation |
|---|---|
| קוּם | to arise, arising |
| בּוֹא | to come, coming |
| שִׁית | to put, putting |

There are no changes when suffixes are added.

## Stems other than Qal

In the stems other than Qal the form of the infinitive construct is usually the same as the form of the ms imperative. The **Hiphil** often has הַשְׁמֵר for the ms imperative and הַשְׁמִיר for the infinitive construct, but occasionally הַשְׁמֵר also appears to be an infinitive construct. The **Piel** ms imperative and infinitive construct are both שַׁמֵּר.

The Hiphil and Piel infinitive construct forms of roots with weak letters will be outlined in Chapter 29.

## Use and Meaning of the Infinitive Construct

A common use of the infinitive construct is with the prefixed prepositions beth (-בְּ), kaph (-כְּ) and lamed (-לְ).

Clauses expressing time, called **temporal clauses**, often use the preposition beth (-בְּ) or kaph (-כְּ). According to Ernst Jenni, the bet (-בְּ) expresses the closeness of two events ("When..."), whereas the kaph (-כְּ) expresses the time immediately before an event ("As soon as..."). *direct causality*

בֶּן־שְׁלֹשִׁים שָׁנָה דָּוִד
בְּמָלְכוֹ

David was thirty years old
*when he became king* (2 Sam 5:4)

וַיְהִי כְמָלְכוֹ
הִכָּה אֶת־כָּל־בֵּית
יָרָבְעָם

*as soon as he became king,*
he killed the whole house
of Jeroboam (1 Kgs 15:29)

Separable prepositions used with the infinitive construct to introduce temporal clauses are עַד "until," אַחֲרֵי / אַחַר "after," and מִן "from."

Temporal clauses may use the infinitive construct, or use כַּאֲשֶׁר, כְּמוֹ or כִּי with a finite verb. They may begin with וַיְהִי for the past, as in the previous example, and וְהָיָה for the future, as in the next example.

וְהָיָה כִּי־תָבֹאוּ אֶל־הָאָרֶץ      *when you enter the land*
אֲשֶׁר יִתֵּן יְהוָה לָכֶם ...        that the LORD will give
                                  to you ... (Exod 12:25)

The infinitive construct with a prefixed lamed (-לְ) has a wide range of uses that complete or explain another verb by answering the implied questions why, what, or how. For example, it may answer the question why and express purpose, result, or intention.

סָר לִרְאוֹת      he turned aside *to see*
                 (Exod 3:4)

The vowels under the lamed (-לְ) are due to the rule of sheva.

לִרְאוֹת > לִרְאוֹת*

Second, the infinitive construct with lamed (-לְ) may complete a verb by answering the question what?

מִי יוּכַל לַעֲמֹד לִפְנֵי יְהוָה      Who is able *to stand* before the
                                  LORD? (1 Sam 6:20)

Third, it may explain a verb by answering the question how?

כִּי־יַסִּית אֶתְכֶם לֵאמֹר      when he tempts you *by saying*, the
יְהוָה יַצִּילֵנוּ׃           LORD can deliver us (2 Kgs 18:32)

beginning of
direct quote

These uses of the infinitive construct with lamed (-לְ) are adverbial. An adverb modifies a verb. In addition, the infinitive construct may function as a verb or a noun. The use of the infinitve construct with beth and kaph in temporal clauses is an example of the use of the infinitive construct as a **verb**.

Other types of clauses may use the infinitive construct as a verb with prefixed or independent prepositions, including clauses expressing **cause** ("because") and **result** ("that").

בְּשִׂנְאַת יְהוָה אֹתָנוּ

because the LORD *hates* us (Deut 1:27)

As a verb, the infinitive construct may have a **modal** meaning in clauses with יֵשׁ ("is") or אֵין ("is not"), and without another verb. A variety of prepositions may be used, but most common are -לְ (indicating possibility or permission) or עַל (indicating obligation or permission).

מֶה לַעֲשׂוֹת לָךְ
הֲיֵשׁ לְדַבֶּר־לָךְ
אֶל־הַמֶּלֶךְ

What can be done for you?
May one speak for you
before the king? (2 Kgs 4:13)

When the infinitive construct has **suffixed pronouns**, they may be either the subject or the object of the verb.

עָזְבֵךְ אֶת־יְהוָה

*your abandoning* the LORD (Jer 2:17)

לְעָזְבֵךְ לָשׁוּב מֵאַחֲרָיִךְ

*to abandon you* by turning back from following you (Ruth 1:16)

In addition to its uses as an adverb and verb, the infinitive construct can play any role in a sentence that a **noun** would.

טוֹב לְהֹדוֹת¹ לַיהוָה    to give thanks to the LORD is good (Ps 92:2)

The infinitive construct is usually negated with בִּלְתִּי. A lamed is prefixed to בִּלְתִּי rather than to the infinitive construct.

צִוִּיתִיךָ לְבִלְתִּי אֲכָל־מִמֶּנּוּ    I commanded you *not* to eat from it (Gen 3:11)

The infinitive construct may be charted in the following manner (using לְעָזְבֵךְ from Ruth 1:16 as an example):

| Root | Stem | Conjugation | PGN | Special Features |
|------|------|-------------|-----|------------------|
| עזב | Qal | infinitive construct | | prefixed preposition: לְ <br> 2fs pronoun suffix: ךְ |

## Vocabulary

| | |
|---|---|
| יוֹאָב | Joab |
| *כָּסָה | (Pi) cover, conceal |
| לְבַד | alone (adv); besides (prep) |
| מָוֶת | death |
| נֶגֶד | opposite, before (noun, prep, adv) |
| נָגַע | touch, reach; come to |
| נָסַע | depart |

---

¹ This is a Hiphil infinitive construct. The root ידה here is both doubly weak (the he² has disappeared and the yod has changed) and defective in spelling (the ḥolem vav typical of Hiphil forms has reduced to a ḥolem).

| | |
|---|---|
| עֵדָה | congregation |
| פַּר  פָּרָה | young bull (m); cow (f) |
| פָּתַח | open; (Pi) loosen, free |
| צְדָקָה | righteousness |
| צָפוֹן | north |
| רֹב | multitude, abundance |
| שָׂמַח | rejoice; (Pi) gladden |
| שָׂנֵא | hate; (Qal and Pi part) adversary, enemy |

## Exercises

1. Read aloud and translate the following. Chart the verbs.

(Gen 2:19) וַיִּצֶר יְהוָה אֱלֹהִים ᵃ מִן־הָאֲדָמָה ᵇ כָּל־חַיַּת
הַשָּׂדֶה וְאֵת כָּל־עוֹף הַשָּׁמַיִם וַיָּבֵא אֶל־הָאָדָם
לִרְאוֹת מַה־יִּקְרָא־לוֹ וְכֹל אֲשֶׁר יִקְרָא־לוֹ
הָאָדָם ᶜ נֶפֶשׁ חַיָּה ᶜ הוּא שְׁמוֹ:

(ᵃ 𝔊 + עוֹד ‖ ᵇ ins c 𝔊 אֵת ‖ ᶜ⁻ᶜ frt add)

(Gen 2:15) וַיִּקַּח יְהוָה אֱלֹהִים אֶת־הָאָדָם
וַיַּנִּחֵהוּ בְגַן־עֵדֶן לְעָבְדָהּ וּלְשָׁמְרָהּ:

2. Read and translate Deuteronomy 6:1–9. Chart the verbs.

# Chapter 28

## Hebrew Narrative

In his 1968 Presidential Address to the Society of Biblical Literature in the United States, James Muilenburg suggested that biblical scholars should pay more attention to the art of composition. This address was an early signal of a shift in biblical studies away from the intention of the author as the source of the meaning of a passage, and toward the passage itself and the reader as the sources of meaning. The shift moves away from historical investigation in order to determine the intention of the author and toward literary study of the text and how it affects the reader. For many this is a shift in emphasis rather than a choice of one or the other.

Since Muilenberg, the number of newer, literary studies of both prose and poetry is steadily increasing. A later chapter will focus on poetry. This chapter focuses on one type of prose, that is, narrative. A **narrative** tells a story or a series of events, either real or imagined.

Many of those writing current, literary studies of Hebrew narrative call their work **narrative criticism.** Although they use a variety of different literary theories, they analyze plot, character, setting, narrator, point of view, and style.

## Plot

In literary studies, the **plot** is the principle(s) that connect(s) all the incidents in a story, and creates a beginning, middle, and end. The incidents in a story may or may not occur in chronological order. Literary critics often analyze the conflict that drives a plot, including the climax and resolution of the conflict. David Gunn suggests that the plot of a story can also be uncovered by asking: "Who desires what and when? When are their desires fulfilled?" This way of asking about plot, he says, frees the interpreter from the question of who is the main character determining the interpretation.[1] It also makes the connection, widely recognized and debated in literary studies, between plot and character.

## Character

Literary criticism distinguishes between flat characters, round characters, and agents. Flat characters have only one or two personality traits (such as greed or kindness). Round characters are more complex, possibly changing as the narrative progresses. Agents are present merely to play a role in advancing the plot.

The Hebrew Bible rarely describes the physical features, or psychological characteristics or motives of the characters in a narrative. This contrasts with European novels that often provide detailed descriptions of characters. Hebrew narrative uses a high proportion of dialogue between characters. There are normally only two characters in a dialogue. Different styles of speech may correspond to different characters, for example, using long, flowing speeches, or being silent, or speaking briefly or abruptly. The relation of speech to action also brings out character. The large amount of dialogue in Hebrew narrative is a dramatic and realistic way of portraying characters.

Although the narrator says little, sometimes there are clues to the narrator's interpretation of the story.

## Narrator and Point of View

The narrator is the person who tells the story. The narrator may or may not be identical with the author, and may or may not be a character in the story. The narrator may tell the story in first or third person. In the Hebrew Bible, the narrator often is not identified with a particular character, but speaks in the third

---

[1] "Narrative Criticism," in *To Each Its Own Meaning*, eds. Steven L. McKenzie and Stephen R. Haynes (Louisville: Westminster/John Knox, 1999), 180.

person, and seems to be all knowing. This "god-like" narration gives the Bible authority and influences our interpretations.

A closely related issue in interpretation is **point of view**, also called frame, perspective, or focalization. Point of view is similar to the limited field of view of a television camera. I once attended a protest demonstration in a large park. In the expanses of the park the crowd seemed small and disappointing to me. When I saw the protest on television that evening, the cameras focused on the crowd. No empty spaces were visible. The impression was quite different and a vivid illustration to me of the way television influences our interpretation of events.

Similarly, the narrator frames a story, decides what we see and do not see, what is in focus and what is out of focus. The point of view of the narrator influences and guides our interpretation.

## Setting

In literature the setting is the time, place, and environment of a story or play. Rain, for example, often reflects a somber mood. Biblical stories often occur in places associated with religious and political significance.

## Style and Rhetorical Criticism

Every culture has rules for communicating. We have already seen some of these rules in our study of genre or form. The title of Muilenburg's address is "Form Criticism and Beyond." In addition to studying genre, he wanted to study rules of composition or style. Muilenburg named this art of composition rhetoric and its analysis **rhetorical criticism**. Within biblical studies some people use rhetorical criticism in the narrow sense of analyzing how an author attempts to persuade an audience. Muilenburg and others use it in the broader sense of analyzing the compositional features a text uses to communicate meaning.

Among the habits or rules of Hebrew narrative composition are various types of **repetition**. One that requires some Hebrew to identify is what is known as a *Leitwort* (German for "guide word"). A *Leitwort* is a word that, because of its repetition and prominence, gives structure and emphasis to a passage. For example,

2 Samuel 7 plays on the meanings of the Hebrew word for house. After David builds a "house" (palace), God rejects David's desire to build a "house" (temple), but promises to build David a "house" (dynasty).

Also characteristic of Hebrew storytelling are omissions or **gaps**. A gap is an essential word or piece of information that is left out.

Muilenburg's student, Phyllis Trible, is well known for her use of this method in her books *Texts of Terror*, *God and the Rhetoric of Sexuality* and, more recently, *Rhetorical Criticism*.

In *Rhetorical Criticism*, Trible outlines a method for doing rhetorical criticism.[2] This method includes looking for plot and character (already discussed above). What is of interest here is how she goes about studying the composition or style of a passage. As she reads the passage many times, she looks for the repetition of sounds, words, phrases, and sentences.

Two rhetorical features that biblical writers seemed to like were chiasmus and inclusio. **Chiasmus** literally means "crossing" and refers to the repetition of elements in reverse order. This crossing may occur in a single verse or in longer passages. For example, Psalm 103:22 says:

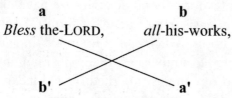

**a**            **b**
*Bless* the-LORD,     *all*-his-works,

**b'**             **a'**
in-*all*-places of-his-realm,    *bless* the-LORD, O-my-soul.

In the above example both form and content cross over. The chiasmus reinforces the meaning as blessing surrounds God's actions.

This is also an example of inclusio because Psalm 103 begins and ends with "Bless the LORD, O my soul." **Inclusio** is the

_____

[2] Pp. 101–106.

repetition of the same word, phrase, or sentence at the beginning and end of a passage.

Chiasmus may also occur over larger passages. For example, Trible, following Lohfink, sees a chiasm in Chapter 1 of Jonah:

**A**    Framework (1:4–6)
    **B**    Two speeches by the sailors (1:7–8)
        **Center**    Confession of Jonah (1:9–10a)
    **B'**   Two speeches by the sailors (1:10a–11)
**A'**   Framework (1:12–16)

This kind of literary structure often displays or sets off the material in the center, like a fine gem set on a ring.

Trible also notices **word order**. Deviations from normal word order, such as putting the subject before the verb in Hebrew, are for emphasis. In addition, the placement of small **particles** like כִּי, הִנֵּה, and לָכֵן are important signs of movement and emphasis in Hebrew narrative.

When you are studying a passage, you may want to make copies, and mark or highlight elements you notice. As you read, also look for narrative and rhetorical features already discussed above.

As a way of seeing rhetorical features and helping others see them (particularly if they do not know Hebrew), you may want to make a word-for-word translation. (A dynamic translation into English would obscure the Hebrew patterns.) As in the example above, Trible joins with hyphens English words that are a single Hebrew word. She then uses different types of underlining to highlight repetitions. This visual presentation should be accompanied by an explanation of the patterns and how they relate to the content and meaning of the passage.

**Exercise**

Translate Exodus 3:8–15 and discuss the literary features of Exodus 3:1–15. (You read Exodus 3:1–7 in Chapter 26.)

# Chapter 29

## Infinitive Absolute

### Form of the Qal Infinitive Absolute

The form of the Qal infinitive absolute is:

שָׁמוֹר

III-he³ roots, as well as II-vav and II-yod roots, have unique forms of the infinitive absolute. Note the Qal infinitive absolute of **III-he³** verbs:

גָּלוֹ

or

גָּלֹה

The Qal infinitives absolute of **II-vav** and **II-yod** verbs have the same form:

| Root | Infinitive Absolute |
|------|---------------------|
| קוּם | קוֹם |
| שִׂים | שׂוֹם |

The infinitive absolute does not take prefixes or suffixes.

### Use and Meaning

The infinitive absolute most often comes before or after a finite verb. Although some grammars distinguish between the meanings depending on the position of the infinitive absolute, there is no convincing evidence for this distinction. The use of the

*[handwritten margin notes:]*
① for emphasis — "surely," "indeed" — with the same verb

② by itself — instead of a finite verb of legal texts of imv.

③ adverbial (root meaning) + -ly

infinitive absolute before or after a finite verb emphasizes the *intensity* or *certainty* of the finite verb.

מוֹת יָמוּת     he will *surely* die
(1 Sam 14:39)

The infinitive absolute may also be used as an **imperative**:

זָכוֹר אֶת־יוֹם הַשַּׁבָּת     *Remember* the Sabbath day
(Exod 20:8)

Intermediate and advanced reference grammars list other less frequent uses of the infinitive absolute.

## Piel and Hiphil Infinitives

Piel infinitives construct and absolute have the same form. The form of both **Piel infinitives** is the same as the ms Piel imperative. As with the imperative, the **indicator** of the Piel infinitive is a pataḥ under the first root letter. When the second root letter is a guttural or resh, the pataḥ may or may not lengthen to a qamets. The Piel infinitive construct of III-heʾ verbs adds an נֹ– ending that distinguishes it from the absolute.

| Root | | Infinitive Absolute | Infinitive Construct |
|---|---|---|---|
| Strong | גדל | גַּדֵּל | גַּדֵּל |
| II-resh | ברך | בָּרֵךְ | בָּרֵךְ |
| II-guttural | בער | בַּעֵר | בַּעֵר |
| III-heʾ | צוה | צַוֵּה | צַוּוֹת |

The **Hiphil infinitive absolute** usually has the same form as the ms imperative. As shown in the table below, the **construct** tends to have a ḥireq yod instead of a tsere under the middle root letter. Like the Piel, the Hiphil infinitive construct of III-heʾ verbs has an נֹ– ending.

| Root | | Infinitive Absolute | Infinitive Construct |
|---|---|---|---|
| Strong | שׁמד | הַשְׁמֵד | הַשְׁמִיד |
| III-heʾ | גלה | הַגְלֵה | הַגְלוֹת |
| I-nun | נגד | הַגֵּד | הַגִּיד |
| I-vav | ישׁב | הוֹשֵׁב | הוֹשִׁיב |
| Hollow | קום | הָקֵם | הָקִים |

**Vocabulary**

| | |
|---|---|
| אָז | then (adv) |
| מֵאָז | formerly, since (adv, prep) |
| זֶבַח | slaughter, sacrifice; (Pi) sacrifice |
| חָכָם | wise (adj) |
| חָנָה | encamp |
| יַחַד | community (noun) |
| יַחְדָּו | together, at the same time (adv) |
| יַיִן | wine |
| יָמִין | right hand/side; south |
| יֵשׁ | there is, there are |
| כְּמוֹ | just like (relative particle) |
| כִּסֵּא | seat, throne |
| מִסְפָּר | number (noun) |
| מַעַל | upwards (adj); above (prep) |
| מִשְׁכָּן | dwelling, tabernacle |
| נוּחַ | rest, settle down, make quiet; (Hi) lay, deposit |
| רָעָב | hunger, famine |
| שֶׁ– שָׁ– שַׁ– | who, which, that (prefixed relative particle; the following consonant takes a dagesh) |

## Exercises

1. Read aloud and translate the following. Chart the verbs.

אֶל⁻[a]הָאִשָּׁה אָמַר הַרְבָּה אַרְבֶּה עִצְּבוֹנֵךְ וְהֵרֹנֵךְ[b] (Gen 3:16)
בְּעֶצֶב[c] תֵּלְדִי בָנִים [d]וְאֶל⁻אִישֵׁךְ תְּשׁוּקָתֵךְ וְהוּא יִמְשָׁל⁻בָּךְ[d]: ס

([a] l c 𝔐𝔊𝔖𝔙 וְאֶל ‖ [b] frt l c 𝔐 וְהֵרְיוֹנֵךְ; 𝔊 καὶ τὸν στεναγμόν σου = וְהֶגְיֹנֵךְ ‖ [c] 𝔐 בעצבון ‖ [d-d] cf 4,7[b-b])

2. Read aloud and translate Ecclesiastes 3:1–8. Chart the verbs.

# Chapter 30
## Niphal

### Perfect

The **indicator** of the Niphal perfect is a nun prefixed to the three root letters.

The 3ms Niphal perfect is:

נִשְׁמַר          he was kept (passive); *or*
                he kept himself (reflexive)

The suffixes of the perfect are the same as in the Qal stem.

With **I-nun** verbs, the nun assimilates into the following root letter.

| Qal Perfect 3ms | Niphal Perfect 3ms |
|---|---|
| נָשָׂא | נִשָּׂא |

I-vav verbs keep the original vav after the nun.

| Qal Perfect 3ms | Niphal Perfect 3ms |
|---|---|
| יָדַע | נוֹדַע |

**Hollow** verbs have a qamets under the nun prefix (compare the Qal imperfect of hollow verbs). With suffixes that begin with consonants (that is, all the second and first person forms), the vowel under the prefix reduces to a sheva and there is a holem vav before the suffix.

| PGN | Qal Perfect | Niphal Perfect |
|-----|-------------|----------------|
| 3ms | רָם | נָרוֹם |
| 2ms | רַמְתָ | נְרוֹמֹתָ |

Fortunately, hollow verbs are rare in Niphal.

With **I-gutturals** the pointing under the nun can be נֶ, נַ or נֱ.

נֶעֱזַב

Note: The Niphal perfect 3ms can have the same form as the Qal imperfect 1cp with III-guttural (נִשְׁמַע) and III-ʾaleph (נִמְצָא) roots and a similar form with III-heʾ roots (Qal: נִגְלֶה Niphal: נִגְלָה). For the first two roots, only context tells you which one it is. With III-heʾ roots, the qamets (ָ) under the second root letter is characteristic of the Niphal.

**Imperfect**

The **indicator** of the Niphal imperfect is a dagesh in the first root letter and a qamets under it. The nun prefix assimilates into the first root letter with the addition of imperfect prefixes.

יִשָּׁמֵר    → preformative
                has its own syllable

The dagesh is missing with **I-gutturals**, but the qamets under the first root letter continues to identify the Niphal imperfect.

יֵעָזֵב

The indicators are also present with I-nun and I-vav verbs. The first nun of the root remains in **I-nun** verbs.

יִנָּצֵל

The original vav appears in **I-vav** verbs.

יֻלַד (from ילד)

**Hollow** verbs do not have a qamets under the first root letter.

יִכּוֹן

## Imperative and Infinitives

The Niphal infinitive construct has the same form as the 2ms imperative. The **indicator** of the Niphal imperative and infinitive construct is ‑הִ. The other indicators seen in the imperfect—the doubling of the first root letter with a qamets under it—distinguish the Niphal imperative and infinitive from the Hiphil perfect, which also begins with ‑הִ.

הִשָּׁמֵר

The **indicator** of the Niphal **infinitive absolute** is a holem between the second and third root letters. The form is either:

נִשְׁמוֹר

or

הִשָּׁמוֹר

## Participle

| ms | נִשְׁמָר | mp | נִשְׁמָרִים |
|---|---|---|---|
| fs | נִשְׁמָרָה<br>נִשְׁמֶרֶת | fp | נִשְׁמָרוֹת |

## Meaning of the Niphal

If you look back at the chart of the meaning of verb stems in Chapter 15, you will see that Niphal is the passive or reflexive form corresponding to the Qal. (Grammarians debate what is the original or basic meaning of the Niphal.) In order to express the reflexive or passive (or middle) of a Qal verb, Hebrew most often uses the Niphal stem.

Compare the following English sentences:

| Active: | She | saved | him |
| | (subject) | (verb) | (object) |
| Passive: | She | was saved | by him. |
| | (subject) | (verb) | (agent) |
| Reflexive: | She | saved | herself. |
| | (subject) | (verb) | (subject as own agent) |

Passive verbs in English usually involve some form of the verb "to be," such as "was" in the above example. In Hebrew **passive** means that the subject receives the action of the verb. The agent of the action may be explicit or implicit, and the passive may be used personally or impersonally.

| וַיִּפְתַּח אֶת־פִּי ... | And he opened my mouth ... |
| וַיִּפָּתַח פִּי | so my mouth *was opened* |
| | (Ezek 33:22) |

| עַל־כֵּן יֵאָמַר בְּסֵפֶר | Thus *it is said* in the book |
| מִלְחֲמֹת יְהוָה | of the wars of the LORD (Num 21:14) |

Related to the passive are **stative** uses of the Niphal.

| נִשְׁבְּרוּ בְרִיחֶיהָ׃ | Its bars *are broken* (Jer 51:30) |

**Reflexive** means that the subject acts on itself. Related to the reflexive are the **middle, tolerative** and **reciprocal** meanings. In the middle, the object acts by itself. In the tolerative, the subject lets the action of a verb happen to it. In the reciprocal, the subjects act together.

Reflexive:

תִּשָּׁמֵרוּ

*you should watch over yourself* (Exod 23:13)

Middle:

נִפְתְּחוּ הַשָּׁמַיִם

the heavens *opened*[1] (Ezek 1:1)

Tolerative:

נִדְרַשְׁתִּי לְלוֹא שָׁאָלוּ

*I allowed myself to be sought* by those who did not ask [for me] (Isa 65:1)

Reciprocal:

וַיֹּאמֶר הֵאָסְפוּ

he said *gather yourselves together* (Gen 49:1)

## Vocabulary

| | |
|---|---|
| אוֹר | light |
| אֱמֶת | trustworthiness, stability, truth |
| אַף | also, even, the more so (conj) |
| בַּד בַּד | separation; alone, by (one)self (with –לְ) |
| בּוֹשׁ | be ashamed |
| מַרְאֶה | sight, appearance |
| נַחַל | torrent, valley, wadi |
| נְחֹשֶׁת | copper, bronze |
| סוּס סוּסָה | horse; mare |

---

[1] Examples of the middle in the Hebrew Bible could often also be translated as passives: "The heavens were opened." The difference depends on whether one interprets the subject as being acted on (passive) or acting by itself (middle).

| | |
|---|---|
| עֲבוֹדָה | service |
| עָפָר | dry earth, dust |
| עֶ֫רֶב | evening |
| פָּנָה | turn about, turn aside |
| קָרָא | happen; against (inf cstr as prep) |
| רָדַף | pursue, persecute |
| שָׁבַר | break |
| שֶׁ֫מֶשׁ | sun |

## Exercises

1. Read aloud and translate the following. Chart the verbs.

(Gen 2:9) וַיַּצְמַ֨ח יְהוָ֣ה אֱלֹהִים֮ מִן־הָ֣אֲדָמָ֔ה כָּל־עֵ֛ץ נֶחְמָ֥ד
לְמַרְאֶ֖ה וְט֣וֹב לְמַאֲכָ֑ל וְעֵ֤ץ הַֽחַיִּים֙ בְּת֣וֹךְ הַגָּ֔ן וְעֵ֕ץ הַדַּ֖עַת
ט֥וֹב וָרָֽע׃

2. Translate Genesis 2:15–25. Chart the verbs.

Verse 15

וַיַּנִּחֵ֫הוּ   The הוּ– on the end is a suffixed pronoun. Notice the ḥireq under the nun. If you wrote the full spelling with a ḥireq yod it might be easier to recognize the root, which is one of your vocabulary words in the last chapter.

Verse 17

אֲכָלְךָ   This is one of the alternate forms of the infinitive construct before a suffixed pronoun.

Verse 18

כְּנֶגְדּוֹ   Once you remove the prefixed preposition and the suffixed pronoun, you should have no trouble finding the root.

### Verse 19

וַיִּצֶר ᵖ | This is an exception to the indicator for I-yod verbs. The root is יצר.

### Verse 23

לֻקֳחָה | "she was taken" (You have not had this stem yet, but should recognize the root.)

### Verse 25

יִתְבֹּשָׁשׁוּ | Don't worry about this form and its root. "They were ashamed."

# Chapter 31

## Hitpael

The Hitpael **stem indicator** is an **infixed tav**. Infixed means that a tav is fixed inside the word. Hitpael, like Piel, has as an **indicator** the doubling of the middle root letter. (Hitpael and Piel have related meanings and forms.) As in the Piel, the middle root letter may lose the dagesh when a sheva comes under it.

## Perfect

In the Hitpael perfect, the tav is fixed between a prefixed he⁾ (like the Hiphil) and the three root letters.

הִתשׁמּר

The full vowel pointing of the Hitpael perfect, 3ms is:

הִתְשַׁמֵּר

## Imperfect

The Hitpael imperfect loses the prefixed he⁾ when adding the prefixes of the imperfect. The prefixes and suffixes are the same as for other stems and **indicate** an imperfect. The **stem indicators** remain the same as for the perfect: an infixed tav and doubling. The 3ms form is:

יִתְשַׁמֵּר

## Imperative and Infinitive

The form of the 2ms imperative, the infinitive absolute, and the infinitive construct are the same:

הִתְשַׁמֵּר

## Participle

As in the Piel and Hiphil, the Hitpael participle prefixes a mem. The ms form is:

מִתְשַׁמֵּר

## Missing Letters and other Peculiarities

The missing letters are by now predictable. **I-vav** verbs may either return to original vav or substitute a yod and appear like I-yod verbs. No Hitpael forms of **I-yod** verbs occur in the Bible. **III-he'** may be missing or replaced by a yod or a tav. **II-gutturals** do not accept doubling (a dagesh) and may lengthen the preceding vowel.

In the Hitpael a series of other peculiarities can make it difficult to identify the root. As languages develop, the pronunciation of words changes over time. The linguistic term for one such change is **metathesis**, which means that two letters switch places. In the Hebrew Hitpael, roots that begin with one of the "s" sounds (ס צ שׂ שׁ), called **sibilants**, switch places with the infixed tav.

וָאֶשְׁתַּמֵּר מֵעֲוֹנִי      *I kept myself* from guilt
(Ps 18:24 ET 23)

The root is שׁמר. The shin and tav have changed places.

When the first root letter is צ, not only does it change places with the tav, it also causes the tav to change to a ṭet (ט).

וּמַה־נִּצְטַדָּק How can *we declare ourselves righteous?* (Gen 44:16)

The root is צדק, which is a Hitpael stem.

When the first root letter is ד or ט or ת, the infixed tav will assimilate. These three letters are called **dentals** because they are pronounced with the teeth (from the Latin *dens*, for tooth).

וַיִּשְׁמַע אֶת־הַקּוֹל he heard the voice

מִדַּבֵּר אֵלָיו *speaking* to him (Num 7:89)

The dagesh in the dalet (ד) is the assimilated tav (ת). Assimilation occurs sometimes with other dentals.

הִנַּבְּאוּ בַבַּעַל they prophesied by Baal (Jer 23:13)

The dagesh in the nun is the assimilated tav.

**Hishtaphel**

וְנִשְׁתַּחֲוֶה *that we may worship*

וְנָשׁוּבָה אֲלֵיכֶם and may return to you (Gen 22:5)

The first verb in the example above looks as if it might be a Hitpael from the root שׁחה "to bow." (This would be an example of shin and tav changing places, as mentioned above.) This is, in fact, the root under which BDB lists such verb forms. However, from what we have seen of other III-heᵓ verbs, we do not expect the heᵓ to go back to an original vav and to have another heᵓ appear at the end (as in the verb above). Modern grammarians tend to see this as an example of a shin-tav infix in Hebrew, either from the root חוה or חיה. The first root occurs in Ugaritic as a sheen-tav infix with the meaning "to throw oneself down (striking the earth)." The second occurs in the same stem with the meaning "to cause oneself to live (by worship)."[1]

## Vocabulary

| | |
|---|---|
| בְּכֹר בְּכוֹר | firstborn |
| גָּדַל | be(come) strong, great; (Pi) bring up, let grow, nourish |
| *חָוָה | (Hishtaphel stem) bow down |
| חוֹמָה | (city) wall |
| חִזְקִיָּהוּ | Hezekiah (short form: חִזְקִיָּה) |
| חֵמָה | heat; rage, wrath; poison |
| חֲצִי | half |
| חֹק | prescription, law, due, decree |
| חָשַׁב | account, regard, value |
| כֶּבֶשׂ כִּבְשָׂה (כֶּשֶׂב כִּשְׂבָּה) | young ram; ewe-lamb |
| כֹּחַ | strength, power |
| *כָּפַר | (Pi) cover over, expiate (כִּפֶּר) |
| לָכַד | seize, capture |
| נָגַשׁ | draw near, approach |
| נָשִׂיא | prince |
| עֶצֶם | bone(s) |
| פַּעַם | foot(step), occurrence, time |
| שָׁכַח | forget |

---

[1] *UT* § 19.847.

**Exercise**

Read aloud and translate Genesis 3:1–13. Chart the verbs.

Verse 1

אַף כִּי־   "Did...?" ("Is it that...?")

Verse 4

תְּמֻתוּן   The sheva under the tav makes this look like a Piel, but מוּת does not appear in Piel (indeed, *very* few hollow verbs do), and the sheva is a vowel reduction caused by the addition of the suffix.

Verse 6

וַתֵּרֶא   Normally, the tsere under the imperfect prefix is a sign of a I-vav or I-yod verb. But sometimes the loss of the third he⁾ and the moving back of the accent causes the lengthening of the vowel under the imperfect prefix in III-he⁾ verbs. The root is רָאָה.

Verse 7

וַיִּתְפְּרוּ   Hint: This is not a Hitpael. The dagesh in the peh is weak because it is not preceded by a short vowel.

Verse 8

Notice the Hitpael verbs in this verse. What is the meaning of the Hitpael in each case?

Verse 9

אַיֶּכָּה   The ending of this word is the long form of the 2ms suffixed pronoun, "you." You can now look up the remaining two letters. (Why is there a dagesh in the kaph?)

## Verse 11

לְבִלְתִּי      Hebrew uses this word to negate an infinitive. "Not to [+infinitive]"

# Chapter 32
## Hebrew Poetry

**Parallelism**

Anyone who reads the Psalms or one of the prophets will notice that the writers seem to repeat themselves. This repetition is one of the characteristics of Hebrew poetry. The balancing of thought between two lines is called parallelism.

לַיהוָה הָאָרֶץ וּמְלוֹאָהּ
To the LORD belongs the Earth and its fullness,

תֵּבֵל וְיֹשְׁבֵי בָהּ:
the world and those who dwell in it. (Ps 24:1)

Each line is called a **colon** (plural, cola). Two parallel lines are called a **bicola** and three are a **tricola**. Also used are the terms stich for one line, distich for two, and tristich for three parallel lines.

Since Bishop Robert Lowth first described Hebrew poetic parallelism, it has been traditional to speak of three types of parallelism.

**Synonymous parallelism** occurs when the second colon repeats the thought of the first colon (see above verse as an example).

**Antithetic parallelism** happens when the second colon states the opposite or contrasting thought to the first colon. The two cola are usually joined by a vav adversative translated as "but." This type of parallelism is characteristic of Proverbs.

דֶּרֶךְ אֱוִיל יָשָׁר
בְּעֵינָיו
The way of a fool is right in his own eyes,

וְשֹׁמֵעַ לְעֵצָה חָכָם:     but one who listens to counsel
is a wise person. (Prov 12:15)

**Synthetic parallelism** occurs when there is no balancing of thoughts but of word order and rhythm.

The problem with this traditional way of naming Hebrew parallelism is that verses are more often synthetic than synonymous. Recent research tends to follow two directions. The first tendency is to classify many more types of synthetic parallelism, including parallelism of word order, grammatical forms, and sound. The second tendency is to develop one definition of parallelism that includes all types, and is probably the most helpful for beginning students of Hebrew poetry. Berlin suggests that a colon may substitute for, continue, or advance, the thought of the previous colon, or both. Similarly, Kugel says that when A is the first colon and B is the second colon, then "B typically *supports* A, carries it further, backs it up, completes it, goes beyond it." He describes the basic idea of Hebrew poetic parallelism as "A is so, *and what's more* B is so."

As you read Hebrew poetry, look for the many ways the subsequent lines substitute, nuance, underscore, add, specify, elaborate, expand, identify, or give examples. Look for parallels and contrasts of meaning, word order, grammatical forms, and sound. In combination, these various types of parallelism may set up complex and profound patterns of interaction.

While parallelism is perhaps the most obvious and studied feature of Hebrew poetry, it is not the only element that makes a biblical passage poetic. (Parallelism occurs also in Hebrew narrative (Gen 22:17). Some lines in Hebrew poetry show no parallelism. Meter or rhythm also creates poetry in Hebrew, as do other literary features (see below for discussion). Both Hebrew narrative and poetry may contain any of these elements. As in many cultures, prose and poetry are on a continuum. These features make a narrative text sound "poetic." Greater and more effective concentrations of these features make a passage into poetry. The effective *concentration* of parallelism, rhythm, and literary features creates Hebrew poetry.

## Meter or Rhythm

For centuries scholars have claimed that biblical poetry has a meter. **Meter** is the ordering of accented and unaccented syllables according to a regular pattern.

Scholars, however, still cannot agree on what exactly Hebrew poetic meter is. There are two ways of counting meter, neither of them entirely satisfactory. Some scholars count the number of Masoretic accents in a colon, although the Masoretic vowel points and accents were added long after the text was first written. Others count the number of syllables in a colon, which involves counting not the Masoretic vowels but reconstructing the vowels of a hypothetical, earlier stage of the Hebrew language. Sometimes the vowel counts are not regular or require changes to the consonantal text to create regularity. Since neither system is entirely adequate, talk of meter in Hebrew poetry remains open to question.

The length of the cola in Hebrew poetry does often seem roughly equal. For this reason, Petersen and Richards prefer to speak of **rhythm** rather than meter. They understand rhythm as being similar to meter, but as a broader term indicating greater freedom and variation, and less clearly defined regularity. The lines of Hebrew poetry exhibit both regularity of colon length and creative variation of length that might be called rhythm.

## Literary Features

Literary features are those techniques that make for good literature. Like parallelism and meter they are also present in narrative. Since they have already been discussed in the chapter on Hebrew narrative, this chapter will review only a few of these features.

Discussions of Hebrew poetry sometimes mention stanzas or strophes, which can mean the same thing. Since strophe can refer specifically to a type of stanza in Greek literature, stanza as the more general term is more appropriate for discussing Hebrew poetry. A **stanza** is a unit of meaning in poetry, as a paragraph is in narrative.

Some think there are no stanzas in Hebrew. But readers will almost certainly divide a poem into units of meaning as they read.

And the Hebrew poets seem to provide certain indications of division, such as changes in rhythm or speaker, or the repetition of the same line at the beginning and end.

**Inclusio** is the repetition of a word or words at the beginning and end of a verse, stanza, or longer passage. Several hymns in the Psalms have the same call to praise at the beginning and end (see Ps 8).

**Chiasmus** means crossing over.

> a                    b
> "My-God, my-God, why-have you-abandoned-me,
> b'                    a'
> so-far from-my-deliverance, the-words of-my-crying?"
>
> (Ps 22:1 [ET 2])

The first phrase is the cry of the psalmist and the last phrase mentions "crying" so we call them *a* and *a'* ("a prime"). "Abandoned" and "far away" are related thoughts so we can call these phrases *b* and *b'*. The elements of the two cola, therefore, cross over. Notice that in line with Kugel's analysis the second colon specifies, expands, and nuances the first in a number of ways.

Hebrew poetry uses many types of repetition. **Alliteration** is the repetition of the initial sound in several words of a phrase or line. **Assonance** is a repetition of the same or similar sounds in a series of syllables or words.

**Metaphor** and **simile**, comparisons of one thing to another, are common in poetry. Similes use "like" or "as." Metaphors state that one thing "is" something else.

These are only a few of the most common literary features. For others consult books on Hebrew poetry and narrative, such as those listed in this book's bibliography.

**Exercise**

Read aloud and translate Psalm 1. Study and be prepared to discuss its poetic and literary qualities.

# Chapter 33

## Other Passive Stems

So far, we have studied the Niphal, which is the passive stem corresponding to the meaning of the Qal stem. It is the most common passive stem. But there are also passive stems corresponding to the meaning of the Piel and Hiphil, as well as another passive corresponding to the Qal. These other passive stems are dealt with in this chapter. They occur only occasionally and are easy to recognize.

**Pual** *- passive of Piel*

The passive stem corresponding in meaning to the Piel is the Pual. Thus Pual has the same type of meaning as the Piel but expressed as a passive—translated with a form of the verb "to be" in English.

... כִּי־כֵן צֻוֵּיתִי:          ... for thus I have been
                                commanded (Lev 8:35)

The **stem indicators** of the Pual are the doubling of the second root letter and a u-class vowel under the first root letter.

שֻׁמַּר

The same prefixes and suffixes identify the **perfect** and **imperfect** as in other stems. The prefix of the **participle** is the same as the Piel: מְ–. There is only one occurrence of the Pual infinite absolute and one of the infinitive construct in the Bible. The only Pual **infinitive absolute** is found in Genesis 40:15:

גֻּנֹּב גֻּנַּבְתִּי          I was indeed stolen

The only Pual **infinitive construct** is in Psalm 132:1. It is from a III-heʾ root and has the typical ‏וֹת‎– ending:

‏עֻנּוֹתוֹ‎ his being afflicted

As in other stems the heʾ is missing or replaced by a yod or tav in **III-heʾ** verbs.

**II-gutturals** and **resh** do not take doubling and may or may not lengthen the preceding vowel from silluq to ḥolem.

‏בֹּרַךְ‎

Here is a summary of Pual verbs:

| Root | Perfect | Imperfect | Participle |
|---|---|---|---|
| ‏בקש‎ | ‏בֻּקַּשׁ‎ | ‏יְבֻקַּשׁ‎ | ‏מְבֻקַּשׁ‎ |
| ‏ברך‎ | ‏בֹּרַךְ‎ | ‏יְבֹרַךְ‎ | ‏מְבֹרַךְ‎ |
| ‏גלה‎ | ‏גֻּלָּה‎ | ‏יְגֻלֶּה‎ | ‏מְגֻלֶּה‎ |

## Hophal

The Hophal is the passive stem corresponding to the Hiphil.

‏הֲלוֹא הֻגַּד‎ Has it not been told? (Isa 40:21)

The **stem indicator** of the Hophal is a u-class vowel under a prefix. The u-class vowel is normally qamets ḥatuph ( ָ ), pronounced "o" and sometimes ḥolem ( ֹ ), but qibbuts ( ֻ ) for I-nun verbs and shureq ( וּ ) for I-vav or I-yod and hollow verbs.

The prefix for the **perfect** is a heʾ as in the Hiphil.

‏הָשְׁמַר‎

The heʾ is lost in the imperfect and the participle, and the u-class vowel is under the prefix.

**imperfect** ‏יָשְׁמַר‎    **participle** ‏מָשְׁמָר‎

There are only two Hophal **imperatives** in the Bible:

| Root | Imperative | Translation |
|---|---|---|
| פנה | הָפְנוּ | Be turned back (Jer 49:8) |
| שׁכב | הָשְׁכְּבָה | Be laid down (Ezek 32:19) |

The **infinitive absolute** has a tsere under the second root letter (unlike the perfect, which has an a-class vowel).

הָשְׁמֵר

The **infinitive construct** has a patah under the middle root letter:

הָשְׁמַר

The **I-vav/yod** and **hollow** verbs have shureq ( וּ ) after prefixes, as mentioned above. The **III-heʾ** is missing in the same places as in other stems. **I-nun** verbs show assimilation of the nun.

The table below is a summary of Hophal verb forms:

| Root | Perfect | Impf. | Inf. Abs. | Inf. Cstr. | Part. |
|---|---|---|---|---|---|
| שׁמר | הָשְׁמַר | יָשְׁמַר | הָשְׁמֵר | הָשְׁמַר | מָשְׁמָר |
| ירד | הוּרַד | יוּרַד | הוּרֵד | הוּרַד | מוּרָד |
| סור | הוּסַר | יוּסַר | הוּסֵר | הוּסַר | מוּסָר |
| נגשׁ | הֻגַּשׁ | יֻגַּשׁ | הֻגֵּשׁ | הֻגַּשׁ | מֻגָּשׁ |
| גלה | הָגְלָה | יָגְלֶה | הָגְלֵה | הָגְלוֹת | מָגְלֶה |

## Qal Passive

In the history of the Hebrew language, Niphal took over the function of an earlier Qal passive. There are still some Qal passives pointed as Puals or Hophals. We know that they are Qal passives and not Puals or Hophals when the verbal root does not occur in the Piel or Hiphil, respectively, and the use has a simple Qal meaning rather than a Piel or Hiphil meaning.

BDB was written before scholars recognized the existence of the Qal passive, so BDB incorrectly lists these forms as Puals or Hophals.

Since they are pointed as Puals or Hophals, they have the same indicators. When such a verb does not occur in Piel or Hiphil and does not have a Piel or Hiphil meaning, it is a Qal Passive.

... כִּי מֵאִישׁ ...     ... because from a man

לֻקֳחָה־זֹּאת:     *was taken* this one. (Gen 2:23)

The dagesh drops out when a sheva appears under it. So the pointing of the above form is like the Pual, but the root does not appear in the Piel and there is no secondary subject. Therefore, this is a Qal passive.

## Vocabulary

| | |
|---|---|
| אָחוֹת | sister |
| אָמַן* | (Ni) be firm, reliable, trustworthy; (Hi) trust, believe |
| בָּטַח | trust |
| בָּכָה | weep |
| יָדָה* | (Pi) throw, cast; (Hi, Hitp) thank, praise, confess |
| יָטַב | be good |
| יָשָׁר | straight, right, upright (adj) |
| כָּבֵד | be heavy, honored |
| לָבַשׁ | put on, clothe |
| נֶגֶב | south, Negev; the dry country |
| נָחַם* | (Ni) be sorry, repent; (Pi) comfort, console |
| פֶּן- | lest (conj) |
| קָבַץ | assemble |

קָבַר      bury

קָהָל      assembly, congregation

שָׁאַר      remain; (Ni, Hi) be left over

שָׁכֵן      tent, dwell, settle (verb)

שָׁלַךְ*      (Hi) throw, cast

## Exercises

1. Read and translate Genesis 3:14–24. Chart the verbs.

2. If you would like additional practice identifying passive stems, translate the following and chart the verbs.

(Num 36:2) וַיֹּאמְרוּ אֶת־אֲדֹנִי צִוָּה יְהוָה לָתֵת אֶת־הָאָרֶץ בְּנַחֲלָה
בְּגוֹרָל לִבְנֵי יִשְׂרָאֵל ᵃוַאדֹנִי צֻוָּה בַיהוָהᵃ לָתֵת אֶת־נַחֲלַת צְלָפְחָד
אָחִינוּ לִבְנֹתָיו:
(ᵃ⁻ᵃ prp וְאֹתָנוּ צִוָּה יְ vel וַיְצַו בְּשֵׁם יְ)

(Lev 6:23 ET 30) וְכָל־חַטָּאת אֲשֶׁר יוּבָאᵃ מִדָּמָהּ אֶל־אֹהֶל
מוֹעֵד לְכַפֵּר בַּקֹּדֶשׁ לֹא תֵאָכֵל בָּאֵשׁ תִּשָּׂרֵף:
(ᵃ יָבוֹא ש)

(Gen 45:19) וְאַתָּה צֻוֵּיתָהᵃ זֹאת עֲשׂוּ קְחוּ־לָכֶם מֵאֶרֶץ
מִצְרַיִם עֲגָלוֹת לְטַפְּכֶם וְלִנְשֵׁיכֶם וּנְשָׂאתֶם אֶת־אֲבִיכֶם וּבָאתֶם:
(ᵃ צַוֵּה אֹתָם l? cf 𝔊𝔖)

(Judg 6:28) וַיַּשְׁכִּימוּ אַנְשֵׁי הָעִיר בַּבֹּקֶר וְהִנֵּה נֻתַּץ מִזְבַּח הַבַּעַל
וְהָאֲשֵׁרָה אֲשֶׁר־עָלָיו כֹּרָתָה וְאֵת הַפָּר הַשֵּׁנִיᵃ הֹעֲלָה עַל־הַמִּזְבֵּחַ
הַבָּנוּי:
(ᵃ הַשֵּׁנִי l cf 𝔊* et 25ᵃ⁻ᵃ)

# Chapter 34
## Geminate Verbs

The name geminate is related to the word *Gemini,* or "twins." Geminate verbs have the same last two root letters, as in סבב "go around." When you are reading Hebrew, the **indicator** of a geminate root is the same last two root letters (סָבְבוּ), often represented by a strong dagesh (תַּמּוּ from the root תמם).

### Qal Stem

In the **perfect,** a second **indicator** of a geminate verb is a holem vav before suffixes beginning with a consonant (סַבּוֹתָ). Only the third masculine singular of one type of geminate verb (תַּם) lacks the two indicators above. This form is similar to the Qal perfect 3 ms of a hollow verb (שָׁב), but has a pataḥ rather than a qamets. The table below illustrates the two types of geminate verbs in the Qal perfect.

| PGN | Type I (Example: סבב) | | Type II (Example: תמם) | |
|---|---|---|---|---|
| 3ms | סָבַב | he went around | תַּם | he was complete |
| 3fs | סָבְבָה | she went around | תַּמָּה | she was complete |
| 2ms | סַבּוֹתָ | you went around | תַּמּוֹתָ | you were complete |
| 2fs | סַבּוֹת | you went around | תַּמּוֹת | you were complete |
| 1cs | סַבּוֹתִי | I went around | תַּמּוֹתִי | I was complete |
| 3cp | סָבְבוּ | they went around | תַּמּוּ | they were complete |
| 2mp | סַבּוֹתֶם | you went around | תַּמּוֹתֶם | you were complete |
| 2fp | סַבּוֹתֶן | you went around | תַּמּוֹתֶן | you were complete |
| 1cp | סַבּוֹנוּ | we went around | תַּמּוֹנוּ | we were complete |

Type II, seen in the example, usually has a stative meaning.

When the second and third root consonants are gutturals or resh, which do not accept doubling, the preceding vowel is lengthened, as in רֹעוּ "they are broken" (Jer 11:16) from רעע.

In the Qal **imperfect**, Type I geminate verbs have the appearance and indicators of hollow or I-nun roots. Type II geminate verbs look like I-vav verbs in the imperfect. As you can see from the table below, some forms have the strong dagesh indicating a geminate root, but many have only the indicators of hollow, I-nun, or I-vav roots respectively.

| | Type I | | Type II |
|---|---|---|---|
| PGN | Like hollow | Like I-nun | Like I-vav |
| 3ms | יָסֹב | יִסֹּב | יֵתַם |
| 3fs | תָּסֹב | תִּסֹּב | תֵּתַם |
| 2ms | תָּסֹב | תִּסֹּב | תֵּתַם |
| 2fs | תָּסֹבִּי | תִּסֹּבִי | תֵּתַּמִּי |
| 1cs | אָסֹב | אֶסֹּב | אֵתַם |
| 3mp | יָסֹבּוּ | יִסֹּבוּ | יֵתַּמּוּ |
| 3fp | תְּסֻבֶּינָה | תִּסֹּבְנָה | תֵּתַּמֶּינָה |
| 2mp | תָּסֹבּוּ | תִּסֹּבוּ | תֵּתַּמּוּ |
| 2fp | תְּסֻבֶּינָה | תִּסֹּבְנָה | תֵּתַּמֶּינָה |
| 1cp | נָסֹב | נִסֹּב | נֵתַם |

The Qal **imperatives** remove the prefix of the imperfect. They are, therefore, either סֹב סֹבִי סֹבּוּ סֹבֶנָה or תַּם תַּמִּי תַּמּוּ תַּמְנָה.

The Qal **infinitive absolute** is סָבוֹב. The **infinitive construct** is סֹב and with suffixes סָבִּי.

The Qal **active participle** is סֹבֵב or תַּם.
The Qal **passive participle** is regular: סָבוּב.

## Hiphil and Niphal

Geminate verbs in the Hiphil and Niphal stems continue the mixture of indicators unique to geminates and shared with missing-letter verb roots. The table below summarizes the features of geminates in these stems.

| Conjugation | Niphal | Hiphil |
|---|---|---|
| Perfect | | |
| 3ms | נָסַב | הֵסַב |
| 2ms | נְסַבּוֹתָ | הֲסִבּוֹתָ |
| Imperfect | | |
| 3ms | יִסַּב | יָסֵב |
| 2fs | תִּסַּבִּי | תָּסֵבִּי |
| Imperative | | |
| 2ms | הִסַּב | הָסֵב |
| 2fs | הִסַּבִּי | הָסֵבִּי |
| Participle | | |
| ms | נָסָב | מֵסֵב |
| fs | נְסַבָּה | מְסִבָּה |
| Infinitive | | |
| Construct | הִסּוֹב | הָסֵב |
| Absolute | הִסֵּב | הָסֵב |

Not only do geminate verbs have the form and indicators of other missing-letter verb roots, but for some roots the lexicons list hollow or III-heʾ roots with the same range of meaning. Examples are פּוּר פרר "break out" and רבה רבב "be numerous."

The best advice for the beginner is to remember the **indicators** of the geminate: the ִ and the dagesh in the second letter. Some forms are missing these indicators. When the indicators suggest a III-he, a II-vav/yod, I-nun, or I-vav verb, but you cannot find the root, or the meaning does not make sense in the context, it may be a geminate.

## Other Stems

Geminate verbs appear in the Piel, Pual, and Hitpael stems, but sometimes in the **Pilpel**, **Polpal**, and **Hitpolel** with similar meanings. The repetition of the two letters makes these stems easy to identify.

| Root[1] | Pilpel | Polpal | Hitpalel |
|---------|--------|--------|----------|
| קָלַל | קִלְקֵל | קָלְקַל | הִתְקַלְקֵל |

Some **II-vav/yod** verbs also take these stems. Note that these will be listed in BDB as II-vav/yod verbs, but will show repetition of the first and third root letters in these stems.

The **hollow** verbs occur most often in the Piel, Pual, and Hitpael stems, but also frequently with the same meanings in the **Polel**, **Polal**, and **Hitpolel** stems respectively.

| Root[2] | Polel | Polal | Hitpolel |
|---------|-------|-------|----------|
| קוּם | קוֹמֵם | קוֹמַם | הִתְקוֹמֵם |

## Vocabulary

| | |
|---|---|
| חָלַל* | (Ni) be defiled; (Pi) pollute, profane; (Hi) begin |
| יָתַר* | (Ni, Hi) be left, remain |
| לִקְרַאת | over against, opposite (inf. cstr. used as a prep.) |
| לָשׁוֹן | tongue |
| מִגְרָשׁ | pasture; produce |
| מַמְלָכָה | kingdom |

---

[1] These stems seldom occur, so no verb root actually appears in all three stems.

[2] These stems seldom occur, so no verb root actually appears in all three stems.

| | |
|---|---|
| נָבָא* | (Ni, Hitp) prophesy |
| נָהָר | river |
| עַמּוּד | pillar, column |
| פְּרִי | fruit |
| צֶדֶק | righteousness, what is just |
| קָדוֹשׁ | holy |
| קָטַר* | (Pi) send (an offering) up in smoke; (Hi) make smoke |
| רֶכֶב | chariot |
| שָׂרַף | burn |
| שָׁלֵם | be whole, complete; (Pi) repay; (Hi) make peace with |
| שֹׁמְרוֹן | Samaria |

## Exercises

1. Read aloud and translate Lamentations 1:18–22. Chart the verbs. Most translations understand the first verb in verse 18 as being from the root מרה. Could it be from the root מרר? How would this change what Jerusalem is saying?

## Verse 19

| | |
|---|---|
| לָמוֹ | This is a rare pronoun suffix attached to the preposition לְ. See page 43. For other explanations, see BDB page 555 under מוֹ and page 510 under לְ. |

2. If you would like additional practice identifying geminate stems, translate the following and chart the verbs.

(Ezra 3:6) מִיּוֹם אֶחָד לַחֹדֶשׁ הַשְּׁבִיעִי הֵחֵלּוּ לְהַעֲלוֹת עֹלוֹת לַיהוָה וְהֵיכַל יְהוָה לֹא יֻסָּד:

(Hos 7:2) וּבַל־יֹאמְרוּ לִלְבָבָם כָּל־רָעָתָם זָכָרְתִּי עַתָּה סְבָבוּם מַעַלְלֵיהֶם נֶגֶד פָּנַי הָיוּ:
(ᵃ prp כִּי־)

(1 Kings 1:2) וַיֹּאמְרוּ לוֹ עֲבָדָיו יְבַקְשׁוּ לַאדֹנִי הַמֶּלֶךְ נַעֲרָה בְתוּלָה וְעָמְדָה לִפְנֵי הַמֶּלֶךְ וּתְהִי־לוֹ סֹכֶנֶת וְשָׁכְבָה בְחֵיקֶךְ וְחַם לַאדֹנִי הַמֶּלֶךְ:

(Joel 2:26) יְהוָה אֱלֹהֵיכֶם אֲשֶׁר־עָשָׂה עִמָּכֶם לְהַפְלִיא וְלֹא־יֵבֹשׁוּ עַמִּי לְעוֹלָם:

# Chapter 35

## Oaths

An introductory textbook only explains the most common rules of grammar and syntax. When reading the Hebrew Bible you will encounter exceptions and variations to these rules. Therefore, it is important to know how to consult more lengthy and detailed reference grammars.

### Reference Grammars

The standard reference grammars in English are *Gesenius' Hebrew Grammar*, edited by Kautzsch and translated by Cowley, and Joüon's *Grammar of Biblical Hebrew*, translated and revised by Muraoka. They are commonly referred to by the abbreviations GKC and Joüon. Although called *An Introduction to Biblical Hebrew Syntax*, Waltke and O'Connor's book is actually an intermediate textbook that can be used as a reference grammar. It has many useful examples and references to current research and is typically abbreviated as *IBHS*.

The easiest way to consult reference grammars is to use the index of biblical passages or the index of Hebrew words and forms. For example, if you are studying a passage, you can look it up in the index of biblical passages. If the passage you are studying has unusual or difficult forms or constructions, you may find a discussion of it in a reference grammar.

Suppose you had difficulty translating the infinitive construct in the last exercise of the previous chapter (Joel 2:26). In the "Index of Passages" in GKC, beside Joel 2:26 is §114 o. Typically, reference grammars refer you to the section ( § ). This leads you to the section of the page where there is a reference to Joel 2:26 and can help you understand the relationship of the comment to the broader discussion. If you turn to §114 o, you will notice by the heading on the page or by turning back several pages to the title that section 114 is about uses of the infinitive construct. Subsection o discusses the infinitive construct with lamed as "frequently used in a much looser connexion [sic] . . . to define more exactly." In the case of Joel 2:26, the infinitive construct with lamed (לְהַפְלִיא "wondrously") defines more closely how God "has dealt." Thus this reference grammar explains that the infinitive construct with lamed used in this way is fairly common in Biblical Hebrew and discusses its meaning.

## Curses

You might have to look up curses and oaths in a reference grammar because they are difficult to understand and sometimes not discussed in introductory textbooks. They seem counter intuitive because אִם can be translated "surely not" and אִם־לֹא "surely." Most difficult to translate are certain oaths that only make sense in English if translated this way. We begin with curses because they can be translated literally with "if" for אִם and "if not" for אִם־לֹא although we can also understand how they could be translated אִם "surely not" and אִם־לֹא "surely."

Examine, for example, the following common curses:

| | |
|---|---|
| כֹּה־יַעֲשֶׂה־לִּי אֱלֹהִים | Thus may God do to me |
| וְכֹה יוֹסִף | and add more |
| אִם־יַעֲמֹד רֹאשׁ | if stands the head of Elisha son of |
| אֱלִישָׁע בֶּן־שָׁפָט | Shaphat (= *it will surely not*) |
| עָלָיו הַיּוֹם: | on him today. (2 Kgs 6:31) |
| | |
| כֹּה יַעֲשֶׂה־לִּי אֱלֹהִים | Thus may God do to me |
| וְכֹה יוֹסִיף | and add more |
| אִם־לֹא | if you do not (= *surely you will*) |
| שַׂר־צָבָא תִּהְיֶה | become army commander |
| | (2 Sam 19:14) |

The typical curse, therefore, begins with:

כֹּה יַעֲשֶׂה־לִי אֱלֹהִים וְכֹה יוֹסִיף

and ends with a statement that begins with אִם or אִם־לֹא or occasionally by כִּי translated "surely."

Joüon thinks that "thus" indicates a self-curse that goes unexpressed but, as he suggests, may be indicated by a gesture, such as passing the hand across the throat (§165 a). Reuben's promise to bring Jacob's son Benjamin back from Egypt may provide an example of such a self-curse being expressed.

אֶת־שְׁנֵי בָנַי תָּמִית
אִם־לֹא אֲבִיאֶנּוּ אֵלֶיךָ

My two sons may you kill,
if I do not bring him to you.
(Gen 42:37)

In this kind of statement, if the first part, "my two sons may you kill," began to go unexpressed because it was so shocking, then in the second half אִם־לֹא would be translated in a way similar to many oaths: "Surely, I will bring him to you."

**Oaths**

Oaths typically begin with either the verb נִשְׁבַּע "swear," or with חַי (or חֵי) + name "by the life of ," or with both.

נִשְׁבַּע אֲדֹנָי יְהוִה

The Lord God swears . . .
(Amos 4:2)

חַי־יְהוָה

As the LORD lives . . .
(2 Sam 12:5)

These introductions are followed by statements beginning with כִּי or אִם־לֹא "surely," or אִם "surely not." These are easy enough to translate when they begin with כִּי "surely."

חַי־יְהֹוָה כִּי     As the LORD lives, surely
בֶּן־מָוֶת הָאִישׁ הָעֹשֶׂה זֹאת:     the man who did this is a dead
      man. (2 Sam 12:5)

They are more complicated when the statements begin with אִם־לֹא or כִּי אִם "surely" or אִם "surely not."

נִשְׁבַּע יְהוָה צְבָאוֹת לֵאמֹר     The LORD of Hosts has sworn:
אִם־לֹא כַּאֲשֶׁר דִּמִּיתִי     "Surely, as I designed,
כֵּן הָיָתָה     thus shall it be. (Isa 14:24)

חַי־יְהֹוָה     As the LORD lives,
כִּי אִם־יְהוָה יִגְּפֶנּוּ     surely the LORD will strike him.

חֵי פַרְעֹה     As Pharoah lives,
אִם־תֵּצְאוּ מִזֶּה     you shall surely not leave here.
      (Gen 42:15)

וַיִּשָּׁבַע שָׁאוּל     Saul swore,
חַי־יְהֹוָה     "As the LORD lives,
אִם־יוּמָת:     he shall surely not be put to
      death." (1 Sam 19:6)

According to GKC, the common explanation for the use of אִם and אִם־לֹא in oaths is that oaths suppress a self-curse (§149 b). For example, we would understand 1 Samuel 19:6 above as, "As the LORD lives, [may something terrible happen to me] if he is put to death," which is equivalent to "he shall surely not be put to death." GKC admits a self-curse is difficult to understand when put in the mouth of God, but suggests the origin of the construction may have been forgotten (§149 b). Joüon thinks they are better explained as the result of contamination from curses and vice-versa

(§165 g–h). However, *IBHS* thinks the reasons behind these constructions may be lost to us (§ 40.2.2 a).

In this manner, reference grammars may help you identify and understand unusual forms and constructions.

## Vocabulary

| | |
|---|---|
| בִּלְתִּי | non-existence (noun); not (adv); except (prep) |
| בָּמָה | high place |
| בַּעַד | away from, behind, through, for (the benefit of) (prep) |
| גָּאַל | redeem |
| גִּלְעָד | Gilead (גִּלְעָדִי "Gileadites") |
| חֻקָּה | statute, prescription |
| יָרָבְעָם | Jeroboam |
| שָׁפַּךְ | pour out |
| שֶׁקֶר | lie, deception, falsehood |
| תּוֹעֵבָה | abomination |
| תָּמִיד | continuance (noun); continually, regularly (adv) |

## Exercise

Read aloud and translate Ruth 1:6–18. Chart the verbs.

# Chapter 36

## Overview of Interpretation

This chapter integrates the exegetical methods introduced throughout this book into a method of interpretation. For one of my professors, who was opposed to such outlines of the steps in exegesis, exegesis was not a plodding, systematic method but rather a creative dance. Moreover, different texts required different methods. A one-size-fits-all method could not accommodate the diversity of literature in the Bible. In a postmodern context, I am aware that methods are problematic because of the power dynamics they assume and conceal.

In my experience, however, such a list of exegetical questions and methods that can typically be applied to a passage is much appreciated by students. Not all of the following questions and methods will apply equally to every text or appeal equally to every reader. Furthermore, an interpreter seldom proceeds through the list in a straight line. Rather, questions and insights arise in reading that will cause him or her to revisit a question or method.

Although the following list is not exhaustive, it may seem overwhelming to a beginner. Further questions can be asked and methods applied to find meaning in texts. In the beginning, following all the suggestions may seem too time-consuming and difficult but, with practice, they become easier. As a reader you may discover you favor certain methods and begin to recognize which of them will be most productive for a particular text. Biblical scholars, for example, have found genre criticism particularly useful for the book of Psalms.

Interpretation in biblical studies is in the midst of a paradigm shift. In Chapter 4, I defined exegesis as the methods of historical and literary analysis of a passage that "lead out" meaning. Some readers may have noticed that I did not use the definite article.

Traditionally, exegesis has been defined as determining *the* meaning of a passage. This was based on a modern, nineteenth-century, liberal theory of interpretation that defined the meaning of a text as the meaning intended by the author. Identifying the author and understanding the historical context was essential to understanding the intended meaning. There might be disagreement over the author's intention and differences about how to apply the meaning, but it was assumed that the meaning of a work was the one intended by the author and agreed that the appropriate methods were historical-critical. Over time, this historical-critical method came to dominate in academic, biblical studies.

In literary criticism, however, the focus of interpretation shifted in the twentieth-century from the author to the text and finally to the reader. A growing number of biblical scholars are using newer literary methods oriented toward the text and the reader. From another perspective, an increasing number of liberation, feminist, and post-colonial interpreters in biblical studies also shift the focus toward the experience of the reader as an essential element of interpretation. Some of the exegetical methods presented in this book were historical-critical—source, redaction, genre, and tradition criticism. Other methods were text-oriented—narrative, poetry, and rhetorical criticism. This chapter integrates author- and text-oriented methods with a focus on the reader, influenced by feminist and post-colonial interpretation.

## Locating the Readers

What interpretations of this passage have you heard? What are your immediate reactions?

How do your experience, gender, culture, religion, class, and geographical location influence the way you read this passage? How might people from different cultures, social locations, and experiences, read this passage?

What causes systematic oppression in your context? (Sexism? Racism? Capitalism? Colonialism? Ageism? . . . )

As your study progresses, look for ways these relate to the passage you are studying.

## Text

Set the limits of the passage you will study. This involves thinking about what verse(s) can be considered a self-contained unit and why.

Read the textual apparatus of *BHS*. Are there variant readings that affect the meaning? Using the principles of text criticism establish the best text(s). Write down your reasons for choosing a particular reading.

See what the grammar and word order communicate. Note the usage of stems and their meaning. Do word studies of key words using BDB, concordances, *TDOT*, and *TDNT*.

Make your own translations of the passage: one literal and one dynamic. Read a variety of translations as you look for differences in meaning that may come from different readings or translations of the Hebrew.

## Literary Analysis

Make copies of your passage. Mark up the copies, making charts or outlines in order to note narrative features such as repetition, chiasmus, key words, emphasis, climax, and mood.

Think about the events, plot, characters, and settings.

What is the genre? Compare your passage to other passages of the same genre in the Hebrew Bible and Ancient Near East.

Study the place of your passage in the chapter and book.

How do the passage and larger literary setting illumine each other? Consider the context of the canon, place of the passage in the canon, and relation to the other parts of the canon.

## Historical, Social, and Cultural Analysis

Who wrote the passage? Is there evidence of different sources or redaction?

What is the historical situation?

What is the setting in life of the genre?

What is the history of the tradition(s)?

Do any cultural practices in the passage require further research?

What are the social positions of the characters in the passage, of the author, and of the audience?

What would the ideological functions of the passage have been in its historical context and in the history of interpretation?

What is the history of the interpretation of the passage?

## Engagement

How does your experience contribute to your interpretation? How might someone with a different experience and social location interpret the passage?

Can you read yourself into the story? With whom do you identify? How would it change the meaning to identify with a different character?

What is the theology of the passage? What are the images of God in the passage? What does God say or do?

Which historical, cultural, or social realities in the passage can you put into conversation with contemporary society?

## Evaluation

The many features of a passage lend themselves to various interpretations. But some interpretations are better than others. Some are liberating, whereas others, often unintentionally, oppress or harm the world. Better interpretations account for more features of the text, have richer possibilities of meaning for many people, and are open to reflection and action.

## Exercise

In the English-speaking world Psalm 23 has become a cultural icon, even for those with little or no faith. In fact, this was not always the case. Until modern times it was not so widely known and used. Why has it become so popular? What was its original meaning? Read Psalm 23 in Hebrew and use the questions in this chapter to help find the answers.

After answering as many questions as you can on your own, consult the standard critical commentaries. Particularly useful for the history of interpretation is William Holladay's "The Lord is My Shepherd: Then and Now," and "How the Twenty-third Psalm

Became an American Secular Icon."[1] For Latin American, Asian, and African perspectives on Psalm 23 see the chapters by Croatto, Kinoti, and Moon in *Return to Babel: Global Perspectives on the Bible.*[2]

---

[1] *The Psalms through Three Thousand Years* (Minneapolis: Fortress, 1989), 6–14, 359–371.

[2] Priscilla Pope-Levison and John R. Levison, eds. (Louisville: Westminster/John Knox, 1999), 57–72.

# Appendix A

## Verb Chart Worksheets

| Root | Stem | Conjugation | PGN | Special Features |
|------|------|-------------|-----|------------------|
|      |      |             |     |                  |

| Root | Stem | Conjugation | PGN | Special Features |
|------|------|-------------|-----|------------------|
|      |      |             |     |                  |

| Root | Stem | Conjugation | PGN | Special Features |
|------|------|-------------|-----|------------------|
|      |      |             |     |                  |

| Root | Stem | Conjugation | PGN | Special Features |
|------|------|-------------|-----|------------------|
|      |      |             |     |                  |

| Root | Stem | Conjugation | PGN | Special Features |
|------|------|-------------|-----|------------------|
|      |      |             |     |                  |

| Root | Stem | Conjugation | PGN | Special Features |
|------|------|-------------|-----|------------------|
|      |      |             |     |                  |

| Root | Stem | Conjugation | PGN | Special Features |
|------|------|-------------|-----|------------------|
|      |      |             |     |                  |

| Root | Stem | Conjugation | PGN | Special Features |
|------|------|-------------|-----|------------------|
|      |      |             |     |                  |

| Root | Stem | Conjugation | PGN | Special Features |
|------|------|-------------|-----|------------------|
|      |      |             |     |                  |

| Root | Stem | Conjugation | PGN | Special Features |
|------|------|-------------|-----|------------------|
|      |      |             |     |                  |

| Root | Stem | Conjugation | PGN | Special Features |
|------|------|-------------|-----|------------------|
|      |      |             |     |                  |

| Root | Stem | Conjugation | PGN | Special Features |
|------|------|-------------|-----|------------------|
|      |      |             |     |                  |

| Root | Stem | Conjugation | PGN | Special Features |
|------|------|-------------|-----|------------------|
|      |      |             |     |                  |

| Root | Stem | Conjugation | PGN | Special Features |
|------|------|-------------|-----|------------------|
|      |      |             |     |                  |

| Root | Stem | Conjugation | PGN | Special Features |
|------|------|-------------|-----|------------------|
|      |      |             |     |                  |

| Root | Stem | Conjugation | PGN | Special Features |
|------|------|-------------|-----|------------------|
|      |      |             |     |                  |

| Root | Stem | Conjugation | PGN | Special Features |
|------|------|-------------|-----|------------------|
|      |      |             |     |                  |

| Root | Stem | Conjugation | PGN | Special Features |
|------|------|-------------|-----|------------------|
|      |      |             |     |                  |

# Appendix B
## Stem and Conjugation Indicators

| Stem | Perf. | Impf. | Impv. | Ptc. | Inf. Abs. | Inf. Cstr. |
|------|-------|-------|-------|------|-----------|------------|
| Qal | שָׁמַר | יִשְׁמֹר | שְׁמֹר | שֹׁמֵר | שָׁמוֹר | שְׁמֹר |
| Ni. | נִשְׁמַר | יִשָּׁמֵר | הִשָּׁמֵר | נִשְׁמָר | נִשְׁמוֹר / הִשָּׁמֹר | הִשָּׁמֵר |
| Pi. | שִׁמֵּר | יְשַׁמֵּר | שַׁמֵּר | מְשַׁמֵּר | | שַׁמֵּר |
| Pu. | שֻׁמַּר | יְשֻׁמַּר | | מְשֻׁמָּר | | |
| Hit. | הִתְשַׁמֵּר | יִתְשַׁמֵּר | הִתְשַׁמֵּר | מִתְשַׁמֵּר | הִתְשַׁמֵּר | הִתְשַׁמֵּר |
| Hi. | הִשְׁמִיר | יַשְׁמִיר | הַשְׁמֵר | מַשְׁמִיר | | הַשְׁמִיר / הַשְׁמֵר |
| Ho. | הָשְׁמַר | יָשְׁמַר | | מָשְׁמָר | הָשְׁמֵר | |

# Appendix C
## Verb Charts

With the exception of the first one, the design of each verb chart corresponds to the internal organization of the chapters in this book. The first verb chart shows the forms of the stems on a strong verb. The other verb charts display strong and weak verbs in columns under a stem and its conjugations, just as the chapters present the strong and weak verbs together under a stem and conjugation. The reader can thereby track, on one chart, the indicators of a stem, conjugation, and weak roots presented in the corresponding chapter.

The charts use roots that appear in the Hebrew Bible in those particular stems and conjugations, though not all the forms in each column are attested.

| Strong Verb | | Qal (שָׁמַר) | Niphal (שמר) | Piel (שמר) | Pual (שמר) |
|---|---|---|---|---|---|
| Perf. | 3ms | שָׁמַר | נִשְׁמַר | שִׁמֵּר | שֻׁמַּר |
| | 3fs | שָׁמְרָה | נִשְׁמְרָה | שִׁמְּרָה | שֻׁמְּרָה |
| | 2ms | שָׁמַ֫רְתָּ | נִשְׁמַ֫רְתָּ | שִׁמַּ֫רְתָּ | שֻׁמַּ֫רְתָּ |
| | 2fs | שָׁמַרְתְּ | נִשְׁמַרְתְּ | שִׁמַּרְתְּ | שֻׁמַּרְתְּ |
| | 1cs | שָׁמַ֫רְתִּי | נִשְׁמַ֫רְתִּי | שִׁמַּ֫רְתִּי | שֻׁמַּ֫רְתִּי |
| | 3cp | שָׁמְרוּ | נִשְׁמְרוּ | שִׁמְּרוּ | שֻׁמְּרוּ |
| | 2mp | שְׁמַרְתֶּם | נִשְׁמַרְתֶּם | שִׁמַּרְתֶּם | שֻׁמַּרְתֶּם |
| | 2fp | שְׁמַרְתֶּן | נִשְׁמַרְתֶּן | שִׁמַּרְתֶּן | שֻׁמַּרְתֶּן |
| | 1cp | שָׁמַ֫רְנוּ | נִשְׁמַ֫רְנוּ | שִׁמַּ֫רְנוּ | שֻׁמַּ֫רְנוּ |
| Impf. | 3ms | יִשְׁמֹר | יִשָּׁמֵר | יְשַׁמֵּר | יְשֻׁמַּר |
| | 3fs | תִּשְׁמֹר | תִּשָּׁמֵר | תְּשַׁמֵּר | תְּשֻׁמַּר |
| | 2ms | תִּשְׁמֹר | תִּשָּׁמֵר | תְּשַׁמֵּר | תְּשֻׁמַּר |
| | 2fs | תִּשְׁמְרִי | תִּשָּׁמְרִי | תְּשַׁמְּרִי | תְּשֻׁמְּרִי |
| | 1cs | אֶשְׁמֹר | אֶשָּׁמֵר | אֲשַׁמֵּר | אֲשֻׁמַּר |
| | 3mp | יִשְׁמְרוּ | יִשָּׁמְרוּ | יְשַׁמְּרוּ | יְשֻׁמְּרוּ |
| | 3fp | תִּשְׁמֹ֫רְנָה | תִּשָּׁמַ֫רְנָה | תְּשַׁמֵּ֫רְנָה | תְּשֻׁמַּ֫רְנָה |
| | 2mp | תִּשְׁמְרוּ | תִּשָּׁמְרוּ | תְּשַׁמְּרוּ | תְּשֻׁמְּרוּ |
| | 2fp | תִּשְׁמֹ֫רְנָה | תִּשָּׁמַ֫רְנָה | תְּשַׁמֵּ֫רְנָה | תְּשֻׁמַּ֫רְנָה |
| | 1cp | נִשְׁמֹר | נִשָּׁמֵר | נְשַׁמֵּר | נְשֻׁמַּר |
| Impv. | 2ms | שְׁמֹר | הִשָּׁמֵר | שַׁמֵּר | not |
| | 2fs | שִׁמְרִי | הִשָּׁמְרִי | שַׁמְּרִי | attested |
| | 2mp | שִׁמְרוּ | הִשָּׁמְרוּ | שַׁמְּרוּ | |
| | 2fp | שְׁמֹ֫רְנָה | הִשָּׁמַ֫רְנָה | שַׁמֵּ֫רְנָה | |
| Inf. | Abs. | שָׁמוֹר | נִשְׁמֹר / הִשָּׁמֹר | שַׁמֵּר / שַׁמֹּר | שֻׁמֹּר |
| | Cstr. | שְׁמֹר | הִשָּׁמֵר | שַׁמֵּר | |
| Part. | Act. | שֹׁמֵר | | מְשַׁמֵּר | |
| | Pass. | שָׁמוּר | נִשְׁמָר | | מְשֻׁמָּר |
| Vav consec. | | וַיִּשְׁמֹר | וַיִּשָּׁמֵר | וַיְשַׁמֵּר | וַיְשֻׁמַּר |

|  |  | Hitpael (קדשׁ) | Hiphil (קרב) | Hophal (פקד) |
|---|---|---|---|---|
| Perf. | 3ms | הִתְקַדֵּשׁ | הִקְרִיב | הָפְקַד |
|  | 3fs | הִתְקַדְּשָׁה | הִקְרִיבָה | הָפְקְדָה |
|  | 2ms | הִתְקַדַּשְׁתָּ | הִקְרַבְתָּ | הָפְקַדְתָּ |
|  | 2fs | הִתְקַדַּשְׁתְּ | הִקְרַבְתְּ | הָפְקַדְתְּ |
|  | 1cs | הִתְקַדַּשְׁתִּי | הִקְרַבְתִּי | הָפְקַדְתִּי |
|  | 3cp | הִתְקַדְּשׁוּ | הִקְרִיבוּ | הָפְקְדוּ |
|  | 2mp | הִתְקַדַּשְׁתֶּם | הִקְרַבְתֶּם | הָפְקַדְתֶּם |
|  | 2fp | הִתְקַדַּשְׁתֶּן | הִקְרַבְתֶּן | הָפְקַדְתֶּן |
|  | 1cp | הִתְקַדַּשְׁנוּ | הִקְרַבְנוּ | הָפְקַדְנוּ |
| Impf. | 3ms | יִתְקַדֵּשׁ | יַקְרִיב | יָפְקַד |
|  | 3fs | תִּתְקַדֵּשׁ | תַּקְרִיב | תָּפְקַד |
|  | 2ms | תִּתְקַדֵּשׁ | תַּקְרִיב | תָּפְקַד |
|  | 2fs | תִּתְקַדְּשִׁי | תַּקְרִיבִי | תָּפְקְדִי |
|  | 1cs | אֶתְקַדֵּשׁ | אַקְרִיב | אָפְקַד |
|  | 3mp | יִתְקַדְּשׁוּ | יַקְרִיבוּ | יָפְקְדוּ |
|  | 3fp | תִּתְקַדֵּשְׁנָה | תַּקְרֵבְנָה | תָּפְקַדְנָה |
|  | 2mp | תִּתְקַדְּשׁוּ | תַּקְרִיבוּ | תָּפְקְדוּ |
|  | 2fp | תִּתְקַדֵּשְׁנָה | תַּקְרֵבְנָה | תָּפְקַדְנָה |
|  | 1cp | נִתְקַדֵּשׁ | נַקְרִיב | נָפְקַד |
| Impv. | 2ms | הִתְקַדֵּשׁ | הַקְרֵב |  |
|  | 2fs | הִתְקַדְּשִׁי | הַקְרִיבִי |  |
|  | 2mp | הִתְקַדְּשׁוּ | הַקְרִיבוּ |  |
|  | 2fp | הִתְקַדֵּשְׁנָה | הַקְרֵבְנָה |  |
| Inf. | Abs. | הִתְקַדֵּשׁ | הַקְרֵב | הָפְקֵד |
|  | Cstr. | הִתְקַדֵּשׁ | הַקְרִיב | הָפְקַד |
| Part. | Act. | מִתְקַדֵּשׁ | מַקְרִיב |  |
|  | Pass. |  |  | מָפְקָד |
| Vav consec. |  | וַיִּתְקַדֵּשׁ | וַיַּקְרֵב | וַיָּפְקַד |

| Qal | | Strong (שָׁמַר) | III-heʾ (נלה) | III-gutt. (שלח) | III-ʾaleph (מצא) | II-vav (קום) |
|---|---|---|---|---|---|---|
| Perf. | 3ms | שָׁמַר | גָּלָה | שָׁלַח | מָצָא | קָם |
| | 3fs | שָׁמְרָה | גָּלְתָה | שָׁלְחָה | מָצְאָה | קָמָה |
| | 2ms | שָׁמַׁרְתָּ | גָּלִׁיתָ | שָׁלַחְתָּ | מָצָאתָ | קַׁמְתָּ |
| | 2fs | שָׁמַרְתְּ | גָּלִית | שָׁלַחַתְּ | מָצָאת | קַמְתְּ |
| | 1cs | שָׁמַׁרְתִּי | גָּלִיתִי | שָׁלַחְתִּי | מָצָאתִי | קַׁמְתִּי |
| | 3cp | שָׁמְרוּ | גָּלוּ | שָׁלְחוּ | מָצְאוּ | קָמוּ |
| | 2mp | שְׁמַרְתֶּם | גְּלִיתֶם | שְׁלַחְתֶּם | מְצָאתֶם | קַמְתֶּם |
| | 2fp | שְׁמַרְתֶּן | גְּלִיתֶן | שְׁלַחְתֶּן | מְצָאתֶן | קַמְתֶּן |
| | 1cp | שָׁמַׁרְנוּ | גָּלִינוּ | שָׁלַחְנוּ | מָצָאנוּ | קַׁמְנוּ |
| Impf. | 3ms | יִשְׁמֹר | יִגְלֶה | יִשְׁלַח | יִמְצָא | יָקוּם |
| | 3fs | תִּשְׁמֹר | תִּגְלֶה | תִּשְׁלַח | תִּמְצָא | תָּקוּם |
| | 2ms | תִּשְׁמֹר | תִּגְלֶה | תִּשְׁלַח | תִּמְצָא | תָּקוּם |
| | 2fs | תִּשְׁמְרִי | תִּגְלִי | תִּשְׁלְחִי | תִּמְצְאִי | תָּקוּמִי |
| | 1cs | אֶשְׁמֹר | אֶגְלֶה | אֶשְׁלַח | אֶמְצָא | אָקוּם |
| | 3mp | יִשְׁמְרוּ | יִגְלוּ | יִשְׁלְחוּ | יִמְצְאוּ | יָקוּמוּ |
| | 3fp | תִּשְׁמֹרְנָה | תִּגְלֶׁינָה | תִּשְׁלַׁחְנָה | תִּמְצֶׁאנָה | תְּקוּמֶׁינָה |
| | 2mp | תִּשְׁמְרוּ | תִּגְלוּ | תִּשְׁלְחוּ | תִּמְצְאוּ | תָּקוּמוּ |
| | 2fp | תִּשְׁמֹרְנָה | תִּגְלֶׁינָה | תִּשְׁלַׁחְנָה | תִּמְצֶׁאנָה | תְּקוּמֶׁינָה |
| | 1cp | נִשְׁמֹר | נִגְלֶה | נִשְׁלַח | נִמְצָא | נָקוּם |
| Impv. | 2ms | שְׁמֹר | גְּלֵה | שְׁלַח | מְצָא | קוּם |
| | 2fs | שִׁמְרִי | גְּלִי | שִׁלְחִי | מִצְאִי | קוּמִי |
| | 2mp | שִׁמְרוּ | גְּלוּ | שִׁלְחוּ | מִצְאוּ | קוּמוּ |
| | 2fp | שְׁמֹרְנָה | גְּלֶׁינָה | שְׁלַׁחְנָה | מְצֶׁאנָה | קֹמְנָה |
| Inf. | Abs. | שָׁמוֹר | גָּלֹה | שָׁלוֹחַ | מָצוֹא | קוֹם |
| | Cstr. | שְׁמֹר | גְּלוֹת | שְׁלֹחַ | מְצֹא | קוּם |
| Part. | Act. | שֹׁמֵר | גֹּלֶה | שֹׁלֵחַ | מֹצֵא | קָם |
| | Pass. | שָׁמוּר | גָּלוּי | שָׁלוּחַ | מָצוּא | קוּם |
| Vav consec. | | וַיִּשְׁמֹר | וַיִּגֶל | וַיִּשְׁלַח | וַיִּמְצָא | וַיָּקָם |

| II-gutt. (גאל) | I-nun | | (נתן) | I-vav (ישב) | I-yod (יטב) | I-gutt. (עמד) |
|---|---|---|---|---|---|---|
| | (נגש) | נפל | | | | |
| גָּאַל | נָגַשׁ | נָפַל | נָתַן | יָשַׁב | יָטַב | עָמַד |
| גָּאֲלָה | נָגְשָׁה | נָפְלָה | נָתְנָה | יָשְׁבָה | יָטְבָה | עָמְדָה |
| גָּאַלְתָּ | נָגַשְׁתָּ | נָפַלְתָּ | נָתַתָּ | יָשַׁבְתָּ | יָטַבְתָּ | עָמַדְתָּ |
| גָּאַלְתְּ | נָגַשְׁתְּ | נָפַלְתְּ | נָתַתְּ | יָשַׁבְתְּ | יָטַבְתְּ | עָמַדְתְּ |
| גָּאַלְתִּי | נָגַשְׁתִּי | נָפַלְתִּי | נָתַתִּי | יָשַׁבְתִּי | יָטַבְתִּי | עָמַדְתִּי |
| גָּאֲלוּ | נָגְשׁוּ | נָפְלוּ | נָתְנוּ | יָשְׁבוּ | יָטְבוּ | עָמְדוּ |
| גְּאַלְתֶּם | נְגַשְׁתֶּם | נְפַלְתֶּם | נְתַתֶּם | יְשַׁבְתֶּם | יְטַבְתֶּם | עֲמַדְתֶּם |
| גְּאַלְתֶּן | נְגַשְׁתֶּן | נְפַלְתֶּן | נְתַתֶּן | יְשַׁבְתֶּן | יְטַבְתֶּן | עֲמַדְתֶּן |
| גָּאַלְנוּ | נָגַשְׁנוּ | נָפַלְנוּ | נָתַנּוּ | יָשַׁבְנוּ | יָטַבְנוּ | עָמַדְנוּ |
| יִגְאַל | יִגַּשׁ | יִפֹּל | יִתֵּן | יֵשֵׁב | יִיטַב | יַעֲמֹד |
| תִּגְאַל | תִּגַּשׁ | תִּפֹּל | תִּתֵּן | תֵּשֵׁב | תִּיטַב | תַּעֲמֹד |
| תִּגְאַל | תִּגַּשׁ | תִּפֹּל | תִּתֵּן | תֵּשֵׁב | תִּיטַב | תַּעֲמֹד |
| תִּגְאֲלִי | תִּגְּשִׁי | תִּפְּלִי | תִּתְּנִי | תֵּשְׁבִי | תִּיטְבִי | תַּעַמְדִי |
| אֶגְאַל | אֶגַּשׁ | אֶפֹּל | אֶתֵּן | אֵשֵׁב | אִיטַב | אֶעֱמֹד |
| יִגְאֲלוּ | יִגְּשׁוּ | יִפְּלוּ | יִתְּנוּ | יֵשְׁבוּ | יִיטְבוּ | יַעַמְדוּ |
| תִּגְאַלְנָה | תִּגַּשְׁנָה | תִּפֹּלְנָה | תִּתֵּנָּה | תֵּשַׁבְנָה | תִּיטַבְנָה | תַּעֲמֹדְנָה |
| תִּגְאֲלוּ | תִּגְּשׁוּ | תִּפְּלוּ | תִּתְּנוּ | תֵּשְׁבוּ | תִּיטְבוּ | תַּעַמְדוּ |
| תִּגְאַלְנָה | תִּגַּשְׁנָה | תִּפֹּלְנָה | תִּתֵּנָּה | תֵּשַׁבְנָה | תִּיטַבְנָה | תַּעֲמֹדְנָה |
| נִגְאַל | נִגַּשׁ | נִפֹּל | נִתֵּן | נֵשֵׁב | נִיטַב | נַעֲמֹד |
| גְּאַל | גַּשׁ | נְפֹל | תֵּן | שֵׁב | יְטַב | עֲמֹד |
| גַּאֲלִי | גְּשִׁי | נִפְלִי | תְּנִי | שְׁבִי | יִטְבִי | עִמְדִי |
| גַּאֲלוּ | גְּשׁוּ | נִפְלוּ | תְּנוּ | שְׁבוּ | יִטְבוּ | עִמְדוּ |
| גְּאַלְנָה | גַּשְׁנָה | נְפֹלְנָה | תֵּנָּה | שֵׁבְנָה | יְטַבְנָה | עֲמֹדְנָה |
| גָּאוֹל | נָגוֹשׁ | נָפוֹל | נָתוֹן | יָשׁוֹב | יָטוֹב | עָמוֹד |
| גָּאֹל | נָגֹשׁ / גֶּשֶׁת | נָפֹל | נָתֹן / תֵּת | שֶׁבֶת | יְטֹב | עֲמֹד |
| גֹּאֵל | נֹגֵשׁ | נֹפֵל | נֹתֵן | יֹשֵׁב | יֹטֵב | עֹמֵד |
| גָּאוּל | נָגוּשׁ | נָפוּל | נָתוּן | יָשׁוּב | יָטוּב | עָמוּד |
| וַיִּגְאַל | וַיִּגַּשׁ | וַיִּפֹּל | וַיִּתֵּן | וַיֵּשֶׁב | וַיֵּיטֶב | וַיַּעֲמֹד |

| Niphal | | Strong (שמר) | III-heʾ (גלה) | III-gutt. (שמע) | III-ʾaleph (מצא) | II-vav (כון) |
|---|---|---|---|---|---|---|
| Perf. | 3ms | נִשְׁמַר | נִגְלָה | נִשְׁמַע | נִמְצָא | נָכוֹן |
| | 3fs | נִשְׁמְרָה | נִגְלְתָה | נִשְׁמְעָה | נִמְצְאָה | נָכוֹנָה |
| | 2ms | נִשְׁמַרְתָּ | נִגְלֵיתָ | נִשְׁמַעְתָּ | נִמְצֵאתָ | נְכוּנֹתָ |
| | 2fs | נִשְׁמַרְתְּ | נִגְלֵית | נִשְׁמַעַתְּ | נִמְצֵאת | נְכוּנוֹת |
| | 1cs | נִשְׁמַרְתִּי | נִגְלֵיתִי | נִשְׁמַעְתִּי | נִמְצֵאתִי | נְכוּנוֹתִי |
| | 3cp | נִשְׁמְרוּ | נִגְלוּ | נִשְׁמְעוּ | נִמְצְאוּ | נָכוֹנוּ |
| | 2mp | נִשְׁמַרְתֶּם | נִגְלֵיתֶם | נִשְׁמַעְתֶּם | נִמְצֵאתֶם | נְכוּנוֹתֶם |
| | 2fp | נִשְׁמַרְתֶּן | נִגְלֵיתֶן | נִשְׁמַעְתֶּן | נִמְצֵאתֶן | נְכוּנוֹתֶן |
| | 1cp | נִשְׁמַרְנוּ | נִגְלֵינוּ | נִשְׁמַעְנוּ | נִמְצֵאנוּ | נְכוּנוֹנוּ |
| Impf. | 3ms | יִשָּׁמֵר | יִגָּלֶה | יִשָּׁמַע | יִמָּצֵא | יִכּוֹן |
| | 3fs | תִּשָּׁמֵר | תִּגָּלֶה | תִּשָּׁמַע | תִּמָּצֵא | תִּכּוֹן |
| | 2ms | תִּשָּׁמֵר | תִּגָּלֶה | תִּשָּׁמַע | תִּמָּצֵא | תִּכּוֹן |
| | 2fs | תִּשָּׁמְרִי | תִּגָּלִי | תִּשָּׁמְעִי | תִּמָּצְאִי | תִּכּוֹנִי |
| | 1cs | אֶשָּׁמֵר | אֶגָּלֶה | אֶשָּׁמַע | אֶמָּצֵא | אֶכּוֹן |
| | 3mp | יִשָּׁמְרוּ | יִגָּלוּ | יִשָּׁמְעוּ | יִמָּצְאוּ | יִכּוֹנוּ |
| | 3fp | תִּשָּׁמַרְנָה | תִּגָּלֶינָה | תִּשָּׁמַעְנָה | תִּמָּצֶאינָה | תִּכּוֹנָה |
| | 2mp | תִּשָּׁמְרוּ | תִּגָּלוּ | תִּשָּׁמְעוּ | תִּמָּצְאוּ | תִּכּוֹנוּ |
| | 2fp | תִּשָּׁמַרְנָה | תִּגָּלֶינָה | תִּשָּׁמַעְנָה | תִּמָּצֶאינָה | תִּכּוֹנָה |
| | 1cp | נִשָּׁמֵר | נִגָּלֶה | נִשָּׁמַע | נִמָּצֵא | נִכּוֹן |
| Impv. | 2ms | הִשָּׁמֵר | הִגָּלֵה | הִשָּׁמַע | הִמָּצֵא | הִכּוֹן |
| | 2fs | הִשָּׁמְרִי | הִגָּלִי | הִשָּׁמְעִי | הִמָּצְאִי | הִכּוֹנִי |
| | 2mp | הִשָּׁמְרוּ | הִגָּלוּ | הִשָּׁמְעוּ | הִמָּצְאוּ | הִכּוֹנוּ |
| | 2fp | הִשָּׁמַרְנָה | הִגָּלֶינָה | הִשָּׁמַעְנָה | הִמָּצֶאנָה | הִכּוֹנָה |
| Inf. | Abs. | הִשָּׁמֹר / נִשְׁמֹר | נִגְלֹה / הִגָּלֵה | נִשְׁמוֹעַ / הִשָּׁמֵעַ | נִמְצֹא / הִמָּצֵא | הִכּוֹן |
| | Cstr. | הִשָּׁמֵר | הִגָּלוֹת | הִשָּׁמַע | הִמָּצֵא | הִכּוֹן |
| Part. | | נִשְׁמָר | נִגְלֶה | נִשְׁמָע | נִמְצָא | נָכוֹן |
| Vav consec. | | וַיִּשָּׁמֵר | וַיִּגָּל | וַיִּשָּׁמַע | וַיִּמָּצֵא | וַיִּכּוֹן |

| | | II-guttural (נאל) | I-nun (נצל) | I-vav (ישׁב) | I-guttural (עזב) |
|---|---|---|---|---|---|
| Perf. | 3ms | נִגְאַל | נִצַּל | נוֹשַׁב | נֶעֱזַב |
| | 3fs | נִגְאֲלָה | נִצְּלָה | נוֹשְׁבָה | נֶעֶזְבָה |
| | 2ms | נִגְאַׁלְתָּ | נִצַּׁלְתָּ | נוֹשַׁבְתָּ | נֶעֱזַבְתָּ |
| | 2fs | נִגְאַלְתְּ | נִצַּלְתְּ | נוֹשַׁבְתְּ | נֶעֱזַבְתְּ |
| | 1cs | נִגְאַׁלְתִּי | נִצַּׁלְתִּי | נוֹשַׁבְתִּי | נֶעֱזַבְתִּי |
| | 3cp | נִגְאֲלוּ | נִצְּלוּ | נוֹשְׁבוּ | נֶעֶזְבוּ |
| | 2mp | נִגְאַלְתֶּם | נִצַּלְתֶּם | נוֹשַׁבְתֶּם | נֶעֱזַבְתֶּם |
| | 2fp | נִגְאַלְתֶּן | נִצַּלְתֶּן | נוֹשַׁבְתֶּן | נֶעֱזַבְתֶּן |
| | 1cp | נִגְאַׁלְנוּ | נִצַּׁלְנוּ | נוֹשַׁבְנוּ | נֶעֱזַבְנוּ |
| Impf. | 3ms | יִגָּאֵל | יִנָּצֵל | יִוָּשֵׁב | יֵעָזֵב |
| | 3fs | תִּגָּאֵל | תִּנָּצֵל | תִּוָּשֵׁב | תֵּעָזֵב |
| | 2ms | תִּגָּאֵל | תִּנָּצֵל | תִּוָּשֵׁב | תֵּעָזֵב |
| | 2fs | תִּגָּאֲלִי | תִּנָּצְלִי | תִּוָּשְׁבִי | תֵּעָזְבִי |
| | 1cs | אֶגָּאֵל | אֶנָּצֵל | אִוָּשֵׁב | אֵעָזֵב |
| | 3mp | יִגָּאֲלוּ | יִנָּצְלוּ | יִוָּשְׁבוּ | יֵעָזְבוּ |
| | 3fp | תִּגָּאַׁלְנָה | תִּנָּצַׁלְנָה | תִּוָּשַׁבְנָה | תֵּעָזַׁבְנָה |
| | 2mp | תִּגָּאֲלוּ | תִּנָּצְלוּ | תִּוָּשְׁבוּ | תֵּעָזְבוּ |
| | 2fp | תִּגָּאַׁלְנָה | תִּנָּצַׁלְנָה | תִּוָּשַׁבְנָה | תֵּעָזַׁבְנָה |
| | 1cp | נִגָּאֵל | נִנָּצֵל | נִוָּשֵׁב | נֵעָזֵב |
| Impv. | 2ms | הִגָּאֵל | הִנָּצֵל | הִוָּשֵׁב | הֵעָזֵב |
| | 2fs | הִגָּאֲלִי | הִנָּצְלִי | הִוָּשְׁבִי | הֵעָזְבִי |
| | 2mp | הִגָּאֲלוּ | הִנָּצְלוּ | הִוָּשְׁבוּ | הֵעָזְבוּ |
| | 2fp | הִגָּאַׁלְנָה | הִנָּצַׁלְנָה | הִוָּשַׁבְנָה | הֵעָזַׁבְנָה |
| Inf. | Abs. | נִגְאוֹל | הִנָּצֵל | הִוָּשֵׁב | נַעֲזוֹב/הֵעָזֵב |
| | Cstr. | הִגָּאֵל | הִנָּצֵל | הִוָּשֵׁב | הֵעָזֵב |
| Part. | | נִגְאָל | נִצָּל | נוֹשָׁב | נֶעֱזָב |
| Vav consec. | | וַיִּגָּאֵל | וַיִּנָּצֵל | וַיִּוָּשֵׁב | וַיֵּעָזֵב |

| Piel | | Strong (שמר) | III-heʾ (גלה) | III-guttural (שלח) | III-ʾaleph (מצא) | II-vav (קום) |
|---|---|---|---|---|---|---|
| Perf. | 3ms | שִׁמֵּר | גִּלָּה | שִׁלַּח | מִצֵּא | קִיֵּם |
| | 3fs | שִׁמְּרָה | גִּלְּתָה | שִׁלְּחָה | מִצְּאָה | קִיְּמָה |
| | 2ms | שִׁמַּרְתָּ | גִּלִּיתָ | שִׁלַּחְתָּ | מִצֵּאתָ | קִיַּמְתָּ |
| | 2fs | שִׁמַּרְתְּ | גִּלִּית | שִׁלַּחַתְּ | מִצֵּאת | קִיַּמְתְּ |
| | 1cs | שִׁמַּרְתִּי | גִּלִּיתִי | שִׁלַּחְתִּי | מִצֵּאתִי | קִיַּמְתִּי |
| | 3cp | שִׁמְּרוּ | גִּלּוּ | שִׁלְּחוּ | מִצְּאוּ | קִיְּמוּ |
| | 2mp | שִׁמַּרְתֶּם | גִּלִּיתֶם | שִׁלַּחְתֶּם | מִצֵּאתֶם | קִיַּמְתֶּם |
| | 2fp | שִׁמַּרְתֶּן | גִּלִּיתֶן | שִׁלַּחְתֶּן | מִצֵּאתֶן | קִיַּמְתֶּן |
| | 1cp | שִׁמַּרְנוּ | גִּלִּינוּ | שִׁלַּחְנוּ | מִצֵּאנוּ | קִיַּמְנוּ |
| Impf. | 3ms | יְשַׁמֵּר | יְגַלֶּה | יְשַׁלַּח | יְמַצֵּא | יְקַיֵּם |
| | 3fs | תְּשַׁמֵּר | תְּגַלֶּה | תְּשַׁלַּח | תְּמַצֵּא | תְּקַיֵּם |
| | 2ms | תְּשַׁמֵּר | תְּגַלֶּה | תְּשַׁלַּח | תְּמַצֵּא | תְּקַיֵּם |
| | 2fs | תְּשַׁמְּרִי | תְּגַלִּי | תְּשַׁלְּחִי | תְּמַצְּאִי | תְּקַיְּמִי |
| | 1cs | אֲשַׁמֵּר | אֲגַלֶּה | אֲשַׁלַּח | אֲמַצֵּא | אֲקַיֵּם |
| | 3mp | יְשַׁמְּרוּ | יְגַלּוּ | יְשַׁלְּחוּ | יְמַצְּאוּ | יְקַיְּמוּ |
| | 3fp | תְּשַׁמֵּרְנָה | תְּגַלֶּינָה | תְּשַׁלַּחְנָה | תְּמַצֶּאנָה | תְּקַיֵּמְנָה |
| | 2mp | תְּשַׁמְּרוּ | תְּגַלּוּ | תְּשַׁלְּחוּ | תְּמַצְּאוּ | תְּקַיְּמוּ |
| | 2fp | תְּשַׁמֵּרְנָה | תְּגַלֶּינָה | תְּשַׁלַּחְנָה | תְּמַצֶּאנָה | תְּקַיֵּמְנָה |
| | 1cp | נְשַׁמֵּר | נְגַלֶּה | נְשַׁלַּח | נְמַצֵּא | נְקַיֵּם |
| Impv. | 2ms | שַׁמֵּר | גַּלֵּה | שַׁלַּח | מַצֵּא | קַיֵּם |
| | 2fs | שַׁמְּרִי | גַּלִּי | שַׁלְּחִי | מַצְּאִי | קַיְּמִי |
| | 2mp | שַׁמְּרוּ | גַּלּוּ | שַׁלְּחוּ | מַצְּאוּ | קַיְּמוּ |
| | 2fp | שַׁמֵּרְנָה | גַּלֶּינָה | שַׁלַּחְנָה | מַצֶּאנָה | קַיֵּמְנָה |
| Inf. | Abs. | שַׁמֹּר | גַּלֵּה | שַׁלֵּחַ | מַצֵּא | קַיֹּם |
| | | שַׁמֵּר | גַּלֵּה | שַׁלַּח | מַצֵּא | קַיֵּם |
| | Cstr. | שַׁמֵּר | גַּלּוֹת | שַׁלַּח | מַצֵּא | קַיֵּם |
| Part. | Act. | מְשַׁמֵּר | מְגַלֶּה | מְשַׁלֵּחַ | מְמַצֵּא | מְקַיֵּם |
| Vav consec. | | וַיְשַׁמֵּר | וַיְגַל | וַיְשַׁלַּח | וַיְמַצֵּא | וַיְקַיֵּם |

| | | II-gutt. (גאל) | I-nun (נצל) | I-vav (ישב) | I-yod (יטב) | I-gutt. (עמד) |
|---|---|---|---|---|---|---|
| Perf. | 3ms | גָּאַל | נִצַּל | יָשַׁב | יָטַב | עָמַד |
| | 3fs | גָּאֲלָה | נִצְּלָה | יָשְׁבָה | יָטְבָה | עָמְדָה |
| | 2ms | גָּאַלְתָּ | נִצַּלְתָּ | יָשַׁבְתָּ | יָטַבְתָּ | עָמַדְתָּ |
| | 2fs | גָּאַלְתְּ | נִצַּלְתְּ | יָשַׁבְתְּ | יָטַבְתְּ | עָמַדְתְּ |
| | 1cs | גָּאַלְתִּי | נִצַּלְתִּי | יָשַׁבְתִּי | יָטַבְתִּי | עָמַדְתִּי |
| | 3cp | גָּאֲלוּ | נִצְּלוּ | יָשְׁבוּ | יָטְבוּ | עָמְדוּ |
| | 2mp | גְּאַלְתֶּם | נִצַּלְתֶּם | יְשַׁבְתֶּם | יְטַבְתֶּם | עֲמַדְתֶּם |
| | 2fp | גְּאַלְתֶּן | נִצַּלְתֶּן | יְשַׁבְתֶּן | יְטַבְתֶּן | עֲמַדְתֶּן |
| | 1cp | גָּאַלְנוּ | נִצַּלְנוּ | יָשַׁבְנוּ | יָטַבְנוּ | עָמַדְנוּ |
| Impf. | 3ms | יִגְאַל | יִנָּצֵל | יוֹשֵׁב | יִיטַב | יַעֲמֹד |
| | 3fs | תִּגְאַל | תִּנָּצֵל | תּוֹשֵׁב | תִּיטַב | תַּעֲמֹד |
| | 2ms | תִּגְאַל | תִּנָּצֵל | תּוֹשֵׁב | תִּיטַב | תַּעֲמֹד |
| | 2fs | תִּגְאֲלִי | תִּנָּצְלִי | תּוֹשְׁבִי | תִּיטְבִי | תַּעֲמְדִי |
| | 1cs | אֶגְאַל | אֶנָּצֵל | אוֹשֵׁב | אִיטַב | אֶעֱמֹד |
| | 3mp | יִגְאֲלוּ | יִנָּצְלוּ | יוֹשְׁבוּ | יִיטְבוּ | יַעֲמְדוּ |
| | 3fp | תִּגְאַלְנָה | תִּנָּצַלְנָה | תּוֹשַׁבְנָה | תִּיטַבְנָה | תַּעֲמֹדְנָה |
| | 2mp | תִּגְאֲלוּ | תִּנָּצְלוּ | תּוֹשְׁבוּ | תִּיטְבוּ | תַּעֲמְדוּ |
| | 2fp | תִּגְאַלְנָה | תִּנָּצַלְנָה | תּוֹשַׁבְנָה | תִּיטַבְנָה | תַּעֲמֹדְנָה |
| | 1cp | נִגְאַל | נִנָּצֵל | נוֹשֵׁב | נִיטַב | נַעֲמֹד |
| Impv. | 2ms | גְּאַל | נִצֵּל | שֵׁב | יְטַב | עֲמֹד |
| | 2fs | גַּאֲלִי | נַצְּלִי | שְׁבִי | יַטְבִי | עִמְדִי |
| | 2mp | גַּאֲלוּ | נַצְּלוּ | שְׁבוּ | יַטְבוּ | עִמְדוּ |
| | 2fp | גְּאַלְנָה | נַצֵּלְנָה | שֵׁבְנָה | יְטַבְנָה | עֲמֹדְנָה |
| Inf. | Abs. | | | יָשׁוֹב | | |
| | | גָּאֹל | נָצֹל | יָשֹׁב | יָטֹב | עָמֹד |
| | Cstr. | גְּאֹל | נְצֹל | יָשֹׁב | יָטֹב | עֲמֹד |
| Part. | Act. | גֹּאֵל | נֹצֵל | מוֹשֵׁב | מֵיטֵב | עֹמֵד |
| Vav consec. | | וַיִּגְאַל | וַיִּנָּצֵל | וַיּוֹשֶׁב | וַיִּיטַב | וַיַּעֲמֹד |

| Pual | | Strong (שמר) | III-heʾ (נלה) | III-gutt. (שלח) | III-ʾaleph (מלא) | II-vav |
|---|---|---|---|---|---|---|
| Perf. | 3ms | שֻׁמַּר | גֻּלָּה | שֻׁלַּח | מֻלָּא | rare and |
| | 3fs | שֻׁמְּרָה | גֻּלְּתָה | שֻׁלְּחָה | מֻלְּאָה | usually |
| | 2ms | שֻׁמַּרְתָּ | גֻּלֵּיתָ | שֻׁלַּחְתָּ | מֻלֵּאתָ | with |
| | 2fs | שֻׁמַּרְתְּ | גֻּלֵּית | שֻׁלַּחַתְּ | מֻלֵּאת | doubly |
| | 1cs | שֻׁמַּרְתִּי | גֻּלֵּיתִי | שֻׁלַּחְתִּי | מֻלֵּאתִי | weak |
| | 3cp | שֻׁמְּרוּ | גֻּלּוּ | שֻׁלְּחוּ | מֻלְּאוּ | roots |
| | 2mp | שֻׁמַּרְתֶּם | גֻּלֵּיתֶם | שֻׁלַּחְתֶּם | מֻלֵּאתֶם | |
| | 2fp | שֻׁמַּרְתֶּן | גֻּלֵּיתֶן | שֻׁלַּחְתֶּן | מֻלֵּאתֶן | |
| | 1cp | שֻׁמַּרְנוּ | גֻּלֵּינוּ | שֻׁלַּחְנוּ | מֻלֵּאנוּ | |
| Impf. | 3ms | יְשֻׁמַּר | יְגֻלֶּה | יְשֻׁלַּח | יְמֻלָּא | |
| | 3fs | תְּשֻׁמַּר | תְּגֻלֶּה | תְּשֻׁלַּח | תְּמֻלָּא | |
| | 2ms | תְּשֻׁמַּר | תְּגֻלֶּה | תְּשֻׁלַּח | תְּמֻלָּא | |
| | 2fs | תְּשֻׁמְּרִי | תְּגֻלִּי | תְּשֻׁלְּחִי | תְּמֻלְּאִי | |
| | 1cs | אֲשֻׁמַּר | אֲגֻלֶּה | אֲשֻׁלַּח | אֲמֻלָּא | |
| | 3mp | יְשֻׁמְּרוּ | יְגֻלּוּ | יְשֻׁלְּחוּ | יְמֻלְּאוּ | |
| | 3fp | תְּשֻׁמַּרְנָה | תְּגֻלֶּינָה | תְּשֻׁלַּחְנָה | תְּמֻלֶּאנָה | |
| | 2mp | תְּשֻׁמְּרוּ | תְּגֻלּוּ | תְּשֻׁלְּחוּ | תְּמֻלְּאוּ | |
| | 2fp | תְּשֻׁמַּרְנָה | תְּגֻלֶּינָה | תְּשֻׁלַּחְנָה | לְאָנָה | |
| | 1cp | נְשֻׁמַּר | נְגֻלֶּה | נְשֻׁלַּח | הוֹרֻדוּ | |
| | | | | | תֻּמַ | |
| | | | | | נְמֻלָּא | |
| Inf. | Abs. | שֻׁמֹּר | none | none | none | none |
| | Cstr. | none | גֻּלּוֹת | | | |
| Part. | Pass. | מְשֻׁמָּר | מְגֻלֶּה | מְשֻׁלָּח | מְמֻלָּא | |
| Vav consec. | | וַיְשֻׁמַּר | וַיְגֻל | וַיְשֻׁלַּח | וַיְמֻלָּא | |
| Jussive | | יְשֻׁמַּר | יְגֻל | יְשֻׁלַּח | יְמֻלָּא | |

|  |  | II-gutt. (רחץ) | I-nun (נתץ) | I-vav/yod (ילד) | I-gutt. (חלק) |
|---|---|---|---|---|---|
| Perf. | 3ms | רֻחַץ | נֻתַּץ | יֻלַּד | חֻלַּק |
|  | 3fs | רֻחֲצָה | נֻתְּצָה | יֻלְּדָה | חֻלְּקָה |
|  | 2ms | רֻחַצְתָּ | נֻתַּצְתָּ | יֻלַּדְתָּ | חֻלַּקְתָּ |
|  | 2fs | רֻחַצְתְּ | נֻתַּצְתְּ | יֻלַּדְתְּ | חֻלַּקְתְּ |
|  | 1cs | רֻחַצְתִּי | נֻתַּצְתִּי | יֻלַּדְתִּי | חֻלַּקְתִּי |
|  | 3cp | רֻחֲצוּ | נֻתְּצוּ | יֻלְּדוּ | חֻלְּקוּ |
|  | 2mp | רֻחַצְתֶּם | נֻתַּצְתֶּם | יֻלַּדְתֶּם | חֻלַּקְתֶּם |
|  | 2fp | רֻחַצְתֶּן | נֻתַּצְתֶּן | יֻלַּדְתֶּן | חֻלַּקְתֶּן |
|  | 1cp | רֻחַצְנוּ | נֻתַּצְנוּ | יֻלַּדְנוּ | חֻלַּקְנוּ |
| Impf. | 3ms | יְרֻחַץ | יְנֻתַּץ | יְיֻלַּד | יְחֻלַּק |
|  | 3fs | תְּרֻחַץ | תְּנֻתַּץ | תְּיֻלַּד | תְּחֻלַּק |
|  | 2ms | תְּרֻחַץ | תְּנֻתַּץ | תְּיֻלַּד | תְּחֻלַּק |
|  | 2fs | תְּרֻחֲצִי | תְּנֻתְּצִי | תְּיֻלְּדִי | תְּחֻלְּקִי |
|  | 1cs | אֲרֻחַץ | אֲנֻתַּץ | אֲיֻלַּד | אֲחֻלַּק |
|  | 3mp | יְרֻחֲצוּ | יְנֻתְּצוּ | יְיֻלְּדוּ | יְחֻלְּקוּ |
|  | 3fp | תְּרֻחַצְנָה | תְּנֻתַּצְנָה | תְּיֻלַּדְנָה | תְּחֻלַּקְנָה |
|  | 2mp | תְּרֻחֲצוּ | תְּנֻתְּצוּ | תְּיֻלְּדוּ | תְּחֻלְּקוּ |
|  | 2fp | תְּרֻחַצְנָה | תְּנֻתַּצְנָה | תְּיֻלַּדְנָה | תְּחֻלַּקְנָה |
|  | 1cp | נְרֻחַץ | נְנֻתַּץ | נְיֻלַּד | נְחֻלַּק |
| Inf. | Abs. Cstr. | not attested | not attested | not attested | not attested |
| Part. | Pass. | מְרֻחָץ | מְנֻתָּץ | מְיֻלָּד | מְחֻלָּק |
| Vav consec. |  | וַיְרֻחַץ | וַיְנֻתַּץ | וַיְיֻלַּד | וַיְחֻלַּק |

| Hitpael | | Strong (קדש) | III-heʾ (נלה) | III-gutt. (שלח) | III-ʾaleph (מצא) |
|---|---|---|---|---|---|
| Perf. | 3ms | הִתְקַדֵּשׁ | הִתְגַּלָּה | הִשְׁתַּלַּח | הִתְמַצֵּא |
| | 3fs | הִתְקַדְּשָׁה | הִתְגַּלְּתָה | הִשְׁתַּלְּחָה | הִתְמַצְּאָה |
| | 2ms | הִתְקַדַּ֫שְׁתָּ | הִתְגַּלִּ֫יתָ | הִשְׁתַּלַּ֫חְתָּ | הִתְמַצֵּ֫אתָ |
| | 2fs | הִתְקַדַּ֫שְׁתְּ | הִתְגַּלִּית | הִשְׁתַּלַּחַתְּ | הִתְמַצֵּאת |
| | 1cs | הִתְקַדַּ֫שְׁתִּי | הִתְגַּלֵּ֫יתִי | הִשְׁתַּלַּ֫חְתִּי | הִתְמַצֵּ֫אתִי |
| | 3cp | הִתְקַדְּשׁוּ | הִתְגַּלּוּ | הִשְׁתַּלְּחוּ | הִתְמַצְּאוּ |
| | 2mp | הִתְקַדַּשְׁתֶּם | הִתְגַּלִּיתֶם | הִשְׁתַּלַּחְתֶּם | הִתְמַצֵּאתֶם |
| | 2fp | הִתְקַדַּשְׁתֶּן | הִתְגַּלִּיתֶן | הִשְׁתַּלַּחְתֶּן | הִתְמַצֵּאתֶן |
| | 1cp | הִתְקַדַּ֫שְׁנוּ | הִתְגַּלִּ֫ינוּ | הִשְׁתַּלַּ֫חְנוּ | הִתְמַצֵּ֫אנוּ |
| Impf. | 3ms | יִתְקַדֵּשׁ | יִתְגַּלֶּה | יִשְׁתַּלַּח | יִתְמַצֵּא |
| | 3fs | תִּתְקַדֵּשׁ | תִּתְגַּלֶּה | תִּשְׁתַּלַּח | תִּתְמַצֵּא |
| | 2ms | תִּתְקַדֵּשׁ | תִּתְגַּלֶּה | תִּשְׁתַּלַּח | תִּתְמַצֵּא |
| | 2fs | תִּתְקַדְּשִׁי | תִּתְגַּלִּי | תִּשְׁתַּלְּחִי | תִּתְמַצְּאִי |
| | 1cs | אֶתְקַדֵּשׁ | אֶתְגַּלֶּה | אֶשְׁתַּלַּח | אֶתְמַצֵּא |
| | 3mp | יִתְקַדְּשׁוּ | יִתְגַּלּוּ | יִשְׁתַּלְּחוּ | יִתְמַצְּאוּ |
| | 3fp | תִּתְקַדֵּ֫שְׁנָה | תִּתְגַּלֶּ֫ינָה | תִּשְׁתַּלַּ֫חְנָה | תִּתְמַצֶּ֫אנָה |
| | 2mp | תִּתְקַדְּשׁוּ | תִּתְגַּלּוּ | תִּשְׁתַּלְּחוּ | תִּתְמַצְּאוּ |
| | 2fp | תִּתְקַדֵּ֫שְׁנָה | תִּתְגַּלֶּ֫ינָה | תִּשְׁתַּלַּ֫חְנָה | תִּתְמַצֶּ֫אנָה |
| | 1cp | נִתְקַדֵּשׁ | נִתְגַּלֶּה | נִשְׁתַּלַּח | נִתְמַצֵּא |
| Impv. | 2ms | הִתְקַדֵּשׁ | הִתְגַּלֵּה | הִשְׁתַּלַּח | הִתְמַצֵּא |
| | 2fs | הִתְקַדְּשִׁי | הִתְגַּלִּי | הִשְׁתַּלְּחִי | הִתְמַצְּאִי |
| | 2mp | הִתְקַדְּשׁוּ | הִתְגַּלּוּ | הִשְׁתַּלְּחוּ | הִתְמַצְּאוּ |
| | 2fp | הִתְקַדֵּ֫שְׁנָה | הִתְגַּלֶּ֫ינָה | הִשְׁתַּלַּ֫חְנָה | הִתְמַצֶּ֫אנָה |
| Inf. | Abs. | הִתְקַדֵּשׁ | | הִשְׁתַּלֵּחַ | הִתְמַצֵּא |
| | Cstr. | הִתְקַדֵּשׁ | הִתְגַּלּוֹת | הִשְׁתַּלֵּחַ | הִתְמַצֵּא |
| Part. | Act. | מִתְקַדֵּשׁ | מִתְגַּלֶּה | מִשְׁתַּלֵּחַ | מִתְמַצֵּא |
| Vav consec. | | וַיִּתְקַדֵּשׁ | וַיִּתְגַּל | וַיִּשְׁתַּלַּח | וַיִּתְמַצֵּא |

|  |  | II-guttural | I-nun | I-vav | I-guttural |
|---|---|---|---|---|---|
| Perf. | 3ms | הִתְרַחֵץ | הִתְנַדֵּב | Rare and only on doubly weak roots. (ידה, ידע) | הִתְחַזֵּק[1] |
|  | 3fs | הִתְרַחֲצָה | הִתְנַדְּבָה |  | הִתְחַזְּקָה |
|  | 2ms | הִתְרַחַצְתָּ | הִתְנַדַּבְתָּ |  | הִתְחַזַּקְתָּ |
|  | 2fs | הִתְרַחַצְתְּ | הִתְנַדַּבְתְּ |  | הִתְחַזַּקְתְּ |
|  | 1cs | הִתְרַחַצְתִּי | הִתְנַדַּבְתִּי |  | הִתְחַזַּקְתִּי |
|  | 3cp | הִתְרַחֲצוּ | הִתְנַדְּבוּ |  | הִתְחַזְּקוּ |
|  | 2mp | הִתְרַחַצְתֶּם | הִתְנַדַּבְתֶּם |  | הִתְחַזַּקְתֶּם |
|  | 2fp | הִתְרַחַצְתֶּן | הִתְנַדַּבְתֶּן |  | הִתְחַזַּקְתֶּן |
|  | 1cp | הִתְרַחַצְנוּ | הִתְנַדַּבְנוּ |  | הִתְחַזַּקְנוּ |
| Impf. | 3ms | יִתְרַחֵץ | יִתְנַדֵּב |  | יִתְחַזֵּק |
|  | 3fs | תִּתְרַחֵץ | תִּתְנַדֵּב |  | תִּתְחַזֵּק |
|  | 2ms | תִּתְרַחֵץ | תִּתְנַדֵּב |  | תִּתְחַזֵּק |
|  | 2fs | תִּתְרַחֲצִי | תִּתְנַדְּבִי |  | תִּתְחַזְּקִי |
|  | 1cs | אֶתְרַחֵץ | אֶתְנַדֵּב |  | אֶתְחַזֵּק |
|  | 3mp | יִתְרַחֲצוּ | יִתְנַדְּבוּ |  | יִתְחַזְּקוּ |
|  | 3fp | תִּתְרַחֵצְנָה | תִּתְנַדֵּבְנָה |  | תִּתְחַזֵּקְנָה |
|  | 2mp | תִּתְרַחֲצוּ | תִּתְנַדְּבוּ |  | תִּתְחַזְּקוּ |
|  | 2fp | תִּתְרַחֵצְנָה | תִּתְנַדֵּבְנָה |  | תִּתְחַזֵּקְנָה |
|  | 1cp | נִתְרַחֵץ | נִתְנַדֵּב |  | נִתְחַזֵּק |
| Impv. | 2ms | הִתְרַחֵץ | הִתְנַדֵּב |  | הִתְחַזֵּק |
|  | 2fs | הִתְרַחֲצִי | הִתְנַדְּבִי |  | הִתְחַזְּקִי |
|  | 2mp | הִתְרַחֲצוּ | הִתְנַדְּבוּ |  | הִתְחַזְּקוּ |
|  | 2fp | הִתְרַחֵצְנָה | הִתְנַדֵּבְנָה |  | הִתְחַזֵּקְנָה |
| Inf. | Abs. | הִתְרַחֵץ | הִתְנַדֵּב |  | הִתְחַזֵּק |
|  | Cstr. | הִתְרַחֵץ | הִתְנַדֵּב |  | הִתְחַזֵּק |
| Part. | Act. | מִתְרַחֵץ | מִתְנַדֵּב |  | מִתְחַזֵּק |
| Vav consec. |  | וַיִּתְרַחֵץ | וַיִּתְנַדֵּב |  | וַיִּתְחַזֵּק |

[1] Often in the perfect and sometimes in the imperfect, I-guttural roots have an a-class rather than the expected i-class vowel under the second root letter. This is the case with the root חזק.

| Hiphil | | Strong (קרב) | III-heʾ (גלה) | III-gutt. (שלח) | III-ʾaleph (מצא) | II-vav (קום) |
|---|---|---|---|---|---|---|
| Perf. | 3ms | הִקְרִיב | הִגְלָה | הִשְׁלִיחַ | הִמְצִיא | הֵקִים |
| | 3fs | הִקְרִיבָה | הִגְלְתָה | הִשְׁלִיחָה | הִמְצִיאָה | הֵקִימָה |
| | 2ms | הִקְרַבְתָּ | הִגְלִיתָ | הִשְׁלַחְתָּ | הִמְצֵאתָ | הֲקִימֹותָ |
| | 2fs | הִקְרַבְתְּ | הִגְלִית | הִשְׁלַחַתְּ | הִמְצֵאת | הֲקִימֹות |
| | 1cs | הִקְרַבְתִּי | הִגְלִיתִי | הִשְׁלַחְתִּי | הִמְצֵאתִי | הֲקִימֹותִי |
| | 3cp | הִקְרִיבוּ | הִגְלוּ | הִשְׁלִיחוּ | הִמְצִיאוּ | הֵקִימוּ |
| | 2mp | הִקְרַבְתֶּם | הִגְלִיתֶם | הִשְׁלַחְתֶּם | הִמְצֵאתֶם | הֲקִימֹותֶם |
| | 2fp | הִקְרַבְתֶּן | הִגְלִיתֶן | הִשְׁלַחְתֶּן | הִמְצֵאתֶן | הֲקִימֹותֶן |
| | 1cp | הִקְרַבְנוּ | הִגְלִינוּ | הִשְׁלַחְנוּ | הִמְצֵאנוּ | הֲקִימֹונוּ |
| Impf. | 3ms | יַקְרִיב | יַגְלֶה | יַשְׁלִיחַ | יַמְצִיא | יָקִים |
| | 3fs | תַּקְרִיב | תַּגְלֶה | תַּשְׁלִיחַ | תַּמְצִיא | תָּקִים |
| | 2ms | תַּקְרִיב | תַּגְלֶה | תַּשְׁלִיחַ | תַּמְצִיא | תָּקִים |
| | 2fs | תַּקְרִיבִי | תַּגְלִי | תַּשְׁלִיחִי | תַּמְצִיאִי | תָּקִימִי |
| | 1cs | אַקְרִיב | אַגְלֶה | אַשְׁלִיחַ | אַמְצִיא | אָקִים |
| | 3mp | יַקְרִיבוּ | יַגְלוּ | יַשְׁלִיחוּ | יַמְצִיאוּ | יָקִימוּ |
| | 3fp | תַּקְרֵבְנָה | תַּגְלֶינָה | תַּשְׁלַחְנָה | תַּמְצֶאנָה | תְּקִמֶינָה |
| | 2mp | תַּקְרִיבוּ | תַּגְלוּ | תַּשְׁלִיחוּ | תַּמְצִיאוּ | תָּקִימוּ |
| | 2fp | תַּקְרֵבְנָה | תַּגְלֶינָה | תַּשְׁלַחְנָה | תַּמְצֶאנָה | תְּקִמֶינָה |
| | 1cp | נַקְרִיב | נַגְלֶה | נַשְׁלִיחַ | נָמְצִיא | נָקִים |
| Impv. | 2ms | הַקְרֵב | הַגְלֵה | הַשְׁלַח | הַמְצֵא | הָקֵם |
| | 2fs | הַקְרִיבִי | הַגְלִי | הַשְׁלִיחִי | הַמְצִיאִי | הָקִימִי |
| | 2mp | הַקְרִיבוּ | הַגְלוּ | הַשְׁלִיחוּ | הַמְצִיאוּ | הָקִימוּ |
| | 2fp | הַקְרֵבְנָה | הַגְלֶינָה | הַשְׁלַחְנָה | הַמְצֶאנָה | הָקֵמְנָה |
| Inf. | Abs. | הַקְרֵב | הַגְלֵה | הַשְׁלֵחַ | הַמְצֵא | הָקֵם |
| | Cstr. | הַקְרִיב | הַגְלֹות | הַשְׁלִיחַ | הַמְצִיא | הָקִים |
| Part. | | מַקְרִיב | מַגְלֶה | מַשְׁלִיחַ | מַמְצִיא | מֵקִים |
| Vav consec. | | וַיַּקְרֵב | וַיֶּגֶל | וַיַּשְׁלַח | וַיַּמְצֵא | וַיָּקֶם |

|  |  | II-gutt. (גאל) | I-nun (נצל) | I-vav (ישב) | I-yod (יטב) | I-gutt. (עמד) |
|---|---|---|---|---|---|---|
| Perf. | 3ms | הִגְאִיל | הִצִּיל | הוֹשִׁיב | הֵיטִיב | הֶעֱמִיד |
|  | 3fs | הִגְאִילָה | הִצִּילָה | הוֹשִׁיבָה | הֵיטִיבָה | הֶעֱמִידָה |
|  | 2ms | הִגְאַלְתָּ | הִצַּלְתָּ | הוֹשַׁבְתָּ | הֵיטַבְתָּ | הֶעֱמַדְתָּ |
|  | 2fs | הִגְאַלְתְּ | הִצַּלְתְּ | הוֹשַׁבְתְּ | הֵיטַבְתְּ | הֶעֱמַדְתְּ |
|  | 1cs | הִגְאַלְתִּי | הִצַּלְתִּי | הוֹשַׁבְתִּי | הֵיטַבְתִּי | הֶעֱמַדְתִּי |
|  | 3cp | הִגְאִילוּ | הִצִּילוּ | הוֹשִׁיבוּ | הֵיטִיבוּ | הֶעֱמִידוּ |
|  | 2mp | הִגְאַלְתֶּם | הִצַּלְתֶּם | הוֹשַׁבְתֶּם | הֵיטַבְתֶּם | הֶעֱמַדְתֶּם |
|  | 2fp | הִגְאַלְתֶּן | הִצַּלְתֶּן | הוֹשַׁבְתֶּן | הֵיטַבְתֶּן | הֶעֱמַדְתֶּן |
|  | 1cp | הִגְאַלְנוּ | הִצַּלְנוּ | הוֹשַׁבְנוּ | הֵיטַבְנוּ | הֶעֱמַדְנוּ |
| Impf. | 3ms | יַגְאִיל | יַצִּיל | יוֹשִׁיב | יֵיטִיב | יַעֲמִיד |
|  | 3fs | תַּגְאִיל | תַּצִּיל | תּוֹשִׁיב | תֵּיטִיב | תַּעֲמִיד |
|  | 2ms | תַּגְאִיל | תַּצִּיל | תּוֹשִׁיב | תֵּיטִיב | תַּעֲמִיד |
|  | 2fs | תַּגְאִילִי | תַּצִּילִי | תּוֹשִׁיבִי | תֵּיטִיבִי | תַּעֲמִידִי |
|  | 1cs | אַגְאִיל | אַצִּיל | אוֹשִׁיב | אֵיטִיב | אַעֲמִיד |
|  | 3mp | יַגְאִילוּ | יַצִּילוּ | יוֹשִׁיבוּ | יֵיטִיבוּ | יַעֲמִידוּ |
|  | 3fp | תַּגְאֵלְנָה | תַּצֵּלְנָה | תּוֹשֵׁבְנָה | תֵּיטֵבְנָה | תַּעֲמֵדְנָה |
|  | 2mp | תַּגְאִילוּ | תַּצִּילוּ | תּוֹשִׁיבוּ | תֵּיטִיבוּ | תַּעֲמִידוּ |
|  | 2fp | תַּגְאֵלְנָה | תַּצֵּלְנָה | תּוֹשֵׁבְנָה | תֵּיטֵבְנָה | תַּעֲמֵדְנָה |
|  | 1cp | נַגְאִיל | נַצִּיל | נוֹשִׁיב | נֵיטִיב | נַעֲמִיד |
| Impv. | 2ms | הַגְאֵל | הַצֵּל | הוֹשֵׁב | הֵיטֵב | הַעֲמֵד |
|  | 2fs | הַגְאִילִי | הַצִּילִי | הוֹשִׁיבִי | הֵיטִיבִי | הַעֲמִידִי |
|  | 2mp | הַגְאִילוּ | הַצִּילוּ | הוֹשִׁיבוּ | הֵיטִיבוּ | הַעֲמִידוּ |
|  | 2fp | הַגְאֵלְנָה | הַצֵּלְנָה | הוֹשֵׁבְנָה | הֵיטֵבְנָה | הַעֲמֵדְנָה |
| Inf. | Abs. | הַגְאֵל | הַצֵּל | הוֹשֵׁב | הֵיטֵב | הַעֲמֵד |
|  | Cstr. | הַגְאִיל | הַצִּיל | הוֹשִׁיב | הֵיטִיב | הַעֲמִיד |
| Part. |  | מַגְאִיל | מַצִּיל | מוֹשִׁיב | מֵיטִיב | מַעֲמִיד |
| Vav consec. |  | וַיַּגְאֵל | וַיַּצֵּל | וַיּוֹשֶׁב | וַיֵּיטֶב | וַיַּעֲמֵד |

| Hophal | | Strong (פקד) | III-heʾ (נלה) | III-guttural (מלח) | II-vav (סור) |
|---|---|---|---|---|---|
| Perf. | 3ms | הֻפְקַד | הֻגְלָה | הֻמְלַח | הוּסַר |
| | 3fs | הֻפְקְדָה | הֻגְלְתָה | הֻמְלְחָה | הוּסְרָה |
| | 2ms | הֻפְקַ֫דְתָּ | הֻגְלֵ֫יתָ | הֻמְלַ֫חְתָּ | הוּסַ֫רְתָּ |
| | 2fs | הֻפְקַדְתְּ | הֻגְלֵית | הֻמְלַחַתְּ | הוּסַרְתְּ |
| | 1cs | הֻפְקַ֫דְתִּי | הֻגְלֵ֫יתִי | הֻמְלַ֫חְתִּי | הוּסַ֫רְתִּי |
| | 3cp | הֻפְקְדוּ | הֻגְלוּ | הֻמְלְחוּ | הוּסְרוּ |
| | 2mp | הֻפְקַדְתֶּם | הֻגְלֵיתֶם | הֻמְלַחְתֶּם | הוּסַרְתֶּם |
| | 2fp | הֻפְקַדְתֶּן | הֻגְלֵיתֶן | הֻמְלַחְתֶּן | הוּסַרְתֶּן |
| | 1cp | הֻפְקַ֫דְנוּ | הֻגְלֵ֫ינוּ | הֻמְלַ֫חְנוּ | הוּסַ֫רְנוּ |
| Impf. | 3ms | יֻפְקַד | יֻגְלֶה | יֻמְלַח | יוּסַר |
| | 3fs | תֻּפְקַד | תֻּגְלֶה | תֻּמְלַח | תּוּסַר |
| | 2ms | תֻּפְקַד | תֻּגְלֶה | תֻּמְלַח | תּוּסַר |
| | 2fs | תֻּפְקְדִי | תֻּגְלִי | תֻּמְלְחִי | תּוּסְרִי |
| | 1cs | אֻפְקַד | אֻגְלֶה | אֻמְלַח | אוּסַר |
| | 3mp | יֻפְקְדוּ | יֻגְלוּ | יֻמְלְחוּ | יוּסְרוּ |
| | 3fp | תֻּפְקַ֫דְנָה | תֻּגְלֶ֫ינָה | תֻּמְלַ֫חְנָה | תּוּסַ֫רְנָה |
| | 2mp | תֻּפְקְדוּ | תֻּגְלוּ | תֻּמְלְחוּ | תּוּסְרוּ |
| | 2fp | תֻּפְקַ֫דְנָה | תֻּגְלֶ֫ינָה | תֻּמְלַ֫חְנָה | תּוּסַ֫רְנָה |
| | 1cp | נֻפְקַד | נֻגְלֶה | נֻמְלַח | נוּסַר |
| Impv. | 2ms | הֻפְקַד | | | |
| | 2fs | | | | |
| | 2mp | | הֻגְלוּ | | |
| | 2fp | | | | |
| Inf. | Abs. | הֻפְקֵד | הֻגְלֵה | הֻמְלֵחַ | הוּסֵר |
| | Cstr. | | | | הוּסַר |
| Part. | Pass. | מֻפְקָד | מֻגְלֶה | מֻמְלָח | מוּסָר |
| Vav consec. | | וַיֻּפְקַד | | | וַיּוּסַר |

|  |  | I-nun (נגשׁ) | I-vav (ירד) | I-yod (יצק) | I-guttural (עמד) |
|---|---|---|---|---|---|
| Perf. | 3ms | הֻגַּשׁ | הוּרַד | הוּצַק | הָעֳמַד |
|  | 3fs | הֻגְּשָׁה | הוּרְדָה | הוּצְקָה | הָעֳמְדָה |
|  | 2ms | הֻגַּשְׁתָּ | הוּרַדְתָּ | הוּצַקְתָּ | הָעֳמַדְתָּ |
|  | 2fs | הֻגַּשְׁתְּ | הוּרַדְתְּ | הוּצַקְתְּ | הָעֳמַדְתְּ |
|  | 1cs | הֻגַּשְׁתִּי | הוּרַדְתִּי | הוּצַקְתִּי | הָעֳמַדְתִּי |
|  | 3cp | הֻגְּשׁוּ | הוּרְדוּ | הוּצְקוּ | הָעֳמְדוּ |
|  | 2mp | הֻגַּשְׁתֶּם | הוּרַדְתֶּם | הוּצַקְתֶּם | הָעֳמַדְתֶּם |
|  | 2fp | הֻגַּשְׁתֶּן | הוּרַדְתֶּן | הוּצַקְתֶּן | הָעֳמַדְתֶּן |
|  | 1cp | הֻגַּשְׁנוּ | הוּרַדְנוּ | הוּצַקְנוּ | הָעֳמַדְנוּ |
| Impf. | 3ms | יֻגַּשׁ | יוּרַד | יוּצַק | יָעֳמַד |
|  | 3fs | תֻּגַּשׁ | תּוּרַד | תּוּצַק | תָּעֳמַד |
|  | 2ms | תֻּגַּשׁ | תּוּרַד | תּוּצַק | תָּעֳמַד |
|  | 2fs | תֻּגְּשִׁי | תּוּרְדִי | תּוּצְקִי | תָּעֳמְדִי |
|  | 1cs | אֻגַּשׁ | אוּרַד | אוּצַק | אָעֳמַד |
|  | 3mp | יֻגְּשׁוּ | יוּרְדוּ | יוּצְקוּ | יָעֳמְדוּ |
|  | 3fp | תֻּגַּשְׁנָה | תּוּרַדְנָה | תּוּצַקְנָה | תָּעֳמַדְנָה |
|  | 2mp | תֻּגְּשׁוּ | תּוּרְדוּ | תּוּצְקוּ | תָּעֳמְדוּ |
|  | 2fp | תֻּגַּשְׁנָה | תּוּרַדְנָה | תּוּצַקְנָה | תָּעֳמַדְנָה |
|  | 1cp | נֻגַּשׁ | נוּרַד | נוּצַק | נָעֳמַד |
| Inf. | Abs. | הֻגֵּשׁ | הוּרֵד | הוּצֵק | הָעֳמֵד |
|  | Cstr. | הֻגַּשׁ | הוּרַד | הוּצַק |  |
| Part. | Pass. | מֻגָּשׁ | מוּרָד | מוּצָק | מָעֳמָד |
| Vav consec. |  | וַיֻּגַּשׁ |  |  |  |

| Minor Stems | | Polel (קוֹם) | Polal (רוֹם) | Hitpolel (בִּין) |
|---|---|---|---|---|
| Perf. | 3ms | קוֹמֵם | רוֹמַם | הִתְבּוֹנֵן |
| | 3fs | קוֹמְמָה | רוֹמְמָה | הִתְבּוֹנְנָה |
| | 2ms | קוֹמַ֫מְתָּ | רוֹמַ֫מְתָּ | הִתְבּוֹנַ֫נְתָּ |
| | 2fs | קוֹמַמְתְּ | רוֹמַמְתְּ | הִתְבּוֹנַנְתְּ |
| | 1cs | קוֹמַ֫מְתִּי | רוֹמַ֫מְתִּי | הִתְבּוֹנַ֫נְתִּי |
| | 3cp | קוֹמְמוּ | רוֹמְמוּ | הִתְבּוֹנְנוּ |
| | 2mp | קוֹמַמְתֶּם | רוֹמַמְתֶּם | הִתְבּוֹנַנְתֶּם |
| | 2fp | קוֹמַמְתֶּן | רוֹמַמְתֶּן | הִתְבּוֹנַנְתֶּן |
| | 1cp | קוֹמַ֫מְנוּ | רוֹמַ֫מְנוּ | הִתְבּוֹנַ֫נּוּ / הִתְבּוֹנַ֫נּוּ |
| Impf. | 3ms | יְקוֹמֵם | יְרוֹמַם | יִתְבּוֹנֵן |
| | 3fs | תְּקוֹמֵם | תְּרוֹמַם | תִּתְבּוֹנֵן |
| | 2ms | תְּקוֹמֵם | תְּרוֹמַם | תִּתְבּוֹנֵן |
| | 2fs | תְּקוֹמְמִי | תְּרוֹמְמִי | תִּתְבּוֹנְנִי |
| | 1cs | אֲקוֹמֵם | אֲרוֹמַם | אֶתְבּוֹנֵן |
| | 3mp | יְקוֹמְמוּ | יְרוֹמְמוּ | יִתְבּוֹנְנוּ |
| | 3fp | תְּקוֹמֵ֫מְנָה | תְּרוֹמַ֫מְנָה | תִּתְבּוֹנֵ֫נָּה |
| | 2mp | תְּקוֹמְמוּ | תְּרוֹמְמוּ | תִּתְבּוֹנְנוּ |
| | 2fp | תְּקוֹמֵ֫מְנָה | תְּרוֹמַ֫מְנָה | תִּתְבּוֹנֵ֫נָּה |
| | 1cp | נְקוֹמֵם | נְרוֹמַם | נִתְבּוֹנֵן |
| Impv. | 2ms | קוֹמֵם | | הִתְבּוֹנֵן |
| | 2fs | קוֹמְמִי | | הִתְבּוֹנְנִי |
| | 2mp | קוֹמְמוּ | | הִתְבּוֹנְנוּ |
| | 2fp | קוֹמֵ֫מְנָה | | הִתְבּוֹנֵ֫נָּה |
| Inf. | Abs. | | not attested | |
| | Cstr. | קוֹמֵם | | הִתְבּוֹנֵן |
| Part. | Act. | מְקוֹמֵם | | מִתְבּוֹנֵן |
| | Pass. | | מְרוֹמָם | |
| Vav consec. | | וַיְקוֹמֵם | וַיְרוֹמָם | וַיִּתְבּוֹנֵן |

# Appendix D

## Transliteration

   Transliteration refers to the writing of Hebrew in the letters used for English with some additional symbols. Transliteration enables the discussion of Hebrew words with readers who do not know Hebrew. The system for transliteration in the right column is from the *SBL Handbook of Style* (p. 26). It is useful for accurately representing the Hebrew of the Bible and reflects the pronunciation of Biblical and Rabbinic Hebrew. It is included here for those who continue in Hebrew.

| Consonant | Transliteration | Consonant | Transliteration |
|:---:|:---:|:---:|:---:|
| א | ʾ | ל | *l* |
| בּ | *b̠* | מ | *m* |
| בּ | *b* | נ | *n* |
| ג | *g* | ס | *s* |
| ג | *g* | ע | ʿ |
| ד | *d̠* | פּ | *p̠* |
| ד | *d* | פּ | *p* |
| ה | *h* | צ | *ṣ* |
| ו | *w* | ק | *q* |
| ז | *z* | ר | *r* |
| ח | *ḥ* | שׁ | *s* |
| ט | *ṭ* | שׁ | *š* |
| י | *y* | ת | *t̠* |
| כ | *k̠* | ת | *t* |
| כ | *k* | | |

| Vowel | Name | Transliteration |
|---|---|---|
| ַ | *pataḥ* | *a* |
| ָ | *qameṣ* | *a* |
| הָ | final *qameṣ hê* | *â* |
| יוָ | 3 ms suff. | *ayw* |
| ֶ | *segol* | *e* |
| ֵ | *ṣerê* | *e* |
| יֵ | *ṣerê yôd* | *ê* ( יֵ = *êy*) |
| יֶ | *segol yod* | *ê* ( יֶ = *êy*) |
| ִ | short *ḥîreq* | *i* |
| ִ | long *ḥîreq* | *i* |
| יִ | *ḥîreq yôd* | *î* ( יִ = *îy*) |
| ָ | *qameṣ ḥatûp* | *o* |
| ֹ | *ḥolem* | *o* |
| וֹ | full *ḥolem* | *ô* |
| ֻ | short *qibbûṣ* | *u* |
| ֻ | long *qibbûṣ* | *u* |
| וּ | *šûreq* | *û* |
| ֳ | *ḥatep qameṣ* | *o* |
| ֲ | *ḥatep pataḥ* | *a* |
| ֱ | *ḥatep segol* | *e* |
| ְ | vocal *šewaʾ* | *e* |

# Appendix E
## Abbreviations of BHS

### Latin Words and Abbreviations

| Abbreviation | Meaning |
|---|---|
| **A** add | added; an addition |
| al | others |
| an | or |
| | |
| **C** c | with |
| cf | compare |
| cj | connect |
| cop | copula |
| | |
| **E** et | and |
| ex | from, out of |
| | |
| **F** frt | perhaps |
| | |
| **G** gl | gloss |
| | |
| **H** huc | to this place; hither |
| | |
| **I** ins | insert |
| invers | order inverted |
| | |
| **L** l | read; a reading |
| | |
| **M** mlt | very many (manuscripts) |

| N | numerus | number |
|---|---------|--------|

| O | ordinat | order, arrangement |
|---|---------|-------------------|

| P | pc | a few (manuscripts) |
|---|-----|---------------------|
|   | pl | plural |
|   | pr | instead of |
|   | prb | probably |
|   | prp | propose; it has been proposed |

| S | Seb | Sebir, Sebirin: a note in the margin indicating the usual word or form when the text is unusual. |
|---|------|------|
|   | sg | singular |
|   | sic | thus, so |
|   | suff | suffix |
|   | stich | stich or colon |

| T | tr | transpose |
|---|------|-----------|
|   | tot | whole |

| U | ut | as well as; as |
|---|-----|----------------|

| V | vel | or |
|---|------|-----|

## Signs

| + | it adds, they add |
|---|-------------------|
| > | is wanting in, is absent in |
| * | the form of the word is a probable hypothesis |
| ' | et cetera, and so forth |

## Manuscripts and Versions

| ℭ | A reading of one or several Hebrew manuscripts from the Cairo Geniza |
|---|---------------------------------------------------------------------|
| Ed, Edd | One or several editions of the HB by Kennicott, de Rossi, and Ginsburg |
| Just | Justin |

| L | Leningrad Codex of the HB |
|---|---|
| 𝔐 | Masoretic Text of the HB |
| Ms, Mss | One or several medieval manuscripts of the HB |
| Pap Nash | Nash Papyrus |
| 𝔔 | A reading of one or several manuscripts from Qumran |
| 𝔚 | Samaritan Pentateuch |
| 𝔊 | Septuagint |
| 𝔊* | Original Greek text of the Septuagint |
| 𝔊ᴬ | Codex Alexandrinus |
| 𝔊ᴮ | Codex Vaticanus |
| 𝔊ᴸ | Lucianic recension. These are biblical quotations in other writers identified as coming from Lucian |
| 𝔊ᴹˢ⁽ˢ⁾ | A manuscript or manuscripts of the Septuagint |
| 𝔊ᴼ | Origen's revision of the Septuagint |
| 𝔊⁻ᴼ | Greek tradition except for Origen |
| 𝔊ᴿ | Codex Veronensis. Greek and Old Latin version of the Psalms. |
| σ' | Symmachus' Greek translation of the HB |
| 𝔖 | Syriac version of the HB |
| 𝔗 | Targum(s) |
| 𝔗ᴶ | Targum Jonathan |
| 𝔗ᴹˢ⁽ˢ⁾ | A manuscript or manuscripts of the Targums |
| 𝔗ᴾ | Palestinian Targum |
| 𝔙 | Vulgate |
| 𝔙ᴹˢ⁽ˢ⁾ | A manuscript or manuscripts of the Vulgate |

## Hebrew Scriptures

| Ex | Exodus |
|---|---|
| 1 R | 1 Kings |
| 1 Ch | 1 Chronicles |

## Books of the New Testament

| Lc | Luke |
|---|---|
| Act | Acts |
| Rm | Romans |

# Appendix F
## Selected Bibliographies

### Word Studies

Barr, James. *The Semantics of Biblical Language.* Oxford: Oxford University, 1961.

Brown, Francis, S. R. Driver, and Charles A. Briggs, eds. *A Hebrew and English Lexicon of the Old Testament.* Oxford: Clarendon, 1907.

Landes, George M. *Building Your Biblical Hebrew Vocabulary: Learning Words by Frequency and Cognate.* Atlanta, GA: Scholars, 2001.

Mitchell, Larry A. *A Student's Vocabulary for Biblical Hebrew and Aramaic.* Grand Rapids: Zondervan, 1984.

*Theological Dictionary of the New Testament.* Edited by Gerhard Kittel and Gerhard Friedrich. Grand Rapids: Eerdmans, 1964–1976.

*Theological Dictionary of the Old Testament.* Edited by G. Johannes Botterweck and Helmer Ringgren. Grand Rapids: Eerdmans, 1981.

Westermann, Claus and Ernst Jenni, *Theological Lexicon of the Old Testament.* Translated by Mark E. Biddle. Peabody: Hendrickson, 1997.

### The Masoretic Text

Dotan, Aron. *Biblia Hebraica Leningradensia.* Peabody: Hendrickson, 2001.

Kelley, Page H, Daniel S. Mynatt, and Timothy G. Crawford. *The Masorah of Biblia Hebraica Stuttgartensia: Introduction and Annotated Glossary.* Grand Rapids: Eerdmans, 1998.

Rüger, Hans Peter. *An English Key to the Latin Words and Symbols of Biblia Hebraica Stuttgartensia.* Stuttgart: German Bible Society, 1985.

Scott, William R. *A Simplified Guide to BHS\*: Critical Apparatus, Masora, Accents, Unusual Letters & Other Markings,* 3$^{rd}$ edition. N. Richland Hills, Texas: BIBAL, 1995.

Wonneberger, Reinhard. *Understanding BHS: A Manual for the Users of Biblia Hebraica Stuttgartensia.* Subsidia Biblica, 8. Rome: Editrice Pontificio Biblico, 1990.

Yeivin, Israel. *Introduction to the Tiberian Masorah.* Translated and edited by E. J. Revell. Masoretic Studies 5. Atlanta: Scholars, 1980.

**Textual Criticism**

McCarter, P. K. *Textual Criticism, Recovering the Text of the Hebrew Bible.* Guides to Biblical Scholarship, Old Testament Series. Philadelphia: Fortress, 1986.

Tov, Emanuel. *Textual Criticism of the Hebrew Bible,* 2$^{nd}$ revised edition. Minneapolis: Augsburg Fortress, 2001. (This is the definitive work. The other two are introductions.)

Vasholz, R. I. *Data for the Sigla of the BHS.* Winona Lake, IN: Eisenbrauns, 1983.

Würthwein, Ernst. *The Text of the Old Testament: An Introduction to the Biblia Hebraica.* Translated by Errol F. Rhodes. Grand Rapids: Eerdmans, 1979.

## Translation

Minkoff, Harvey. *Approaches to the Bible: The Best of Bible Review. Vol. 1: Composition, Transmission and Language.* Washington, DC: Biblical Archaeology Society, 1994. (Particularly Harvey Minkoff, "Concern for the Text versus Concern for the Reader," and "Coarse Language in the Bible: It's Culture Shocking!" 266–284; Marc Brettler, "The Torah, The Prophets and the Writings: A New Jewish Translation," 309–319.)

Nida, Eugene A. and Charles R. Taber. *The Theory and Practice of Translation.* Leiden: E. J. Brill, 1969.

## Sources and Editors

Habel, Norman C. *Literary Criticism of the Old Testament.* Guides to Biblical Scholarship, Old Testament Series. Philadelphia: Fortress, 1971.

McKenzie, Steven L. "Deuteronomistic History." Pages 160–168 in vol. II of *Anchor Bible Dictionary.* Edited by David Noel Freedman, et al. New York: Doubleday, 1992.

## Genre and Tradition

Knight, Douglas A. *Rediscovering the Traditions of Israel.* SBLDS 9. Missoula, Montana: Scholars, 1973.

Koch, Klaus. *The Growth of the Biblical Tradition: The Form-Critical Method.* Translated by S. M. Cupitt. London: Adam & Charles Black, 1969.

Tucker, Gene M. *Form Criticism of the Old Testament.* Guides to Biblical Scholarship, Old Testament Series. Philadelphia: Fortress, 1971.

Westermann, Claus. *Basic Forms of Prophetic Speech.* Translated by Hugh Clayton White. London: Lutterworth, 1967.

———. *Praise and Lament in the Psalms.* Translated by Keith R. Crim and Richard N. Soulen. Atlanta: John Knox, 1981.

## Hebrew Narrative

Alter, Robert. *The Art of Biblical Narrative*. New York: Basic Books, 1981.

Longmann, Tremper, III. *Literary Approaches to Biblical Interpretation*. Foundations of Contemporary Interpretation, vol 3. Grand Rapids: Zondervan, 1987.

Muilenburg, James. "Form Criticism and Beyond." *JBL* 88 (1969), 1–18.

Trible, Phyllis. *Rhetorical Criticism: Content, Method and the Book of Jonah*. Guides to Biblical Scholarship, Old Testament Series. Minneapolis: Fortress, 1994.

## Hebrew Poetry

Alter, Robert. *The Art of Biblical Poetry*. New York: Basic Books, 1985.

Berlin, Adele. *The Dynamics of Biblical Parallelism*. Bloomington: Indiana University, 1985.

Kugel, James L. *The Idea of Biblical Poetry: Parallelism and Its History*. New Haven: Yale, 1981.

Miller, Patrick D., Jr. "Poetry and Interpretation." Pages 29–47 in *Interpreting the Psalms*. Philadelphia: Fortress, 1986.

Petersen, David L. and Kent Harold Richards. *Interpreting Hebrew Poetry*. Guides to Biblical Scholarship, Old Testament Series. Minneapolis: Fortress, 1992.

## Hebrew Reference Grammars

Blau, Joshua. *A Grammar of Biblical Hebrew*. 2nd edition. Porta Linguarium, Band 12. Wiesbaden: Harrassowitz, 1993.

*Gesenius' Hebrew Grammar*. Edited and enlarged by E. Kautsch. 2nd English edition by A. E. Cowley. Oxford: Clarendon, 1910.

Joüon, Paul, S. J. *A Grammar of Biblical Hebrew*. Translated and revised by T. Muraoka. 2 vols. Subsidia Biblica, 14. Roma: Editrice Pontificio Istituto Biblico, 1993.

Lambdin, Thomas O. *Introduction to Biblical Hebrew*. New York: Charles Scribner's Sons, 1971.

Waltke, Bruce K. & M. O'Connor. *An Introduction to Biblical Hebrew Syntax*. Winona Lake: Eisenbrauns, 1990.

Williams, Ronald J. *Hebrew Syntax: An Outline*. 2nd edition. Toronto: University of Toronto, 1976.

**Exegesis**

Alexander, Patrick H. *et al.*, eds. *The SBL Handbook of Style: For Ancient Near Eastern, Biblical and Early Christian Studies*. Peabody: Hendrickson, 1999.

Gorman, Michael J. *Elements of Biblical Exegesis: A Basic Guide for Students and Ministers*. Peabody: Hendrickson, 2001.

Harrington, Daniel. *Interpreting the Old Testament*. Old Testament Message, vol. 1. Wilmington, Delaware: Michael Glazier, 1981.

Hayes, John H. and Carl R. Holladay. *Biblical Exegesis: A Beginner's Handbook*. Revised edition. Atlanta: John Knox, 1987.

McKenzie, Steven L. and Stephen R. Haynes, eds. *To Each Its Own Meaning: An Introduction to Biblical Criticisms and Their Application*. Revised and expanded. Louisville: Westminster/John Knox, 1999.

Steck, Odil Hannes. *Old Testament Exegesis: A Guide to the Methodology*. 2nd edition translated by James D. Nogalski. SBL Resources for Biblical Study 39. Atlanta: Scholars, 1998.

Stuart, Douglas. *Old Testament Exegesis: A Primer for Students and Pastors*. Revised edition. Philadelphia: Westminster, 1984.

Tiffany, Frederick C. and Sharon H. Ringe. *Biblical Interpretation: A Roadmap*. Nashville: Abingdon, 1996.

# Index

Printed in the United States
55163LVS00004B/82-96

9 781589 830868